Leadership Can Be Taught

Leadership Can Be Taught

A Bold Approach for a Complex World

Sharon Daloz Parks

HARVARD BUSINESS SCHOOL PRESS

Boston, Massachusetts

978-1-59139-309-2 (ISBN 13)

Library of Congress Cataloging-in-Publication Data

Parks, Sharon Daloz.
    Leadership can be taught : a bold approach for a complex world /
Sharon Daloz Parks.
        p. cm.
    Includes bibliographical references and index.
    ISBN 1-59139-309-4 (alk. paper)
  1. Leadership. 2. Executive ability. I. Title.
    HD57.7.P3655 2005
    658.4'092--dc22

                                        2005021769

To colleagues
—known and unknown—
whose acts of leadership
create possibility,
build collective strength,
and
inspire a grounded hope
on behalf of the common good.

Contents

Contents

Foreword

The illusion is obstinate and enduring: A mortal is seemingly anointed by the gods, typically at the moment of conception, and is stamped with a unique gift that allows him or her to lead others. This person shines irrepressibly, and other mere mortals are compelled to follow.

As prevalent as this notion is, it is demonstrably false, and any person who has seriously studied leadership has found that it is not a predetermined affair. Many of the most significant shapers of history were themselves shaped gradually, not ready to make an impact on the world until time and the crucible of experience had first performed their duties. Leadership can (and often must) be learned by those who would hope to practice it.

This is not at all to suggest that leadership is easy to *teach*. Ronald Heifetz teaches it exceedingly well, however, and this book is Sharon Daloz Parks's invaluable illumination of the teaching method Heifetz has developed for a diverse range of men and women who come through Harvard's Kennedy School doors.

"The only thing that matters in art is the part that can't be explained," Georges Braque once observed. Perhaps the only thing that matters in leadership is the part that we struggle to capture and bottle. Yet when it is captured, as it is in Heifetz's course and in these pages, it is a remarkable force for change. That makes this volume profitable not solely for scholars and educators, but for leaders and managers themselves: it is a guide for creating a learning-based and leadership-nurturing organization similar to Heifetz's classroom setting.

That environment is unpredictable and exhilarating, a petri dish for human imagination and improvisation. As I read Parks's account of the unconventional manner in which Heifetz launches the course (I will not give it away here), I found myself leaning forward in anticipation, certain that something unusual would happen. I would not be disappointed.

Heifetz's legacy, in my estimation, will relate in some significant way to his work in dispelling the aforementioned, fatalistic illusion of leadership as a trait one is either born with or without. Related to it is the Myth of Charisma, captured by images of a Charlton Heston atop the mountain, a grand figure who dwarfs others.

Charisma, as a leadership factor, has been a false front, and it is a term that I have made it a point to use rarely, if ever. In the 1979 Peter Sellers film, *Being There*, a simple-minded gardener is mistaken for a charismatic genius, and his non sequitur comments are taken as brilliant insights into the state of society. It is a comically telling reminder that charisma is defined not by one's innate abilities, but by whether one's thoughts and actions have *resonance* within the larger group.

Social historian Max Weber exaggerated when he spoke of charisma within leaders as a heavenly "gift of grace"; still, his ideas about charisma have been misunderstood and exaggerated. Weber did not imply that it is merely a one-way power, a beam of energy that transforms any and all in its path. Rather, Weber understood charisma as *arising within relationships*—a function of two-way interaction between the leader and the follower.

This comes closer to the leadership concept that Parks observes in the Heifetz approach. She notes that the most accurate and helpful image of leadership is not a top-down one, but one in which the leader is a "resonant and responsive node in a dynamic network or field of energy and an agent of emergent possibility." The good news is that this is an art that can be practiced, and it is done so splendidly in chapter 5.

Fred Rogers, who in his time as television's Mister Rogers helped educate more American children than all of today's schoolteachers taken together, liked to quote the old Quaker proverb, "attitudes are caught, not taught." That is a meaningful nuance on the concept of inculcating leadership, emotional intelligence, character, or any number of skills involving human potential. Heifetz's "case-in-point" teaching methodology is in itself a positive contagion that spreads throughout the classroom, igniting students' abilities in the area of meaningful reflection, communication, and jazz-like improvisation. Imagine what our organizations could be if they incorporated this approach!

Heifetz and Parks help bring to mind the idea of an energetic dance that binds the leader and followers, in which each side is fully present, active, and able to shape the other. In that sense, the teaching of leadership can—in fact, must—be a life-giving activity. Leadership scholars are not simply scribes jotting down the names of the few persons lucky enough to receive divine appointment; rather, they are engagers of ordinary persons, opening them up to potentials and possibilities that will in turn open still others to new possibilities.

In discussing various approaches to leadership, I often note a distinction made between two nineteenth-century British prime ministers. It was observed that when you had dinner with William Gladstone, you left thinking, "That Gladstone is the wittiest, the most intelligent, the most charming person around." But when you had dinner with Benjamin Disraeli, you left thinking, "*I'm* the wittiest, the most intelligent, the most charming person around!" Gladstone shone, but Disraeli created an environment in which others could shine. The latter is the more powerful form of leadership, an adventure in which the leader is privileged to find treasure within others and put it to good use. That is the manner of adventure that Ronald Heifetz and Sharon Daloz Parks lead us through in these pages, and teachers, leaders, and organizations can be far richer for it.

—Warren Bennis
   University professor and founding chairman of the Leadership Institute at the University of Southern California

Acknowledgments

The creation of a book is rarely the work of an individual alone. Especially in a book of this kind, many people have directly and indirectly made essential contributions. First among these are Craig Dykstra and Susan Wisely at the Lilly Endowment who were from the beginning courageous, wise, and supportive colleagues. At the Kennedy School, Peter Zimmerman served as the official administrator for the study project and offered strategic insights; Dutch Leonard, Mark Moore, Jan Schubert, Edith Stokey, and Sue Williamson also informed the work and my understanding of the context it serves. Richard J. Light, Director of the Harvard Assessment Seminars, served as a colleague with whom I could think through the initial phase of the study. In the final stages of preparing the manuscript, the Center for Public Leadership provided several forms of tangible assistance.

I am particularly grateful to Theresa Monroe who was a primary member of Ronald Heifetz's teaching staff during the initial phase of the study and was the person who first spoke with me about the possibility of my becoming engaged in this work. I am grateful also to Jenny Gelber, who served as the head teaching assistant in the course during two years of the study. Other teaching assistants also informed this work and include: Ann Harbeson, Betsy Hasegawa, Tom Landy, Peter Martynowych, Phyllis Steiner, and Claudia Thompson.

Acknowledgments

For administrative support I am grateful to Scott Webster, Carol Boris, Sheila Blake, Eugenie Moriconi, and Kay Millhon.

There would have been no study, however, apart from the participation of more than sixty students. I promised them anonymity, but each one contributed distinctive elements to the mosaic that has taken form here. I offer special appreciation to those who provided hospitality in their professional settings for the postgraduate portion of the study, and to their colleagues who were willing to be interviewed as I tested the findings.

As much as all of those acknowledged contributed in spirit, insight, and practical support, because this work has an evaluative component, for the study to retain its integrity—it was finally mine alone. I am, therefore, particularly grateful for those who worked with me on my side of the boundary. My primary colleague in this work has been my research associate, Karen Thorkilsen. Karen has been steadfast in her efficient and elegant processing of the enormous amount of interview data that this kind of study generates. Her understanding of the forms of learning described here was invaluable as I worked to interpret the findings to a wider public. More, her editing, which sometimes included contributions from her own talented pen, and her insistence on fidelity to the data as she saw it, as usual provided just the kind of tensive power the evaluative imagination requires. She and I are both grateful for the superior skill that Kate Marrone brings to the transcription of interviews.

A number of colleagues have been especially generous in the development of the full manuscript. First among these are Steve Boyd, Marty Linsky, and Riley Sinder, who at differing points in the process made vital contributions. Others who read the manuscript and who each contributed their own distinctive competence to strengthening this work are Patricia Evans, Tom Ewell, Jerry Millhon, Sherry Nicholson, Tony Robinson, Emily Sander, Jim Shaffer, and Roger Taylor—and also the anonymous readers identified by the Press.

Chapter 8 would not have been possible without the investment of time and commitment on the part of Dean Williams, Win O'Toole, Hugh O'Doherty, Alma Blount, and Al Preble. My respect as well as my gratitude for each of them is immense.

For what I continue to learn about leadership and how to teach it, I am grateful to two particular sets of colleagues: Those with whom I work in Leadership for the New Commons: A Bioregional Leadership Initiative of the Whidbey Institute, especially Larry Daloz, Craig Fleck, Diana Gale, Roger Taylor, and Carol Yamada, along with the many professionals who have participated in the Powers of Leadership seasonal retreats at the Institute; and my faculty colleagues at Seattle University and the participants in the Executive Leadership Program, directed by Marilyn Gist, and in the Pastoral Excellence Program, directed by Marianne LaBarr.

Jeff Kehoe, Senior Editor at Harvard Business School Press, has been exceptional in his artful practice of providing the right mix of challenge and support that an author needs. Marcy Barnes-Henrie and Julia Ely and their colleagues in production and marketing have been professional and gracious. For the final title of the book we are all indebted to Sousan Abidian.

For several forms of professional and personal support, I am indebted to Kim Hanson, Gray Kochhar-Lindgren, Dan Lahey, Sam Magill, Carolyn North, Eloys Mills Parks, Stephanie Ryan, Wes and Joyce Veatch, Cathy Whitmire, and Sheryl Whitney. It has been said that marriage is one long conversation, and I am grateful that my husband, Larry Parks Daloz, welcomed my engagement in this work as a part of the conversation we share—both personal and professional. He endured my absorption in the project at critical times, and he served as both editor and "techie" all along the way.

Finally, I am grateful to Ronald Heifetz for his steadfast respect and support in this enterprise. It cannot be easy to have an evaluator observe every aspect of your teaching for five years and more—sometimes appearing unannounced. I want to pay particular respect to the way in which he so consistently honored the boundary that I had to maintain in carrying out the commitments of this work, while he served also as a gracious host.

—Sharon Daloz Parks
Whidbey Island, Washington

CHAPTER ONE

Leadership for a Changing World

A Call to Adaptive Work

O N A COLD, rainy December afternoon, the last session of a course in leadership had just ended. Seated beside me, a bright, thoughtful young man was intently filling out his course evaluation form. Fourteen weeks earlier, I had observed him on the first day of class and suspected he might not take the course. The course begins in an unconventional manner, and he appeared well prepared to exercise other options. Yet now at the close of the term, here he was.

After he finished the evaluation, I told him I had noticed his skepticism on the opening day, and I wondered now how he felt about the course at the end. He responded immediately that the course had been very valuable. Then I asked, "Do you remember why you decided to stay?" After a long pause, he replied, "That would be hard to say—*leadership is a word that holds a lot of hungers.*"

His response has remained with me because his understated eloquence rang true. We live in a time when the hungers for leadership are strong and deep. As our world becomes more complex, diverse, and morally ambiguous, leadership trainings and programs abound and executive coaching has appeared on the scene. Yet there remains a gnawing awareness that our prevailing myths and many of our assumed practices of leadership match neither the central perils nor the finest aspirations spawned by the forces of dramatic change—affecting every society, institution, corporation, agency, organization, community, neighborhood, task force, or project team.

At least five key hungers conspire to create what is increasingly recognized as a growing crisis in leadership. Two of these are ancient, and three of them arise from the particular conditions of this moment in history: (1) Within every person there is a hunger to exercise some sense of *personal agency*—to have an effect, to contribute, to make a positive difference, to influence, help, build—and in this sense to lead. (2) Throughout human history, within every social group there is a hunger for *authority* that will provide orientation and reassurance, particularly in times of stress and fear. What is new is that there is now a hunger for leadership that (3) can deal with the intensification of systemic *complexity* emerging from the cybernetic, economic, political, and ecological realities that have created a more connected and interdependent world; and (4) can respond adaptively to the depth, scope, and pace of *change* that combined with complexity creates unprecedented conditions. Finally, (5) this new landscape creates a new moral moment in history.[1] Critical choices must be made within significantly changed conditions, a greater diversity of perspectives must be taken into account, assumed values are challenged, and there is a deepened hunger for leadership that can exercise a moral imagination and *moral courage* on behalf of the common good.

Leadership for the Common Good
in a Complex, Changing World

The image at the root of the concept of the common good is "the commons." Aligning command-and-control, trait-based, and other prevailing models of leadership with the common good becomes more difficult as "the commons" is being transformed. The new commons in which we now find ourselves is both global in scope and relentlessly local in impact. In a simpler time, the village green, the market square, Main Street, the wharf, the great plaza, the town, the city, or even the nation offered a sense of a shared life within a manageable frame Today's new commons requires participation in a more dynamic, interdependent, and vast web of life—within a frame growing increasingly *un*manageable.[2] In the complexity and change of this new complex commons, hardworking managers who contribute their best find that success in the past does not necessarily translate into the present as new forces thwart their best intentions. Even highly talented people are vulnerable to finding themselves blindsided and their efforts stymied as the new landscape seems to be a place where "vision" has become problematic and competencies are required that can't be reduced to a toolbox.

Leadership for today's world requires enlarging one's capacity to see the whole board, as in a chess match—to see the complex, often volatile interdependence among the multiple systems that constitute the new commons. This capacity is vital to the best aspirations of democratic societies, for democracy presses toward inclusion but functions poorly without leadership.[3] Because power in democratic systems tends to be more circular than linear, to rest in networks more than in hierarchies, those who would practice effective leadership must practice a high degree of imagination, pragmatism, and trust, without falling prey to naïveté.[4] They must hold steady in the face of uncertainty and threat, while remaining creatively open to the demands of changing circumstances, enabling people who may represent significant differences to create together something that is both workable and worthy. Whether it is being worked out within the life of a corporation or the life of a marginalized community, effective leadership in the service of democratic principles is not an easy practice.

Despite these changes and challenges, a deep ambivalence remains regarding the object of today's hungers for leadership. Are we simply to wait for born leaders to appear? There is a strong temptation (as in every age) simply to look for gifted persons who will hold positions of formal authority and who will make the needed difference. Traditional understandings of leadership akin to this impulse focus on personality characteristics, situation analysis, and transactions of power and influence. Now, however, a growing consensus among leadership theorists and practitioners is that in a networked society with power and information widely distributed, the presumption of "born leaders" along with command-and-control leadership models are inadequate. Yet, though there have been calls for a recomposing of the art and myth of leadership, larger-than-life heroic leaders continue to be studied and offered as models.[5] Why? Because we haven't developed good alternatives—both in content and method.

Can Leadership Be Taught?

If leaders are not simply "born," can leadership be taught? It has been well acknowledged that it is difficult to teach for the world of professional practice. It is particularly difficult to teach for the practice of leadership. Teaching and learning are typically conceived as a matter of transmitting knowledge: teaching as telling. Conventionally, such transfer of knowledge is presumed to occur through a formal or informal process of reading, lecture, or presentation from an expert in the field, perhaps some discussion (primarily involving students' questions and the teacher's answers), note taking, and perhaps also term papers and exams. Within this paradigm of teaching and learning, and across every sector and profession, it is one thing to teach knowledge of the field, and it is quite another to prepare people to exercise the judgment and skill needed to bring that knowledge into the intricate systems of relationships that constitute the dynamic world of practice. It is yet another challenge altogether to prepare someone to practice leadership within the profession and the communities it serves—to prepare a physician, for example, to practice leadership within a hospital system and the regional, national, or world health care systems as well as to care for individual patients.

Learning by Doing and the Artistry of Good Coaching

In his classic, *Educating the Reflective Practitioner*, Donald Schon eloquently argued that people cannot simply be *told* what they need to know in the complexity of practice. They must learn to *see* for themselves. What is needed is access to coaches who initiate the learner into the "traditions of the calling" and help them by "the right kind of telling" to see on their own behalf and in their own way what they most need to see. "We ought, then," he wrote, "to study the experience of learning by doing and the artistry of good coaching. We should base our study on the working assumption that both processes are intelligent and—within limits to be discovered—intelligible. And we ought to search for examples wherever we can find them."[6]

Building on these assumptions, this book affirms that leadership can be taught. We do so by looking in depth at one particular approach to practicing and teaching leadership that responds to Schon's call for "learning by doing and the artistry of good coaching." This is found in the work of Ronald Heifetz, author of *Leadership Without Easy Answers*, and coauthor with Marty Linsky of *Leadership On the Line: Staying Alive Through the Dangers of Leading*.[7] Across more than two decades, Heifetz and his colleagues at Harvard University have pioneered a distinctive, bold approach to learning and teaching leadership, created and practiced in a manner that is responsive to the hungers for a new story about what leadership means and asks—and ways of learning it. Other theorists and practitioners also have begun to explore new understandings of leadership that more adequately honor an interdependent, systemic awareness, and the need for significant shifts in perspective and practice. Fewer, however, have wrestled with the attendant questions: Can leadership be learned? If it can be learned, can it be taught? And, if so, what methods or approaches will work? Is teaching an act of leadership? If leading involves risk, what are the risks involved in teaching leadership? Can new insight move beyond conceptual awakening and actually change leadership behavior at the level of default settings—habitual ways of responding, especially in crisis and under stress?

The response of Heifetz and his colleagues to these questions is an approach that artfully integrates a set of ideas—a framework for understanding a practice of leadership fitting to today's world—with a corresponding teaching methodology that is congruent with those ideas. The methodology is called *case-in-point*.

Case-in-Point

Case-in-point teaching, as Heifetz and his colleagues have developed it, draws on several well-established learning traditions and methods—seminar, simulation, presentation of ideas and perspectives (through lecture, reading, and film), discussion and dialogue, clinical-therapeutic practice, coaching, the laboratory, the art studio, writing as a form of disciplined reflection, and the case study method.

The celebrated case study method pioneered by Harvard's law and business schools is a powerful research methodology (critical to helping scholar-practitioners analyze data and work inductively with concepts that may apply broadly across multiple contexts). It is also a powerful pedagogical tool (giving students multiple situations, concepts, and images to work with as they think about experiences that they haven't yet had).[8]

Educators, at least since John Dewey, have persuasively argued that human beings, and particularly adults, learn best from their own experience. The traditional case study method draws on practical experience, but it is usually somewhat removed from the actual, immediate experience of the student. In the quest of a methodology that can teach further below the neck—to the default settings that people act from in a crisis—case-in-point teaching and learning seeks to make optimal use of the student's own past and immediate experience.

In case-in-point teaching, what goes on in the classroom itself is an occasion for learning and practicing leadership within a social group. The class is recognized as a social system inevitably made up of a number of different factions and acted on by multiple forces. The class also has a clear and challenging purpose—to make progress in understanding and practicing leadership.

The teacher has a set of ideas and frameworks to offer. But instead of presenting a lecture, or starting with a written case from another context that may or may not be relevant to the learning of the people in the class, the teacher waits for a case to appear in the process of the class itself. Every group generates its own set of issues, shaped, in part, by what is set in motion by the context and content provided by the teacher-presenter and the events of the day.

The challenge is to make use of both the explicit and underlying issues that surface in the group by connecting those issues to the course content. The teacher, therefore, must reflect on what is happening in the class *as it is happening*, asking, "Is there any way I can use what is happening right here and now to illustrate the content I want the class to learn today?" In other words, the teacher imagines that what went on in the class for the last ten minutes was a case. Then the teacher works to use it to illustrate the theme, concept, or skill that he or she is trying to present. The work is to create a live encounter between the experience of the learner and the idea.

Everything that happens in the classroom is open to scrutiny—including the actions, inconsistencies, and blind spots of the teacher. The students are encouraged to "be on the dance floor" (that is, in the action) and also to "get on the balcony" to see if they can read the larger patterns of what is going on and figure out how to intervene in ways that will help the group make progress. All the while, the students are being offered concepts, metaphors, and frameworks that assist them in interpreting and naming what they are learning to see and do.

In this approach, the teacher remains the authority in the classroom—providing orientation and maintaining equilibrium in the group. But the teacher is also practicing leadership—skillfully allowing enough disequilibrium (confusion, frustration, disappointment, conflict, and stress) to help the group move from unexamined assumptions about the practice of leadership to seeing, understanding, and acting in tune with what the art and practice of leadership may actually require. In the process, the teacher must be aware of the various factions among the students in the room, the differing points of view that each represents, and then must find ways of recruiting, honoring, and sustaining the attention of each of them.

Four Critical Distinctions

Case-in-point teaching provides a model in real time of the practice of leadership that is being taught in the course. This approach rests on a framework for understanding and practicing leadership that rests in four critical distinctions: authority versus leadership, technical problems versus adaptive challenges, power versus progress, and personality versus presence.

Authority Versus Leadership

Heifetz and his colleagues draw a distinction between *authority* and *leadership*. Most people tend to presume that a leader is a person in a position of formal authority—the boss, CEO, president, chair, captain, supervisor, director—the head, or, similarly, the expert. All organizations depend on such roles and the functions they provide to maintain equilibrium within the social group. The functions of authority include providing orientation and direction, setting norms, resolving conflict, and, when necessary, providing protection. The approach to leadership we describe here, however, recognizes that the functions of authority often play a vital but markedly insufficient role in the practice of leadership.

In this view, the function of leadership is to mobilize people—groups, organizations, societies—to address their toughest problems. Effective leadership addresses problems that require people to move from a familiar but inadequate equilibrium—through disequilibrium—to a more adequate equilibrium. That is, today's complex conditions require acts of leadership that assist people in moving beyond the edge of familiar patterns into the unknown terrain of greater complexity, new learning, and new behaviors, usually requiring loss, grief, conflict, risk, stress, and creativity. Often, deeply held values are both at stake and under review. Seen in this light, authority becomes only one resource and sometimes a constraint in the practice of leadership, and often a leader must act beyond his or her authorization.

Technical Problems Versus Adaptive Challenges

The second distinction at the heart of this approach flows from the first: the distinction between technical problems and adaptive challenges. *Technical problems* (even though they may be complex) can be solved with knowledge and procedures already in hand. In contrast, *adaptive challenges* require new learning, innovation, and new patterns of behavior. In this view, leadership is the activity of mobilizing people to address adaptive challenges—those challenges that cannot be resolved by expert knowledge and routine management alone. Adaptive challenges often appear as swamp issues—tangled, complex problems composed of multiple systems that resist technical analysis and thus stand in contrast to the high, hard ground issues that are easier to address but where less is at stake for the organization or the society.[9] They ask for more than changes in routine or mere preference. They call for changes of heart and mind—the transformation of long-standing habits and deeply held assumptions and values.[10]

Today's adaptive challenges may appear on any scale and within every domain. They include obvious global issues such as the growing vulnerability of all populations to untreatable epidemics, climate change, terrorism, and the widening social-economic divide. Adaptive challenges are equally likely to take the form of what is assumed to be a local, technical challenge but, in fact, requires a new mode of operating within a nonprofit agency, an engineering division, or a long-established product line.[11]

Power Versus Progress

When leadership is understood as an activity—the activity of making progress on adaptive challenges—there is less attention to be paid to the transactions of power and influence and more attention given to the question of whether or not progress is being made on swamp issues. Accordingly, making progress on critical adaptive challenges becomes the basic measure of effective leadership in this approach. Note the shift. When a distinction is made between "authority and technical problems" on the one hand and "leadership and adaptive challenges" on the other, the issue becomes less a matter of personal power—who has it and how they wield it—and shifts to making progress on difficult issues. This third distinction orients the practice of leadership to questions of purpose and reorders the criteria for determining whether or not one is exercising leadership effectively.

Personality Versus Presence

The fourth distinction is closely related to the third. When the focus shifts from authority and technical problems to leadership and making progress on adaptive challenges, the charisma and the traits of the individual personality may become less critical. In this view, acts of leadership depend less on the magnetism and social dominance of heroic individuals and more on the capacities of individuals (who may be located in a wide variety of positions) to skillfully intervene in complex systems. Thus, the multifaceted capacity to be present becomes a key factor in effective leadership: the quality of one's capacity to be fully present, comprehend what is happening, hold steady in the field of action, and make choices regarding when and how to intervene from within the social group (from wherever you sit) in ways that help the group to make progress on swamp issues.

With these four critical distinctions in hand, Heifetz and his colleagues have developed a framework for analysis and intervention within social systems to help make progress on tough, adaptive challenges.

An Assessment

A survey assessment of this approach, published in 1989, found that of the 165 former students who responded, more than half believed this approach to teaching and learning leadership to be either the "most useful" or "much more useful" than their other Harvard courses, and similarly the "most useful" or "much more useful" than previous leadership or management training.[12]

Seeking methods and approaches to leadership education that had depth, wisdom, and the potential to make a significant contribution to the larger good subsequently attracted the Lilly Endowment to this work. I was invited to further study, describe, and assess this approach using qualitative methods. Informed by the earlier survey, the consistently high level of student course evaluations, initial observations of the course, and my own teaching and research in the formation of leadership and ethics in three professional schools, I accepted. This approach was breaking some new ground, consolidating several strands of emergent theory and practice, and exploring ways of learning and practicing leadership more aligned with the emerging experience of complexity and change that characterizes the everyday challenges that managers, executives, project directors, and others face.

After several years of study and assessment, I have come to affirm that this approach provides both a response to today's hungers for leadership and a remarkably effective teaching methodology.[13] As a sustained experiment in rethinking leadership and how to learn it, this approach can spur the imagination of those who practice leadership and especially those who dare to teach leadership—instructors, coaches, supervisors, and mentors working within professional schools, corporate leadership and management training programs, undergraduate leadership programs, community development initiatives, or issue-oriented endeavors.

The Terrain Ahead

The purpose of this book, therefore, is to describe, interpret, and assess this particular approach as a vivid and effective example of how leadership for the common good—the well-being of today's commons—can be taught in ways that are relevant across all sectors.

Building on observation, interviews, and analysis, this approach is explored along several sight lines: the content (the theory), the way it is taught (the method), the experience of the students, and the experience of teachers and coaches who have effectively taken up this approach. Chapter 2 steps right into the classroom, immersing the reader in the actual dynamics of the opening session of the course as taught at Harvard. Like the students themselves, you may emerge from this experience both intrigued and disoriented, asking "what's really going on here?" Chapters 3 through 5 seek to answer that question by looking at key features of the theory and the course design.

Chapter 3 explains how the case-in-point approach may be used to develop skills for identifying issues and factions within any social group and intervening strategically on behalf of some larger purpose. This chapter also explores the deeper significance of the cognitive and emotional shift that the achievement of systemic awareness represents for the practice of leadership.

Chapter 4 reveals how the students' own leadership failures are brought into disciplined dialogue with the theory to generate insight into personal blind spots and open a broader repertoire of creative responses for the next time.

Then, challenging the conventional assumption that personality is all and that leadership charisma is something one must be born with, chapter 5 conveys how this approach offers pathways for developing the more valuable quality of *presence*—the ability to intervene, to hold steady, inspire a group, and work in both verbal and nonverbal realms.

After the essence and structure of the approach are laid out in the first half of the book, another set of questions is taken up in the second half. These include two challenges in the transferability of the approach. First, how readily do the lessons of this approach transfer back into the workplace? Courses or training sessions may seem powerful in the moment, but often quickly fade when participants return to business as usual. What kind of staying power does this approach have? Second, how readily can it be picked up by other teacher-practitioners? Can its essential elements be used in quite different settings to good effect? In short, what are the prospects for cultivating the leadership now needed by broadening the reach of this promising approach?

Chapter 6 seeks to answer the first of these questions by following former students back into their workplaces and listening to them describe how they continue to use the insights of this approach. A key finding is that learning distilled into images and metaphors has remarkable staying power, even to the point of affecting people's behavioral default settings.

Chapters 7 and 8 address the development and transferability of this approach from a teacher's perspective. First, what does it feel like to create and practice a way of teaching that keeps the teacher on the edge of new learning and under constant scrutiny? Chapter 7 offers a rare opportunity to hear Ronald Heifetz reflect on the genesis of this approach and his own experience of learning to teach in this mode. Then, chapter 8 introduces several other teachers who have successfully adopted this approach and describes how it is modified and evolves when transferred into markedly different contexts—other institutions, executive coaching, professional consulting, undergraduate leadership development, and other cultures.

To fully assess the potential contribution of this approach, chapter 9 offers one additional perspective—a reconsideration of our culture's myth of leadership itself. It unveils a deeper level of what is really going on here. By comparing today's prevailing command and control models of leadership with an alternative model drawn from the creative process of artists, I will show how this approach helps us all make progress on what is arguably a central adaptive challenge of our time: the transformation of the prevailing myth of leadership. I believe that the mix of intrigue, disorientation, and hope that many experience when first encountering this approach to teaching and learning leadership stems precisely from this challenge. Our times call for a reconfigured understanding of the art of leadership because inherent in our ideas about leadership are deep assumptions about the social contract and how progress gets made. We are in the midst of creating a new understanding, birthing new images even as we learn to act in alignment with them.

Finally, chapter 10 reflects on the strengths and limits of this approach as a whole and its possible trajectories into the future.

Setting the Scene

Teaching and learning the art of leadership occurs in a wide range of places, both formal and informal. The approach described here has been cultivated primarily in the context of a professional school—the Kennedy School of Government at Harvard University, where the work is now anchored in the school's Center for Public Leadership. The Kennedy School is dedicated to enhancing the effectiveness of people who exercise leadership in public life, a function that necessarily places it in direct partnership with the other professional schools at the university—Business, Dentistry, Design, Divinity, Education, Law, Medicine, and Public Health.

The school seeks students who have demonstrated potential for leadership, managerial capability, analytical talent, and ethical sensitivity. These students come from the United States and the wider international community. Some are elected officials and legislators; some are military officers; others are present or prospective heads of government agencies, for-profit, or nonprofit organizations; still others are policy analysts or journalists. The students range in age from twenty-three to sixty (most are in mid-career), and they are enrolled in several degree and other special programs. Collectively they represent a broad field of experience, perspectives, ideologies, hopes, and concerns. Many of their courses focus on policy and analysis. They necessarily deal also with the questions of meaning, ethics, and leadership.

The scope and vitality of the school's work is revealed, in part, in the activity of the Forum—an imaginatively designed, multipurpose space at the center of the school. Three floors of classroom, seminar, and office space open into a rotundalike area that continually hums with conversation—among the clusters of students that spill out of the surrounding classrooms, in the gatherings over coffee or lunch on the first level, in the soft-seating areas adjacent to the open stairways, and in the study group carrels that ring the perimeter of the second and third levels. Several times a week, this space is transformed into a formal amphitheater where national and international figures debate critical issues, and electronic media bring the life of the wider global commons into the heart of the school. The Forum promotes both informal meeting and deliberative dialogue across the differences of geography, gender, ethnicity, culture, ideology, and moral commitment. At the edge of this Forum, a set of double doors on the south side opens into a multitiered classroom with places for ninety students. This is the primary setting in which this approach to teaching leadership has been developed and practiced for the past two and a half decades.

Luxury and Necessity

The opportunity to learn the art and practice of leadership in such a setting might be perceived as a luxury far removed from the experience of most people who aspire to practice or teach leadership. Relatively few imagine that they have either the time or the financial resources to invest in learning something that is, after all, regarded by many as simply a gift or talent. But taking a closer look in the way this book provides leads to the discovery that this approach is not a luxury and need not be confined to any single setting.

Rather, it can be used to reveal essential features of a practice of leadership that can be learned and used throughout today's new commons. This approach, necessarily translated into other settings and expressions, is offered here as one powerful form of learning vital aspects of the art of leadership, a critical feature of the art of life—and a necessity in an increasingly interdependent, complex, dangerous, and demanding world.

Now, we step into the classroom.

CHAPTER TWO

How Do We Begin?

Differing Expectations

I T IS SEPTEMBER. Cambridge is all blue sky and leaves ready to turn into flame. High spirits and purposefulness abound as the pace quickers in Harvard Square and classes get under way across the university, including PAL 101—Exercising Leadership: Mobilizing Group Resources.

Close to the appointed hour, there is a steady hubbub of talk among the ninety students who have found a seat in six horseshoe-shaped tiers of desks. Sitting in the aisles, up the steps, and on the radiators across the back of the room are almost another hundred students plus their book bags, jackets, and briefcases. These students have arrived on time, but all the chairs have been filled, so they are wedging themselves onto whatever perches they can find. Some are certain they want this course; for others the course is still on trial. Everyone is wondering how many students will be admitted.

Two teaching assistants (TAs) are setting up a tape recorder and checking the microphones.[1] Another is passing around syllabi. Still another is informally fielding questions about if and how students will be admitted to the course. About ten minutes after the hour, the instructor, Ronald Heifetz, steps to the front of the room.

He is carefully groomed, wearing a trim, classic, comfortable suit and tie. He is in his forties, slim, not very tall, has dark hair, and bears a mix of seriousness and anticipation. As the rustling subsides into the conventional opening-of-class silence, he just stands there, simply looking back at the class, making eye contact around the room, not speaking. The silence lengthens uncomfortably. No one is quite as sure as they were a few moments earlier about who they are and what they are doing. In that pause, the expected conventions are broken open.

The pause is finally ended by the instructor, who asks a question:

"How many of you have been in a position where you were given a new role, some kind of responsibility and authority, and then walked into a room for the first time where people were gathered for a meeting, and they expected you to be responsible for how they would proceed?"

Most of the students, ranging in age from mid-twenties to sixty, raise their hands. Then he says, "Well, then many of you know something about the position I'm in right now." (There is quiet laughter of recognition around the room.) "So," he continues, "maybe we can begin learning about leadership and authority by studying the position I'm in right now." There is another pause.

Then he says,

"What are my options? How should I be thinking strategically about my first moves and second moves and third moves? Is that first moment—when you walk in and a group of people are doing what people usually do to somebody who they haven't met before who's in a position of authority in relationship to them, that is, largely checking him or her out—is that moment important? What have you done when you have been in that situation?"

If the class needs more prompting, he suggests, "What do other teachers do?"

A series of suggestions and responses ensues:

"You could tell a joke."

"Why would I do that?"

"To build rapport with the class—to put people at ease."

"Yes, and would that be a good thing to do?"

"Might be."

"Yes, it might be, but rapport and learning aren't necessarily the same. This is a class on learning leadership, and most of you have been exercising leadership already, which is why you are here. I have too much respect for the scars you already have on your back from trying to do that."

There is another pause as the truth of what he has just said sinks in, and the class recognizes that something more than a class may be at stake here.

"So," he continues, "I am reluctant to begin with a joke. What else might I do?"

"You need to gain respect."

"Yes, that would be nice. How would I do that?"

"You don't need to do that; you're at Harvard."

"But we all know that being a teacher at Harvard only gets you about ten minutes."

(Laughter)

"You could tell us what we can expect in the course."

"Yes, you come with a set of expectations, don't you? And

already I have countered some of your expectations. What are the risks of that?"

"We may find it interesting, or we may be disappointed."

"So what would be the right move?"

A woman named Gretchen suggests,

"At some point I think it's important to say that I have some concern, because I understand the course enrollment will be limited. I don't know how that's going to be handled. So it might be important to hear from you about that."

"So what you would like to see is that I very quickly read what is going to be a dominant issue in the group, and if I don't speak to that concern right away, then there is going to be disappointment, and I would lose some credibility. Let's say, for example, that I never spoke to your concern. Let's say I was really lame. Let's say you asked me a question about it, and I said, that's not in the script, that's not what we're doing in this first session."

"Then you ought to be a politician!" a student calls out from the back of the room.

"Politicians are generally pretty good at assessing the current concern and speaking to it," the instructor responds.

"They speak to something," says a student sitting directly in front of the instructor in the second row, "but it's not usually the real concern. They prevaricate, they hedge, they work around the system, but they don't address the question directly if it's something they don't want to answer."

"And why would they do that, do you think?" asks the instructor.

."They're serving their interest. They don't want to be put on the spot. They don't want to be painted into a corner."

"Well, whose interest—?"

"And they also want to address the topics that they have on their agenda," says the student, obviously wanting to be sure *he* isn't painted into a corner.

The professor leans forward, hands on the desk, and says directly, clearly, and also with a sense of exploration,

"To commit is to alienate. So when you say 'their self-interest,' their self-interest is complicated because they need to win votes. So that means here they are, and there's this large group of people—two hundred people who show up for a class of a hundred. They'd like to make everybody happy. I mean, what else would make a politician happy other than making everybody happy? But everybody isn't the same. Some people want one thing," he gestures toward one side of the room, "and other people want something else—right?" he asks, eyeing the other side of the room. "You have factions, each of which is pulling this politician in a different direction. So one faction poses a question and the politician immediately does this internal calculation: How is this going to play with my other factions? Can I afford to alienate them? I'd better hedge here. So, you are right, they're always hedging. Now is it because they themselves are just constitutionally predisposed to be liars? To not commit to anything?"

(Laughter)

Another student speaks up:

"If they had the choice, they'd section off one section of the room, talk to that group, turn to the next section, tell them what they want to hear, and turn to the next section—they talk out of three sides of their mouth."

"Yes, it often seems that way, doesn't it?" responds Heifetz.

"Politicians are the links between the various divisions in our society and the decisions and policies we need to make to live together. Helping people to face painful choices and to learn new ways of being without losing credibility is difficult work. Talking to each faction alone is pretty attractive, but even that is hard to do, isn't it? Look at the position I'm in. We all have a lot in common. But there are people of different ages, and perhaps thirty countries, plus at least ten subcultures within the United States represented in this room. How am I going to understand and meet your expectations?"

"You could ask us what our expectations are, what we want?"

"And what would be the risk of doing that?"

"We might want very different things," one student reflects, and another adds, "We might want things that do not correspond with what you want to do with the class."

"It's important for you to listen to us," a woman says with quiet, clear certainty.

"Yes, some of you probably value that very highly. But if I do that, others of you may think that I don't know what I'm doing. What else should I do?"

"You could help people know whether or not they want to take the course."

"What would I tell them? What do you think people want to know?"

"People want to know the outline of the course—and whether or not they can trust you."

"The outline of the course is in the syllabus, which you have—but how are you going to know whether or not you can trust me?"

"Everyone knows about your book, so you are already credible," quips a confident male voice from the far left of the room.

"Well, that's very nice, but a lot of you have been in the classes of professors who have written books, and you have decided in the first five minutes that you don't want to take the course."

There is a murmur of confirmation, and then a woman in the back speaks up, a bit tentatively but displaying also a kind of savvy:

"Just to go back to your original question, I think the initial thing we all want from you is some form of entertainment. You can build a unity or a collective reaction by entertaining us initially—maybe entertainment is the wrong word—but you need to grab us."

"Oh, I think entertainment is quite accurate—and you imply that fun is one of the performance criteria. Now fun doesn't mean it's going to be humorous. Sometimes people have fun watching mysteries and gladiator fights—people have weird notions of what's fun. Learning can be fun—they don't have to be mutually exclusive, although learning often has moments that are also painful. Important learning—good learning, deep learning, the kind of learning that takes place in here—has many facets."

Another woman speaks clearly and compellingly across the room:

"I would like you to tell us what you think your course is about and what type of people you think should be involved with it. I mean, it's one full term, there's a lot of time put into it, there's a lot of reading, there's a lot of effort required, so I would like to have an idea of what you think we would be getting out of it."

"Well," responds the instructor, "what's already clear from our discussion so far is that there are many different kinds of people in here, different values, and different purposes. So my aim is to design a course—with a teaching staff that provides critical help—that enables you to learn what you're ready to learn. But that's going to be different for this guy over here, or for the fun-loving woman in the back, or the woman concerned with enrollment here. Different people have different things to learn, and by the end of the term, my aim would be for people to have learned a lot that was relevant to them in regard to their own capacity to mobilize their communities or their organizations to make progress on the hardest of problems, which is what I think leadership is about—mobilizing people to make progress on the hardest of problems."

"So if leadership is about getting people to tackle tough problems, what that's going to look like in your hands—in the context you choose to operate in—may be very different from somebody in a different country or a different organization with a different set of problems. Furthermore, where she comes into this conversation is different from where you come into this conversation at this moment in time. Both of you are sitting in this class, but you have different things to learn about the tasks of leadership. The complexity of this job is to try to meet you at your level of readiness, with the issues that would be next for you."

Peter asks,

"To roll two questions into one, how many people do you plan to be able to meet at their level of readiness?" (Laughter)

"Ninety percent of the people who take the course. There will be some people we fail with."

Peter persists,

"I don't mean of the people who are accepted into the course, how many will have their needs met. I mean how many people now sitting or standing in the room—what percentage of those will be accepted into the course?"

"Ah, Gretchen got an ally," says the professor with a smile. "Let me speak to this concern." (Laughter)

The professor describes in some detail how the enrollment-selection process will occur, pointing out also that since not everyone presently in the room will finally choose to take the class, it is quite possible that there will not be an enrollment problem—and in any case, things will be clearer at the next meeting of the class.

When there seems to be a new level of clarity and satisfaction on this matter, the professor continues,

"So we've begun to explore two things at once. First of all, we've begun to illustrate one of the teaching methods that we'll be using in this class, which is to use ourselves as a 'case-in-point.' By that I mean that the dynamics that take place in this classroom, including the dynamics between you and me and amongst you, will be available for us to examine."

"You need to be aware of what is going on in the room. Jesuits call it 'contemplation in action'—I speak of it as getting on the balcony so you can see the dance floor, and you need to get there several times a day. Reflection in action. It's very difficult to do."

"For example, why is it that one person is paid attention to and another person who says the same thing isn't paid attention to? Why is it that Peter has already begun to take on a particular role in this class? How does the group contribute to his playing that role, how do I respond to him? Do I respond effectively or ineffectively, and is he playing his role effectively or ineffectively? Is it a useful role in the work of the group or is it just a personal habit? If it is a personal habit, how would you get sufficient mastery over yourself so you could draw on that habit in strategic moments when it is appropriate—but not at other times when the same behavior is inappropriate? We will ask ourselves those sorts of questions."

"But a second thing that I've introduced in this conversation," says Heifetz, signaling a shift of focus, "is about what expectation does somebody in authority need to meet in order to maintain or gain credibility?"

There is only a slight moment of waiting before a woman speaks up to suggest that he should allow the people in the group to identify with him by revealing a more personal side of himself so that he is not just a one-dimensional authority figure.

"So you would tend to trust me more if I were more self-revealing—perhaps particularly in terms of being vulnerable? But you probably wouldn't like it if I tell you how excited I am about the publication of my book and how proud I am of the endorsements and reviews. It would probably speak to you more if I told you about how worried I felt about the reviews, my sleepless nights, and how I've taken it out on my kids . . . "

The woman interrupts,

"You can't go too far, we don't want you to . . ."

"Isn't that interesting," Heifetz interrupts. "I need to be humble and vulnerable, but I need not to be pathetic. (Laughter) That's not a very big hoop to jump through. Between pathetic on one hand and vulnerable on the other is not much space—and you're saying I have to gauge it just right."

Another says,

"You need to have abilities that I can respect."

"Yes," the instructor confirms. "I need to have some sort of abilities, skills, competence, right? Each of you has in mind, it is my guess, some criteria for competence, but they are not highly explicit criteria. It wouldn't be easy for you to write down on a piece of paper your four criteria and then weight them, and then list the behaviors by which I would manifest them. It's all much more unconscious than that, it's more of a blur and gut reaction, isn't it? We'd have to work pretty hard to make explicit what those criteria are by which you would evaluate me, with only the little bit you can get in these ninety minutes—not a lot of data. I do appreciate that you have a very serious problem, because you can't tell whether or not I'm just conning you, if I'm manipulative, if I'm trustworthy—particularly for an enterprise as personal as leadership development."

He continues,

"So at some level this course requires taking a risk. Leadership does too."

A student asks,

"What kinds of risks would we be taking here?"

"Well, if we use ourselves as a case-in-point and our process of working together becomes more transparent, we will analyze how we are operating, what's effective about it, what's brilliant about it, and what's sloppy about it, so that we can each become more effective. We will do that not only in here but also in small groups. Each of you will be in a small group that will meet every week. In these groups each of you will present a case of your own leadership failure, and the rest of the people in your group will be consultants to you so that you can see how you might have done things differently or maybe couldn't have done things differently."

"But," he goes on, "in that process of helping each other learn—both in this big class and in the small groups—we may be mixed in our effectiveness so that a person comes away with 60 percent good stuff, forty percent bad stuff, and maybe some hurt feelings because we didn't operate with enough finesse in providing good feedback."

"Can you define what kind of a leader you think you are?" asks a woman who sounds curious, discerning, and a bit like a frustrated participant in a game of twenty questions. "What is your leadership style, how do you think of your self as a leader?"

"No, I couldn't."

"Why couldn't you answer that question if you're teaching a course—?"

"Well, let's think about that."

Another student picks up this new thread of thought:

"A person is not a leader all the time. In fact, I wouldn't think that an instructor is necessarily a leader. I think that there are certain situations when certain talents and skills come into play and leadership is necessary. That's why you can't answer that question—that's not a fair question to ask somebody that's a bright instructor in front of a class."

Another student jumps in:

"Yes, it is. Here's a class on leadership. I'm trying to get a sense of what this guy thinks leadership is about."

The previous student says,

"But right now I would say this person is not a leader right now. This person is an instructor right now."

Yet another student joins in:

"Well, can't instructors be leaders?"

A student who has not previously spoken earnestly leans into the conversation and speaks up authoritatively:

"I don't think he can answer the question because he may be able to lead me, but he may not be a very good leader for you. I see him very much as a leader right now. The question is whether he's a good leader for me or for somebody else in this classroom."

There follows a series of comments from a broad scattering of students:

"I also think he wants us to learn from ourselves. Maybe he wants us to figure it out."

"You can have an assessment of yourself that may not match what everyone else thinks about you."

"But the question is, what is his assessment of himself?"

Realizing that this might be an important question, another student reflects,

"I may think I'm a fair leader. I listen to people, and all this stuff. But everybody else may say, 'That's absolutely not true.'" Then turning to the instructor he says, "So you can tell us what kind of leader you are, but the best way is to show us. I also think that you're right about an instructor. The leadership may be part of the skills you bring to bear on the classroom, but it's only one thing. So the only thing I want to know about you is how you teach—and I know that just by watching you teach."

"But look at what we're doing," says a man in the top row with a mixture of dismay and insight in his voice. "We're answering on his behalf. All of a sudden we're talking third person." Then, looking directly at the instructor he demands, "I want to hear from you."

The instructor responds respectfully,

"I think that if I were to answer her question, it would be a trap. So can somebody analyze why it would be a trap?"

"The two over there, they actually answered the question," asserts a student on the fourth row off to the right side. The woman said that she found you to be a leader, but the other one didn't perceive you to be a leader. So it's individuals who determine 'leadership.'"

The instructor picks up the beat reflectively:

"So we're back in this kind of situation where I suppose one person will want me to perform this way, and another that way, and another yet another way, and before your know it, anything I say is going to immediately upset two-thirds of the people here. Furthermore, if I answered the question, I would be validating a set of assumptions that some people hold about leadership, without making those assumptions explicit so we can then analyze them. Then each of you would go about having your private conversation in your own mind, evaluating and weighing what I had said without my having any opportunity to engage you regarding your criteria, your definitions of leadership, and whether your conceptions of leadership were even useful as a frame of reference. My job isn't to let you carry on these discussions about something so central as, 'What is a leader?' in the privacy of your own mind. My task is to surface those assumptions so we can begin scrutinizing them to see which of them you really want to hold on to and which you want to begin to discard."

He pauses. And then he continues, speaking with a kind of earnestness that is difficult to ignore—that sense again that something more than a course is at stake:

"And that is the most significant trap. One is a trap in terms of just upsetting two-thirds of you. I'm not so afraid of doing that—though every instructor is tempted to perform according to your expectations, even at the loss of challenging you to learn. But the more significant trap, in terms of my purpose (which is for you to learn how to exercise leadership more effectively)—is that I would be undermining that purpose if I answered the question. A third of you might leave the room for entirely the wrong reasons, reasons that we didn't even have available to analyze."

He pauses again, and then takes up the question in another light:

"But if what you're really trying to do is figure out, 'Should you trust me?'—which is, I think, where your question is coming from, I would suggest to you that the greatest teachers of the great masters of the violin of this century were two people. One was a Russian named Leopold Auer, who taught in the Moscow conservatory before the Russian revolution—the first Russian revolution. The second master was a man named Ivan Galamian, an Armenian man, who taught at Julliard. Neither of them could play the violin very well, but they trained all the masters. So whether or not I'm your ideal type of a leader may not be the right competency, if my task is to help you learn how to be most competent."

There is a pause as this piece of complexity seeks a toehold in people's imaginations.

A woman remarks reflectively,

"It seems to me that some people want the answer from you—"

And the instructor chimes in,

"Isn't that intriguing?"

(Laughter)

"And other people," she continues, "are rather enjoying having us say what leadership is or exploring how do you help us figure out what it is."

"So you are saying," continues the instructor affirmatively, "that different people have different ways of learning. Some people like to learn by the chaos and the fuzz of a discussion, and other people want to learn in a more orderly fashion by hearing a person with authority speak. And I'm sure that those different styles of learning will provide some of the grist for the mill that energizes this course."

A Frenchman raises his hand, and when the professor nods in his direction, he hesitantly offers,

"I do not know if you have this game in English—cat and mouse? It seems like we are playing that game."

The instructor responds immediately,

"Yes, we do have that game in this culture. And it is a bit like that, isn't it? It's hard to know which is which in the territory of authority relationships. Am I the cat or the mouse? And which one are you? In authority relationships we might think that as the instructor, I am the cat. But since I only have authority if students give it to me, the students are the cat, and I am the mouse. It is very ambiguous in an interesting sort of way."

This exchange seems to help the class feel more comfortable with their sense of being somehow off balance, and a man who looks to be mid-career and is at once both open and calculating says,

"My opinion is that you, right now, are being a very effective leader in terms of the definition of leadership that you gave before. Because you said earlier that leadership assists in mobilizing a group to make a hard decision. Now, this is a group that needs to make a decision about whether or not we're going to take this course. And you are leading us to discuss among ourselves what is it about your style of giving the presentation here that is going to entice us to stay or leave. So that's what you're doing. You are exercising leadership according to your definition of leadership. But we also have to figure out whether or not this is a definition of what we would like to be as a leader and whether this is what we're wanting to learn."

The instructor responds,

"That's true. Some of you may not be here with the purpose of learning how to more effectively mobilize people in a community or an organization to take on important problems. You may be here primarily to find out how you can get people to give you more authority or to confer more power upon you. Now, I think that's a valid reason to be in this course, but not a valid reason totally by itself. Because I think knowing how to gain power, to work with power, and how to work with authority is one of the areas that we have to investigate in thinking about leadership. But it's not the whole of it. That's only investigating the instruments. We also have to figure out how to play the instruments. And if you're not interested fundamentally in making music, that is, in serving your communities or serving your organizations or serving your society so as to tackle the tough problems, if really all you're interested in is the instruments, then this course will probably frustrate you."

"Part of my work," acknowledges the instructor, "is to recognize that I am going to frustrate some people's expectations, and I need to do it at a rate they can stand without their killing me off. For example, if you are in a situation where you think people's expectations need to change—let's say, for example, they keep expecting you to behave decisively and to know where you're going. But you realize that the situation calls for experimentation, trying things out, improvisation, the willingness not to know exactly where you're going. Well, how do you get that across to people if people think that means that you're not worthy of authority? In their terminology they'll say, "You're not a leader. You're not being decisive. You're zig-zagging. You're improvising when you're supposed to know where we're going.' So how in that situation, where you don't know where you're going (because nobody does), how are you supposed to say to people, 'Your expectations are wrong. You expect me to know where I'm going. But I need you to trust me to not know where I'm going'?"

An Asian woman asks whether the reading list, which is dominated by white male authors and westerners, suggests that minority members of the class will have to adapt to majority norms.

The instructor responds,

"In the course of this term, you are going to identify all sorts of blind spots, failings, mistakes, and wasted opportunities on my part. And hopefully those will serve as grist for the mill if you learn something about your own blind spots, failure, and wasted opportunities. I don't present myself as having constructed the perfect syllabus or having designed the perfect course, but simply to have provided an environment, a design, that enables all of us to learn from what all of us do."

A woman who appears only partially satisfied with this response joins the conversation:

"I'm very intrigued by this subject, although I have significant concerns with the dynamics that—how close to the dynamic today will the typical class be, or do you usually drive things along more?"

"Sometimes yes, and sometimes less. (Laughter) You have to learn to stomach chaos and confusion if you're going to be leading people in the midst of conflicting values, who are facing hard challenges and engaging in all sorts of avoidance behavior. You're going to have to develop a stomach for that and for not being provided with certainty. So there's a purpose to my letting this be more chaotic than some of you might like."

A man seeking definition says challengingly,

"So this class is about group dynamics as much as leadership?"

The instructor pauses, looks at the challenger with a steady gaze, and responds evenly:

"Being able to diagnose what happens in a social system or in a political system is a critical component of any exercise of leadership. You can't lead without knowing the system you're pushing around."

As the class moves into a second hour, a student over to the left who has been standing in the aisle and leaning against the wall straightens up, takes a step forward, and says,

"I have a problem with some of what we're coming up with. If you look at other kinds of leadership, like if you were to say Jesus was a leader, or any other charismatic type, you wouldn't see characteristics like humility or—well, what I mean is someone like Napoleon, he didn't have a whole lot of humility. You wouldn't describe him as vulnerable or having—and—"

The student seems to be groping but hangs in:

"I think what that goes to is that I don't think I would put 'humility' on my list for this class, because I think in a teaching situation it's not important to me to have a teacher, a professor, who is humble. Maybe self-confidence is more important. But maybe in a work environment, with somebody I work with more interpersonally, humility would be more important."

"Yes," the instructor responds. "We see once again there's not a lot of overlap. One faction wants to see me be humble and another faction wants to see me be self-confident."

"You can be both," says a woman in the first row.

"Well, maybe you can be both," the instructor responds, "but there's not a lot of room for figuring out how to do both. Not in this culture. So what am I supposed to do, invent a new culture quickly?"

The same woman acknowledges, "You can't."

"So I've got to work with what I've got," observes the professor.

A young woman starts to speak, and a student across the room says, "Can't hear you." She starts again at higher volume:

"I guess this goes to maybe another concern I have, and I think it relates to what she is saying—about whether you as the leader or whatever are going to have an open mind about what leadership is and who leaders are. I'm a little concerned from the readings and examples that we're looking at white guys."

She continues,

"I think the majority of the examples in the readings and in class are of people that the press or the history books know about, and I'm sure that there are a lot of leaders that we don't know about in our common culture—"

"So what you're suggesting," responds Heifetz, "is that we ought to make a key distinction between leadership and prominence, or even dominance, or even authority. Leadership is not the same as any of these. That doesn't mean they're mutually exclusive—you might be dominant and exercise leadership. You might even exercise leadership from a position of authority, but you might not—a lot of dominant people don't exercise any leadership. And God knows that a lot of people in positions of authority don't exercise any leadership. But what is leadership if it's not these things when you tend to immediately equate them, as we do in most cultures? People refer to the leadership of the organization, the Congress, the country, or the military—and they are always referring to those people in senior positions of authority. But who knows if they are actually exercising any leadership? All we know is that they have gotten very good at finding out what people expect and how to dive through that hoop where enough peoples' expectations overlap, or at least where the expectations of the critical factions overlap. They know how to gain authority and people give them power.

"Indeed," he continues, "that's all we've been talking about here. We've been talking about what expectations do I need to meet in order to get power from you? If you are going to choose to take this course, you are going to give me some of your attention. Attention is a critical source of power. People vie for attention. You might think of attention as the currency. There are two primary forms of authorization from which you gain attention: the *formal* authorization (in this case of the school), which only gets me in the door, and *informal* authorization that you will or will not choose to give me based on some of the things we have been talking about—competencies and certain sorts of personal accessibility. Humility may not fit for a lot of people. But at least everybody probably will agree that if you're going to give somebody authority, they have to have values that overlap with some of your values. They have to sort of have their heart in the right place. They might be very competent, but they can't abuse your trust."

"But the complexity of authority relationships isn't just a product of the person who's trying to get the authority. What makes authority relationships complicated is that they consist of different publics, constituencies, and factions that each expect you to behave differently and give you authority according to different criteria. (Is he strong? Is he weak? Can she be humble? Will she take a stand and take the punches or will she try to hedge all the time?) So anybody in a position of authority is immediately caught in this bind of whose expectations to frustrate and whose to meet."

A woman in her early thirties thoughtfully asks a question that she seems to have been working on since early in the class session:

"Can you be honest and credible—and effective?"

No hands in the air. The class seems to recognize that an important question has just been laid on the table, and the professor responds in kind:

"If you walk that razor's edge, it can be done. But your feet will get cut up—and you might fall off. Part of our work here is to figure out how to not get too cut up and how not to fall off."

There follows a kind of sober silence, and then a woman sitting on the radiator in the back of the class stands up to make herself visible and heard as she reflects,

"It seems to me that it would be really difficult. I'm just thinking about the position people are in right now, having to think about trying to make a commitment to a course on the basis of something that looks uncertain, given that this is the first day of classes for most people, and we don't know what we're comparing it with. It seems like there are lots of attempts to try and say, give me something that I can put my hands around and say a definite yes or no to. I think that what we're hearing is that doesn't happen; and we're going to each have to struggle to get to our own decision."

The professor responds respectfully:

"Part of the problem is that people know how to learn in particular ways, but this course requires that you stretch how you learn so as to be more similar to the ways you're going to have to learn, or the ways you should have been learning, out in real organizational situations where nobody's telling you what to learn according to an outline, and where *you* have got to put the knowledge together and organize it—because, indeed, there's been a lot of very important ideas that have already been presented here. But for many of you, they've sifted right through your fingers because you don't yet have the capacity to identify those important ideas because they didn't come in a form you were expecting. I didn't present them in a way that could make it a more familiar learning or school process. I didn't say, 'Roman numeral one, [he writes on the board] Authority-Leadership Distinction. Roman numeral two, Influence and Tackling Tough Problems; Roman numeral three, Authority. Point A: A product of expectations. Point B: can be divided into Formal and Informal. You see?' "

A man on the first row heaves a sigh, leans back in his chair, and in a tone of rueful humor says,

"This is how I feel right now. I've just come from a situation where I thought that I was exercising leadership, and I thought that I was accomplishing something that I thought was good for the people I was trying to serve. And everybody hated me [laughter], and I never seemed to do anything that was right. Now I say, 'Well, let me take this leadership course.' (Laughter) And I come in here, and you say to me, 'No, you have to go back through all those things that you were doing wrong in order to learn how to do it right.' So—."

As more tension-releasing laughter ripples across the class, the instructor patiently joins the humor of the moment yet affirms:

"Yes, I know, but I can't think of any encyclopedia for you to learn more from than the encyclopedia of your own failures and successes. If you really can understand what you saw wrong, what you did wrong, what was effective, and what you could have done differently, you'll carry that lesson with you much more than you will carry lessons that are distilled from other people's experiences."

A man who looks maybe forty and very thoughtful observes out loud:

"It dispels the notion that I had—that people had convinced me of—that I was a natural leader, and now I'm really doubting that. And I hear you say, 'No, the notion that leaders are born needs to go out the window.'"

The instructor sends the ball back across the court:

"You're lucky that you're finding this out at a young age."

(Laughter)

The man responds,

"I'm not as young as I look."

(More laughter)

The end of the stated class time is approaching, and a few students begin to leave—either because they have decided this is not the course for them or simply because they have to sprint to the other side of the university for their next class. The instructor acknowledges the legitmacy of people exiting early on the first day, but emphatically lays out some clear ground rules that include arriving on time and not leaving early—"Essential," he says, "in a class in which the class itself is the primary subject matter." He also speaks of "norms of civility" that he trusts the class to operate with.

This causes a woman to remark,

"Related to that question, how about confidentiality, or should we change names and places to respect the people that we worked with and will be talking about during our case studies?"

"That's a tricky question," responds the professor. "I think that would be a good question to take up on Wednesday when we talk in more depth about how the small groups will work and how the case consultations will work."

Then,

"Okay, see you Wednesday."

CHAPTER THREE

What Is Really Going On Here?

Engaging People at the Edge of Learning

"TRICKY" IS WHAT HEIFETZ CALLED the last question put to him in the opening class. Actually, he responded to almost every question as if it were "tricky." What is going on here?

Collision of Worlds

Heifetz and his colleagues have asked the question, Can leadership be taught in a way that comes in under people's long-held habits of thought and action—and under their resistance to what the artistry of adaptive leadership requires? Having taken on the challenge embedded in the question, Heifetz is keenly aware that he is inviting people into a way of understanding and learning leadership that will initially disappoint their expectations.

Thus, what is really going on in the first class session is a collision of worlds. One is the world of "the leader" as typically conceived—a powerful, visionary person in a position of authority who can get people to follow. The other is a practice of leadership that most cannot yet imagine. The instructor is inviting the students into an adventure in which they may learn a completely new understanding of leadership and come to perceive the activity of leadership, and therefore themselves, in a new way. The students bring along a set of expectations that make it tough going.

High, Hard Ground Versus the Swamp

These expectations are embedded in assumptions about what leaders do. Consequently, most people gallop into class on the high, hard ground of an understanding of leadership that is oriented to what Heifetz calls "technical problems"—problems that no matter how complicated can be solved with solutions already in hand.

In contrast, they are being invited to recognize that the challenges they contend with are often best described as "swamp issues." These are the adaptive challenges that contrast with the high, hard ground of technical problems. The students are consistently being invited to discover that increasingly the kind of leadership asked of them is less about power, persuasion, and personality than about the capacity to help a group make progress on the toughest issues that lie in the space between known problems and unknown solutions. These require grappling with competing values, changing attitudes, encouraging new learning, and developing new behavior—among nations, in businesses large and small, in cities, regions, neighborhoods, and other organizations.

Sorting Through Assumptions

In chapter 2, Heifetz frequently refers to the "differing expectations within the group." People are attracted to the subject of leadership for a mix of reasons, and those who teach leadership need to respond to the whole swirling mix. In this context, we find that roughly a third come looking for techniques—skills, tactics, a tool kit. They are interested in what Heifetz calls the instruments" of leadership. They hope to find the right path, discover "how to package the skills I have," or "a recipe that lets you know what you're doing wrong." They hope to learn how to guide and convince according to some yet-unknown formula.

Another third come to sort out career challenges and prospects: Do I have what it takes to move into a larger arena? Which path should I take? Can I learn how to address problems in ways that make a significant difference? (Or simply: Can I get the next promotion or win that office? Can I get people to follow me? Can I prevail?)

The rest include a smaller number who express what others may also feel. They are looking for validation of their competence. If they are still relatively young, they may simply expect further confirmation that they are destined for success as "a leader type." If they are somewhat older, they have practiced leadership as they understand it, but are unsure about how effective they were. They are searching for good company that will affirm their identity and their efforts.

Charisma and Power

Typically, there is also another dynamic at play. Underlying the hope for concrete tools, clues to life questions, and confirming company, there lurks the quiet fear that finally leadership is simply a matter of charisma—an elusive quality you either have or you don't. "Charisma" (meaning graced or favored—even divinely so) is presumed to be a leader's inborn gift, linking leadership with both profound and profane hopes for a more meaningful, successful, animated, and even spiritual life.

Questions of leadership are intimately linked with questions of power, and charisma is one way of talking about power. Along with the needs for belonging and recognition, human beings need some sense of power—the capacity to affect one's world. For some, power is associated with the desire to overcome, dominate, win—a sense of personal freedom and control. Still others settle for vicarious power—association with people perceived as powerful. Human beings are perennially fascinated with claiming power, wresting power away, exercising power, avoiding power, wielding power, sharing power, maintaining power, and handing power over.

Classroom as Studio

Heifetz and his colleagues are wrestling with a somewhat different set of questions. In response, they have concluded that if the new global commons where those who offer leadership must now contend with a myriad of significant challenges is complex, diverse, and fraught with ambiguity, then the space devoted to learning effective leadership for such a world might be usefully similar—a bit of a swamp itself. Accordingly, the learning milieu they have created can be understood best as the combination of a traditional classroom (row upon row of a well-cultivated field) and a laboratory or studio (a less orderly but yeasty place).

Colleen Burke, a business professor and sometime art student, has observed that in contrast to her regular classroom, in the art studio no one expects a lecture. Teachers do not necessarily stand and students do not necessarily sit. Students observe each other's work, exchange insights, and return to their canvases to try again. Mistakes are not seen as failures; they are encouraged and rewarded as inevitable steps in an ongoing learning process that requires trial and error. The teacher moves among the students giving clues that become meaningful knowledge only if they work in the experience of the students.

In the art studio, they are given assignments such as, "paint a matrix of one hundred grays of incremental value and tone, never using black." Burke wonders, "What assignments can I give that would help my business students to see the grays between the inevitable either/or of black-and-white analysis?"

Everything in the art studio seems to reinforce the student's responsibility for learning—and for taking risks. Burke reflects, "My business classroom, several hundred yards across the campus, seems worlds away. Can I carry any piece of this experience across that distance?" [1]

A Bridge Across That Distance

Case-in-point teaching for adaptive leadership works to build a bridge across that distance. Although some aspects of this approach fit within the frame of conventional classroom expectations, others function to create a kind of studio-lab space: a space for practice, experimentation, performance, and learning—a place where a whole range of grays come into view as students work the canvas of their leadership hungers and habits.

Experience and readiness differ, often significantly, among learners. Thus, part of what is going on here rests in the deep conviction that people—and particularly adults—learn from their own experiences at the edge of their own readiness to learn. As it has been developed in this instance, case-in-point teaching seeks to bring action and reflection together in the most immediate way possible for each person. From the beginning, students are encouraged to see the class itself as a social system of which they are a part and a studio-laboratory in which they can practice acts of leadership and learn from their experiments.

The Dance Floor and the Balcony

One of the central metaphors used to anchor the process of this approach is the image of moving between the dance floor and the balcony. "Imagine," Heifetz will suggest, "you are on a dance floor, swept up in the dance, an active participant in a complex scene. There are some things about the dance that you will only know by actually dancing. But if you move to the balcony for a while, you can see things that you can never discover on the dance floor—the larger pattern of interactions of which you are a part. You gain perspective and can make new choices."

This is one way of talking about action and reflection, practice and theory. The learning milieu is designed to encourage students to move continually back and forth between the dance floor and the balcony. The intent is that they will begin to learn what they most need to see in the midst of a dynamic social context and harvest insights that do not present themselves in neat, outline form. Rather they emerge primarily as student-practitioners learn to read in real time the political-economic, cultural-historical, and psychosocial patterns of which they are a part.

In the first session, the instructor is modeling this capacity as he speaks of "identifying the primary concern of the group" and the risks of speaking to it directly. In this case-in-point, there are several primary concerns. One concern is how many people will be admitted to the course and by what process. Another concern is what the course will be like. And just beneath the surface (where the biggest concerns often dwell), there are yet other concerns—particularly questions of whether or not the instructor is qualified as an authority and trustworthy in the practice of teaching leadership.

Indeed, a key feature of what is really going on is that the instructor is mindful that most of the group equate *authority* with *leadership* and depend on his functioning within that expectation. He is working to tease apart this simple equation by frustrating some of their expectations. He does this by giving the work back to the group—without abandoning them. The students are thereby invited to puzzle things out for themselves and strengthen their own capacity for discernment and judgment rather than passively taking in what they expect to hear and blaming others for negative outcomes. They are encouraged to notice the subtle, powerful, and unexamined expectations they hold (and to recognize that those same expectations are present also in most of the situations in which they seek to lead). They discover that they are responsible for a decision they must make themselves, while at the same time the instructor conveys that the decisions they make about leadership in any of its aspects are apt to be very important. He uses humor, but he does not take the subject lightly.

What Is Really Going on Here—the Deep Work

The deep work that underlies all of the learning is a yet more profound shift. This is a shift in epistemology, in how we "know." This shift entails a transformation of the relationship of self and world, a shift of consciousness, a shift in how we see. It includes a shift in how we relate to authority. Across the last several decades, there has been a growing recognition that as human beings continually make meaning (i.e., make sense, compose and recompose reality) across the life span, we may grow in our capacity to apprehend greater degrees of complexity. We may develop a more adequate sense of what is "me and not me"—or what is subject and what is object.[2] We humans do this by developing more comprehensive and integrated structures of thought and feeling that hold and shape what we understand as true and untrue.

Robert Kegan has described these structures of knowing as "orders of consciousness" that evolve in a predictable sequence throughout our lifetimes.[3] We observe this evolution when we watch a grade school child move from concrete knowing (second order of consciousness) to becoming an adolescent who can begin to think more abstractly and symbolically, moving into a larger set of relationships (third order of consciousness), and becoming an adult within the tribe.[4]

It has been normative for most adults—even many who are well educated and trained—to function in this third order of consciousness that I have described elsewhere as "Authority-bound and dependent," and others have described as "received knowledge."[5] In this mode of knowing, people think and work primarily within an interpersonal, tribal frame, and depend on trusted, unexamined Authority. This form of authority may be located in a single person, but it is usually composed from what we receive in our everyday actions with others—conventional thinking mediated by the authority of our social milieu and perceived as simply "the ways things are," as shaped by family, friends, colleagues, the media, religious tradition, cultural norms, school and corporate cultures, and so on.

The challenge in our time is that as our world becomes more complex, the normative ways in which many adults make meaning are increasingly inadequate—whether we are dealing with workplace demands, with questions of how to vote in national elections, or the relationships within our households. More is now asked of us, and as one of Kegan's book titles aptly describes it, we are *In Over Our Heads*.[6] In this new reality, everyone—including and perhaps particularly those in positions of authority—is vulnerable to being merely swept up in a dance of unexamined assumptions and blind to the larger patterns of which we are a part. Swamp issues require us to recognize interdependent systems—to connect more of the dots—opening our eyes to the intricate web of connections among seemingly discrete populations, organizations, actions, and events.

Thus, when Heifetz invites people to get on the balcony to observe larger patterns, he is calling for a major cognitive and affective achievement—the development of a fourth order of consciousness. He is encouraging the development of a critical, systemic, and holistic perspective. He is inviting people out of their own minds—to think about their thinking. He is offering an initiation into a systemic perspective in which everything is hitched to everything else and where a merely interpersonal mode of thinking and acting isn't enough. The unexamined assumption of authoritative control is inappropriate in this new reality, where one must govern and lead though the artful management of a vast net of relationships. As David Gergen, who has served six presidents of the United States, has observed, "A president should see himself as the center of a web." [7]

Thinking Systemically

Peter Senge has written, "Systems thinking is a discipline for seeing wholes. It is a framework for seeing interrelationships rather than things, for seeing patterns of dynamic relationships rather than static 'snapshots' . . . Systems thinking is a sensibility—for the subtle interconnectedness that gives living systems their unique character." [8] Ecological perspectives are teaching us that swamp issues can be best understood as constellations of multiple interdependent systems that are both fragile and often surprisingly resilient. Dealing with only a single element is often not only naive but perilous. Small communities, large corporations, and cities, along with any product, project, or initiative are each a part of a vast web of interdependent systems. [9] Yet every day, leaders within these complex contexts are inclined to focus solely on their project or their sector at most, assuming that they can change things if they could just get the ear of those who seem to be in charge. Their inability to use a more complex and systemic mode of analysis blocks their access to more comprehensive and effective forms of perception, interpretation, and action. They cannot find the leverage points. A practice of leadership that does not include at its heart the capacity to get on the balcony and think systemically is no match for the world in which we now live.[10]

The approach to learning leadership that we are examining here is designed to relentlessly reveal the strengths and the limitations of the individual within social systems and encourage, therefore, a transformation of one's understanding of power within the social group. Everyone has power, but only the power to participate in conscious or unconscious ways in relationship to the profound connectivity of which we are all a part. This way of seeing reveals the illusion of command-and-control assumptions.

It is difficult, however, to develop this awareness at the level of "default settings"—perhaps especially for those who think of themselves as leaders. Our culture tells us we are autonomous. Actually, we are each an integral part of multiple systems. The challenge is to reflect critically on our reality, learn to see the patterns, and recognize how context driven people are, that is, how much people are shaped by the expectations of their social milieu. Within a culture that celebrates individualism, it is easy for people to presume that they are or should be in charge, essentially unaffected by the systems of which they are a part—making their own decisions and shaping their environments rather than being shaped by them.[11] In a prior study, for example, I asked students at Harvard Business School (many of whom were notably context driven) if they thought that people are affected by their social contexts. Typically, they readily affirmed that to be the case. Yet when I asked them if they themselves or their peers were significantly affected by their social context, they quickly reversed this perception, believing that they were exceptions.[12]

Perhaps it is not surprising, therefore, that in my several years of observing students as they worked with Heifetz and his colleagues, nothing was more disturbing to the students as a group than the admittedly provocative suggestion that when they are in a position of formal authority, they have virtually no autonomy. So strong are the forces acting on them to maintain the equilibrium of the social system, they are essentially only puppets on a string. Challenging them, Heifetz would declare, "Thus, you may make only two or three 'free choices' in your lifetime."

In these and other ways, students are given multiple opportunities to discover how they may be, indeed, puppets on a string, swept up in the dance, and acted on by the dramas of others in ways that challenge their assumptions about what is really going on. They also learn that behaviors they assume to be benign may have more effect within the group than they had supposed. This process has the force of disrupting the third order of consciousness. It does so by challenging their unexamined trust in Authority and thus questioning the power and control of the leader as conventionally understood. Authority is no longer ultimate. Whether held by oneself or others, the powers of authority become a significant but limited resource in the practice of leadership. This shift presses toward the development of Kegan's "fourth order of consciousness," or what I have described elsewhere as "critical, inner-dependent, systemic thought."[13] The invitation here is to the formation of conscious commitment in the face of partial knowledge, rather than unexamined certainty within an uncertain world. It constitutes a new way of seeing, thinking, and knowing.

The Cost of New Thinking

This is a profound shift because it fosters a greater capacity to see the big picture, recognize complex patterns, perceive the functions of authority as only one valuable resource in the practice of leadership, and reorder one's sense of power and purpose, but it comes at a cost. In earlier ways of thinking and acting, there is less to take into account. One's world can be perceived as "manageable." In contrast, within a systemic view, one's world becomes larger, more complex, less manageable, and one is vulnerable to feeling overwhelmed, diminished, and less secure.

As this way of seeing and thinking begins to loom into view, one's notions of both leadership and ethics undergo reconstruction. Within an Authority-bound, tribal, and interpersonal frame, one can determine more easily what is true and untrue and who and what is good and bad, harmful or not. In a systemic view, one has to give up the trust that Authority somehow knows and that one can either defer to or aspire to becoming the Authority that knows. Questions of truth and questions of good and evil, right and wrong, dangerous or benign, become more complex and ambiguous. Within an Authority-bound, interpersonal frame, one can imagine one's self as a good self who does not intend harm. Within a systemic, holistic view, one has to give up the good self for the complicit self—an integral, responsible part of the fabric of the wider commons for both good and ill.

One's sense of power begins to be reordered: on the one hand, you are less in charge. Yet, within a radically interdependent world every action has some effect, so one's actions (even when modest) may have more effect than was previously supposed.[14] Thus, one's sphere of responsibility is enlarged. One discovers again and again that the practice of leadership occurs within a more vast, complex, and dynamic world—where knowledge is always partial and the outcomes of one's actions uncertain. For many, this is a step into a new understanding of reality that calls for an enlarged measure of both humility and courage. This way of seeing is increasingly vital to citizenship in democratic societies and to leadership everywhere in our complex world.

A Crucible for Transformative Learning

The process of this deep transformation in the relationship of self and world requires a strong holding environment.[15] There needs to be a sturdy, trustworthy space that can hold the difficult and intimate work of changing one's mind. Thus, despite the seemingly free-wheeling character of case-in-point teaching and learning, a central aspect of what is really going on in chapter 2 is the creation of a holding environment, or what Heifetz describes simply as a "container," designed to serve a process of significant transformation—adaptive work. If people are going to move from one way of seeing and behaving to another, they need to be in a context—in a social culture—that will hold them in a trustworthy way and keep them focused and working on the issues, even and especially when it gets uncomfortable.

In this instance, a part of the holding environment is built on the practice of a traditional classroom—a syllabus, a presiding teacher, teaching assistants, lecture or presentation, films, case studies, discussion, reading assignments, writing assignments, term papers, grades. This structure is further strengthened by the creation of certain norms within the class as a group. For example, near the close of the opening class, Heifetz, who as the instructor and designated authority must be part of the holding environment, lays out clear expectations about students' arriving on time and not leaving early. This is one way of creating the boundaries that form the container that might more accurately be described in relationship to this particular learning process as a crucible, a container that can withstand unusually high heat in the service of transformation.

This crucible for the formation of adaptive leadership is forged also by the artful use of time and space that creates a range of opportunities for both engagement and reflection. The large class (observed in chapter 2) meets for two hours twice a week. But it would be a mistake to assume that this constitutes the course. Rather, these sessions serve as the hub of an ecology of studio-labs—small consultation group meetings and a set of weekly study questionnaires and other written assignments (see chapter 4), extra evening sessions (see chapter 5), informal conversations, and scheduled appointments—all taking place around the large class sessions.

The value of a multifaceted structure is that it provides varying contexts and modes of learning that conspire to meet the needs of differing people for both comfort and stretch. It helps each individual to experience what he or she is prepared to learn next and provides opportunities also to compare the consequences of the same action in differing arenas. Managing this kind of learning milieu is a bit like managing multiple pots on a stovetop. In this instance, it also includes teaching assistant (TA) sessions—a less visible but vital element of the learning ecology and a key girder in the structure of the holding environment.

The Teaching Staff

In this model, a circle of five or six teaching assistants meets with the instructor for an hour before and after every class session.[16] This studio-lab has a dual purpose: (1) to track and support the learning of the students individually and collectively, and (2) to be a locus of ongoing learning for the TAs—and the instructor. Case-in-point teaching requires phenomenal alertness, and it is illusory to believe that one can optimally hold a large group, read the myriad of behaviors accurately, and respond appropriately and productively all by oneself. The TAs provide additional sets of eyes and ears—the balcony to the instructor's dance floor interventions. Over time they learn to intervene more effectively themselves.

When the teaching team gathered before one of the first meetings of the course, Heifetz, conveyed the importance of their role:

> Thank you for joining this team. The course changes every year because the students are different and this team is different. But the constant in the midst of the change, and the reason why the course is important, is that people come here to make a difference out there. People bring passions and purposes. We help them be more effective. We help them develop discipline, analytic awareness, and strategic action.

Our job is to hold people through a process. We structure the course so people can learn from their experiences and from the experience of others. It is not our job to do therapy. We are educational strategists who coordinate resources for these people so as to provide a structure in which they can learn.

People will learn the best depending on how well we work together as a group. We must create a holding environment that they can use It is like a pressure cooker, but it must also be a safe place in which each one can have a voice—and we have to model it. We need to give each other license to enjoy this work and breathe together—not hold our breath. We will make them anxious if we are anxious. They need to take risks, and if the stakes are too high, they can't. The smaller groups will mirror the larger group. We ourselves are a case–in–point. We will gain insight into the larger group as we learn from problem to problem among us.

Throughout the process of the course, the instructor asks the teaching team questions such as these: "What are the (adaptive) challenges that are emerging in the class this week?" "What are the issues among us that may give us clues to what is going on in the class?" or, "How is the theme for this week (e.g. managing conflict, assassination, holding steady, or creativity) manifest in the current life of the class?"

Learning as Theory in Practice

This approach is an ongoing experiment in teaching and learning in a manner that is congruent with the theory of leadership that is being taught. The teaching staff works to serve as a model of what adaptive leadership requires. For example, in the opening class (chapter 2), Heifetz does not respond to the concern about how people would be admitted to the course until after

"Gretchen found an ally." This exchange illustrates what will become an explicit teaching point: adaptive leadership requires partners, allies, and confidants—for perspective, support, information, building coalitions, and sometimes to draw fire. As they work together in the course, the TAs and the instructor are both teaching and modeling the art of partnership.

An Emerging Framework

As this process of case-in-point teaching continues, a framework for analysis, diagnosis, and intervention begins to emerge. It is most visible and focused in the working of student cases in the large class sessions (while the class itself remains a case-in-point). Heifetz invites the student and the class as a whole to reflect on the student's case and to suggest what might have created a more positive outcome. Then, as needed, he speaks directly to the case, using the framework that is being taught, presented primarily in the form of questions, because questions require people to think for themselves rather than deferring to authority. Such questions include these: What is the purpose of the organization, agency, or enterprise? What is the task? Is this a technical problem or an adaptive challenge? Where is the adaptive work located? What are the various factions? Who has formal and informal authority? What forces are acting upon them? Who represents what issues? What is the history of the issue? Where are the partnerships and alliances (actual and possible)? As the student presenting the case and other members of the class work with these questions, the instructor and the chalk go to work, and the system is informally mapped on the board, bringing alternative perspectives and actions into view.

In these and other ways, the teaching staff continually makes accessible the theoretical elements of the approach—concepts and ideas—often distilled as short phrases or metaphors. Some of these are: what needs to be learned and who needs to learn it, thinking politically, focusing attention on the issue, ripening the issue, pacing the work, regulating the heat, taking the heat, walking the razor's edge, holding steady, remaining curious, staying alive, giving the work back to the group, disappointing people at a rate they can bear—thus helping the class to begin to see what they most need to see.[17] As Heifetz has expressed it, "In case-in-point teaching, the concepts are the enzymes for digesting what is happening in the class."

Learning to See the Patterns

This approach to teaching leadership cultivates the practice of learning to read key patterns in social systems that are critical to the art of leadership in a complex world—or as Ellen Schall has put it, "making sense of the mess."[18] Key patterns include the role and functions of authority and the challenges to authority; factions within the social group; regulating the heat required to do the work; work avoidance activity; loss and grief; and challenges to the self.

The Role of Authority and Challenges to Authority

As the class serves as a case-in-point of predicable patterns within a social system, issues that are alive within the group begin to surface, and the expectations that people have of those who are in authority begin to surface. In chapter 2, Heifetz recognized early on that there were both explicit and unarticulated expectations relating to his credibility and competence.

In most adult groups, people are in varying places in the journey from Authority-bound, dependent thinking to critical, inner-dependent thought. Thus there are typically some who strongly feel a need for the person in authority to control the situation, others who want to partner with authority, and still others who are ambivalent.

Remarkably, there is inevitably at least one person who wants to challenge, if not overthrow ("kill off"), the person in the position of formal authority. Sometimes the challenge comes from someone who positions himself or herself directly across from the person holding authority. Other times, the challenge is more akin to sniper fire.

Those who would lead need to become aware of how and when to use the functions of authority to respond to these differing postures. In case-in-point teaching, the instructor cultivates this awareness in students by practicing in real time the functions of authority (e.g., orientation, direction, norm setting, conflict resolution, and protection) that maintain equilibrium in the social system—the learning milieu.

To help students discover both the need for authority in the social group and that authority is only one resource in the practice of leadership, the instructor may step out of the room for a brief period. The students then experience how difficult it is for someone else to establish authority within the group (though several will make the attempt) and the subsequent descent into chaos if there is no authorized governance.

In such a contest, multiple interpretations of "what is really happening" abound, and there is plenty of grist for the learning mill as people muddle and sort out their feelings of frustration, helplessness, desires for authority, resistance to authority, what it takes to gain authority (either formal or informal), their own willingness or unwillingness to take up authority, and how and why they respond as they do. All of this provides good swamp conditions within which one can begin to learn to read critical patterns.

What is really going on here is that the instructor is practicing what leadership requires. In real time, the instructor is doing an analysis of what is happening, using a kind of "sonar" to search out important issues hidden beneath the surface, looking into the depths for what is really taking place, detecting the implicit, unspoken dynamics, and cultivating the ability and poise to risk naming what would otherwise remain unspoken and undigested, yet powerful. The instructor's job is neither to foster dependency on his authority nor to push people away but, rather, to recognize inappropriate dependencies and work to transform them. The instructor both reads the norms and challenges the norms, disappointing expectations but in the process helping people to see what they haven't seen before.

Factions

Another predictable pattern within human groups is the coalescence of individuals into factions in the midst of the seeming chaos. The ability to identify and orchestrate the interaction among the factions is a crucial competence.

As observed in chapter 2, as the instructor "reads the group out loud," he is "teaching" that it is important to recognize the differing factions, each representing distinctive needs and expectations. Students are encouraged to see how the interactions among the factions are more critical than the interaction among individuals per se. (In fact, the instructor presumes that the concern of any single student may represent at least 10 to 20 percent of the class.) Students are encouraged to recognize the various forces that play on each faction, as well as on the people who are trying to manage all those interactions—that is, those in positions of authority and those who are trying to lead.

There is no shortage of factions in a classroom setting, particularly as students begin to use the space as a practice lab. From an instructor point of view,

> there is a faction that wants to challenge you and a faction that wants to defend you. Another faction may be sitting it out as an intellectual activity, and though curious, they aren't learning because they don't have the courage to put their feet into the work. I have to find a way to provoke and

engage them at the risk of alienating them. There is often an ethnic faction that is feeling unheard by some part of the group, and they risk marginalizing themselves instead of engaging and making progress on the issues that matter to them. And there may be another faction with civil rights, military, or executive experience that thinks they know more than anyone else about leadership because of what they have done. Another faction may be upset in response to someone's incendiary remark. There is always a faction that is older, and a faction that is younger. My work as the authority who is also trying to lead is to hold them all, and to respond in ways that surface what is lurking under each faction, help the class to see the class as a system, and keep everyone learning the framework of analysis that we are trying to teach using the class as case-in-point.[19]

Regulating the Heat

The art of adaptive leadership also depends on the ability to regulate the temperature—the heat—required to promote adaptive work. As one discovers the factions and the conflicts among students, the work of leadership is to keep the heat of the conflict within a productive range—a key feature of what is referred to in this approach as *orchestrating the conflict*. If the crucible is something like a pressure cooker and the heat gets too high, the whole thing explodes. If it is too low, no work gets done. Students begin to discover that the instructor regulates the heat in the class in a variety of ways. The heat is turned up by giving people more responsibility than they are comfortable with, bringing conflicts to the surface, and by protecting gadflies and oddballs. The heat can be lowered by such means as addressing technical aspects of the problem, breaking the problem into parts, creating decision rules, using humor, and otherwise slowing down the process of challenging norms and expectations.

One of the ways of orchestrating competing factions into a shared harmonic on behalf of common work is to raise the question of deep purpose and to direct attention to worthy challenges that can enlist everyone's full attention and passion. Again, the leadership classroom is a microcosm of the world at large in this regard. Consider, for instance, the phenomenon of people with impressive resumes who, rather than engaging the hard work of the matter at hand, retreat instead into arrogant and nonproductive demonstrations of their expertise. When similarly a faction in the class acted in this way, reorienting them again to purpose, Heifetz reminded them, "The great challenges of our time such as the globalization of markets, hunger, proliferation of armaments, terrorism, and international health crises are larger and more daunting than anyone in this room (including the instructor) has the capacity to effectively address. This suggests that everyone here could be usefully engaged in learning more about the practice of leadership."

Work Avoidance

The question of purpose creates a perspective from which habits such as focusing on the authority figure begin to be perceived as both relevant and—often—a great distraction. As the instructor continues to identify patterns and make ideas and metaphors available to interpret what is happening in the complex experience of trying to exercise leadership, often a key indicator of what is really going on is *work avoidance activity*—the strong, understandable temptation in the face of the conflict, anxiety, and pain of adaptive work to deflect attention from the real issues and displace responsibility from the stakeholders themselves. This can take forms such as trying to find a technical solution, blaming authority, creating a scapegoat, creating some other distraction, insistence on maintaining established procedures, or simply tuning out. Thus, as Heifetz has put it, "a key question in the practice of leadership becomes:

How can one counteract the expected work avoidances and help people learn despite resistance?" He observes that although adaptive work is typically avoided, it is usually not avoided deliberately. It is often unconscious. So, again, adaptive leadership requires learning to look beneath the surface. The concept of work avoidance activity provides a lens that brings a whole array of seemingly chaotic behaviors into focus as a discernable and powerful pattern and opens a new way of thinking and responding.[20]

Loss and Grief

A major reason for resistance to adaptive work is that it almost always includes loss and grief. Heifetz and Linsky have written, "People do not resist change, per se. People resist loss."[21] It is always a poignant moment when a case is being worked that requires students for the first time to recognize that they have been caught up in various modes of avoiding this aspect of adaptive work. For example, one of the students presented a labor case in which she failed to achieve what she believed the situation truly required. But both she and the class felt stuck in the analysis. As the instructor spoke to what the people in the case were experiencing, the student began to glimpse, along with the class as a whole, that a strategic part of what was needed was the willingness and the ability to deliver bad news, to compassionately help the group to bear disappointment, and to honor a bereavement process without precluding ongoing adaptive work.

For many, recognizing and managing grief and loss is a new concept. In such a moment, Heifetz may pause to let the point sink in, and then deepen it by offering a corresponding example from another conflict, perhaps on another scale and in another time frame. He might, for instance, make reference to the conflict between the Palestinians and Israelis, the adaptive work of building a viable peace, and what Jews and Palestinians will each have to grieve—the loss not only of property, but also deeply held beliefs and precious dreams, including elements of heritage and identity. Students begin to see and experience how adaptive leadership calls, in part, for a skillful blend of both empathy and strategy.

Challenges to the Self

Learning the practice of adaptive leadership presents a distinctive set of challenges to each person. A strength of this approach is that people according to their need and readiness have opportunity to discover some of their particular blind spots, deficits in their experience, and the consequences of acting merely from their own default settings. For example, if a student is constantly speaking, the instructor might remind the student of the importance of getting on the balcony to observe the complex patterns and perhaps speak more strategically as a result. In a yet more confrontational mode, the instructor might interrupt someone who has repeatedly spoken ineffectively and say, "Are you aware that two-thirds of the class isn't listening to you?" Students are also encouraged to "use yourself as a barometer of what is happening in the group." That is, they are invited to notice what they are feeling and perceiving and to test whether this is their experience alone or whether it is an indicator of what is occurring in the system. Thus, if they are bored, agitated, or bewildered, this may be a source of important data, not simply about their own particular state of being, but about the group as a whole or some faction within it.

As students are invited in these ways to learn by moving between the dance floor and the balcony, getting on the dance floor is in itself a challenge for some. One person early in her experience of the course told me, "I find myself on the balcony as an observer, and I'm getting enormous value out of that. But it just looks like such a fray that I'm not so inclined to jump in. Frankly, I think the ability to do that is exactly what would be good for me to develop throughout the rest of the course."

In contrast, another person discovered the value of stepping back from the fray. He realized that in his family he had learned to prevail in an argument through sheer endurance if necessary, talking at the same time as anyone and everyone else. After the course, he reflected, "I found that I couldn't listen, even if I stopped speaking. I found the course tremendously useful because instead of just thinking about what I'm going to say on a particular point, I started developing tactics, which is a lot more fun for one thing, but also a lot more useful. I'm beginning to see that good interventions are a product of good listening." In these and other ways, students learn to recognize the self as a resource—not to be squandered.

Intervening Productively

It is not enough to learn how to read the patterns within a social system and simply make a diagnosis. If someone is going to practice acts of leadership within that system, he or she needs to discover how to intervene to help the organization or community to move to a new place—mobilizing people to address adaptive work productively. This requires learning that within a system there may be many points of leverage, and thus you may be able to exercise leadership understood in these terms from wherever you sit. The art is to be able to analyze the system and then intervene with some word, gesture, or other action (or strategic non-action) that creates productive movement in the life and work of the group—and then to reflect on the consequences in a way that will reliably inform ongoing action.

An African-American woman who works in educational reform recalled a moment in the course, for example, that became a critical turning point for her. As she described it, she had instigated a flare-up in the group by telling "two white guys" that they were taking up too much space and getting off the subject. After her comment, a number of students spoke and she listened, "really wanting to hear what they had to say." "Then," she told us, "it came to a point where I think they had said what they had to say, and Heifetz looked at me, and it was like, 'Do you want to say something now? That would be good.' So, inside myself, I said, 'Yeah.'"

And I began to talk, but I don't remember exactly what I said. I remember I disclosed more about myself than I had before, and about what things meant, and I made connections with the people who had spoken. In that moment, I began to feel that I had been given an opportunity to handle something. I could mess it up, and it wouldn't be so bad, or I could really try to do something with this. And I felt like I really did my best, and I felt great. I felt I had moved to another place, but it wasn't just me. I moved to another place, and the class and I moved to another place—as a group. And that was heaven, because it could have been horrible. But it wasn't.

It helped me become more visible in the group, and it helped me see the group more clearly. The invisibility that I had experienced was one of ignorance. When people don't know a lot about you, they don't have a lot to use against you. That's the protective part. But they also don't know a lot about how to help you either, so no one can stand with you, really . . . You have to be visible in order to get what you want. That was really a major turning point for me. It was like the doors of information had swung open, and I had gotten ten eyeballs-full. It was a whole other way of looking at things, and I can't think of another place where I could have had that experience and learned what I learned, without suffering a tremendous cost.

I asked, "Can you describe your sense of being in a different place—how is the new place different than the place before?"

Well, the place that I moved to was more open. I was feeling really confined, so periodically I would sort of act out because I'd get tired, I would get a cramp, and I would move. But when we *all* moved, the place that I moved to felt much more open. I felt that things were possible—there were possibilities.

And then it was like, "Oh, my God, I can't do these things any more." But then there was a period of sort of going back and forth, holding onto what I had gotten, and letting go of what I couldn't do anymore—what I didn't want to do anymore.

"What was it you didn't want to do anymore?" I asked.

Sort of flippantly incite people, an underhanded work avoidance technique. But that was actually using race in a way that deflected attention from the real race issues at hand, rather than focusing the attention on them constructively . . . The alternative is to try to develop strategies that are connected to what people do that allow me to stay in a place of possibilities instead of descending into an arena of fruitless conflict.

The primary commitment underlying the course design is to enable the discovery of the power of complex social systems and to develop the capacity to recognize, effectively analyze, and strategically intervene to mobilize constructive change. A more complex, artful, and demanding practice of leadership comes into view when one is able to see the interdependent features of a whole field of action as the nature of the reality in which people must act. To know that it is possible to intervene productively even though one cannot fully control the outcome is to discover a new relationship between self and world.

A Bridge Across That Distance

Case-in-point teaching engages people on the lively and disturbing edge of their own learning because it encourages a high degree of active participation. It meets people where they are and then builds a bridge across that distance between the assumptions about leadership that most students hold and a practice of leadership that can more adequately address the adaptive work of complex organizations and societies undergoing dramatic change.

In contrast to teaching as telling, this more interactive approach fosters a discovery process in which essential features of adaptive leadership and what it requires appear as observations, interpretations, concepts, images, metaphors, and stories that are woven into a case-in-point teaching process. Theory emerges from reflection on practice and an analytical framework comes into form, as repeatedly there is an encounter between the students' experience and the idea.

This kind of learning can seem long, confusing, and frustrating. It does require time and practice. It also requires more than the experience of a large group working together as a case-in-point. As will become clear in the following chapter, small group work that focuses on experiences of leadership failure—providing reflection and practice on another scale—also plays a vital role in the art of learning, practicing, and teaching adaptive leadership.

CHAPTER FOUR

Learning from Failure in Public

The Power of Small Group Consultation

I N THE OPENING CLASS, Heifetz sent an important signal when he said, "I can't think of any encyclopedia for you to learn more from than the encyclopedia of your own failures and successes." The conviction that adults learn best from their own experience and that experiences of failure are a potent source of curricular material takes case-in-point teaching to the tender and fertile core where optimal learning dwells.

When a person holding formal authority is presumed to be the leader, there are enormous pressures to finesse failure and rarely, if ever, to admit to making a mistake. Since he or she is expected to maintain or restore equilibrium within the social group, acknowledging failure may appear to threaten that equilibrium by undermining trust and credibility. In a society where expertise is a highly valued coin of the realm and competition is keen, failure puts job security and livelihood in jeopardy and can evoke feelings of shame, guilt, disappointment, powerlessness, bewilderment, and remorse. It can also pose a threat to belonging and inclusion—fundamental human needs. The politics of the market and workplace conspire with one's own defensive powers to build resistance to the opportunity to learn from failure. It appears easier, even apparently required, to seek any available rationale that will place the responsibility and blame elsewhere. So powerful are these forces in some sectors of society that when asked to describe an experience of failure, one successful young man responded: "I think I would have difficulty recognizing failure in my life." Then, with remarkable candor he added, "or at least that is what my wife tells me."[1]

Other sectors of society are less adverse to an engagement with failure. Artists and scientists, for instance, regard it as a natural part of the dialogue with their chosen medium and integral to the pursuit of excellence. Though initially mistakes may be discouraging, they can morph into a gift when they bring to light novel ways of proceeding. Similarly, in the artistry of adaptive leadership, bringing experiences of significant failure into the light of multiple perspectives and a framework of systemic analysis can open up angles of vision that yield new insight, recompose reality, and invite new understanding and action. This process is vital to learning and critical in the formation of adaptive leadership, and there is a need to build a culture that can handle reflection on failure.

Another Scale of Action

Learning at this level of vulnerability requires a smaller scale of social interaction—at least initially. The large class such as was described in chapters 2 and 3 provides a learning forum on a scale that suggests a company, division, legislature, or a hearing at City Hall. The large group provides an arena of confusion and complexity that serves as an initiation into the work of discovering patterns within the big picture and learning how to intervene in a multisystemic field. A small group—ideally six to ten people—is more akin to working with a task force, a board, a small business, a design team, or an executive cabinet where matters are apt to become up close and personal. Most situations calling for adaptive leadership require competence within both scales of action.

Every student, therefore, is required to participate in a small group dedicated to practice, practice, practice. The practice is a blend of experimentation and reflection—both of which are difficult to claim in today's busy societies. A small group provides a concentrated, somewhat more manageable studio-lab in which to reflect critically on one's own practice of leadership both past and present, and to place it in dialogue with the theoretical perspective that is being taught This more concentrated, carefully designed, and highly structured venue serves as a balcony to the large group, and the two in tandem provide a two-dimensional experience of the same approach to learning leadership and thus a more complex field of action and reflection.

The small group appears safer to many, but in a small group, it is also more difficult to just sit it out, thus heightening the possibility of moving from passive observation to real engagement. Students have an opportunity to be in direct, sustained dialogue with other learning colleagues, hearing cases from many different contexts—in this instance from all over the world.

The small groups serve the process of learning the art of adaptive leadership in three primary ways: (1) they set up a dialogue with failure, (2) they require trying out several different roles, (3) they are the focus of disciplined written reflection that sets one's own experience in conversation with the concepts being taught.

Dialogue with Failure

A vital feature of the practice of adaptive leadership is the capacity to take corrective action. This requires continual learning in dialogue with one's own mistakes, missed opportunities, and disappointments that inevitably occur when one is working on the edge of known problems and unclear solutions. Accordingly, for each session, one member of the group is assigned to be a case presenter (CP), presenting a case of his or her own leadership failure.

A Case Study Guide asks the CP to write a brief description of the case and present it as an engaging story, allowing ample time for consultation. In thinking about the case, the CP is encouraged to use suggested questions drawn from the framework that is being taught (another form in which there is the possibility of a meeting between the student's experience and the idea). Students are also encouraged to develop one or two questions that they think will yield the consultation they most need. Thus, the CP has the opportunity to practice distilling relevant material from a complex situation and deciding what critical information the group will need to be able to respond in useful ways. People dealing with swamp issues need to discern what is essential and know how to ask for help. Asking for help runs counter to the heroic myth of leadership, so learning how to ask for and respond to good consultation provides a new and significant domain of learning for many people.

The task of the other members of the small group is to give good consultation so the CP will begin to see new options for diagnosis and action. This also provides an opportunity for every member of the group to learn how to listen, to intervene, and to hold steady to promote the work of the group. Each can test his or her own understanding of what leadership requires, both in relationship to the case being discussed and to the ongoing work of the small group.

Cases of failure are often painful. In the small groups, there is a level of engagement in one another's cases that is different than simply reading and working a case from another context, trying to guess what's on the teacher's mind, and showing off how smart you are by cracking the case in front of your colleagues—as is often the case in the traditional case study method. When someone in the room has his or her real experience on the line, you've got to come up with important questions and good insights. Can they get back in the arena with lessons captured from their own pain and bewilderment? This mode of teaching and learning can cultivate an aliveness in the small group that in turn animates the larger class consultations.

Giving the Work Back

Adaptive leadership requires knowing how to give the work back to the group—that is, to the social system that has to learn, change, and adapt. Consistent with the theory that is being taught, therefore, the learning design departs from the typical academic practice of having students meet in a small group with a teaching assistant (TA) who serves as the authority within the group. Instead, each time the small consultation group meets, a different member of the group serves as the designated authority (DA). (Note that this practice can help to shift the locus of authority from assumed Authority vested in the teaching staff to including oneself in the arena of authority—a key feature of the deep shift to critical-systemic consciousness described in chapter 3.)

Before the meeting, the DA is given a written "Briefing for Designated Authorities." It reminds the DA of the group's purpose and task, the social functions of authority, key principles of leadership, modes of operating—all drawn from the approach the course is teaching (yet another meeting between the experience of the student and the idea). The briefing includes a final section, "After-wards," which suggests, "You might feel successful and elated. You also might feel worked over, chewed up, ignored . . . You have probably conducted more current—energy—than you are aware of." Since each week a different student serves as the DA, every student has the opportunity to reflect on his or her experience of this role—especially in the light of how others in the group take up the same role from week to week.

A teaching assistant is assigned to each small group, but does not attend the small group sessions. (The TAs do meet with students in-dividually.) Thus, each small consultation group is on its own dur-ing the ninety minutes that it meets every week, and the group must manage its needs for the functions of authority. Having a DA for each session not only ensures that every student will have an op-portunity to take up this role, it is also a hedge against the possibil-ity of sheer mayhem.

During the term, each student takes the roles of CP, DA, con-sultant to each case presenter, and, as we shall see, other informal roles that are formed in interaction with the needs of the group and the temperament and habits of each student-practitioner.

Disciplined Written Reflection— Study Questionnaires

A key feature of adaptive leadership is the art of the question. Good questions invite and focus attention, surface important issues, and assist people in learning to see what they most need to see in their own past and emergent experience. In this approach to teaching and learning, a weekly study questionnaire, requiring disciplined writ-ten reflection on the experience of the small group is the central, grounding discipline in the learning process. Writing is a critical part of this discipline because it prompts more depth and precision in reflective thought, yielding more insight than might otherwise be the case. The writing process enables concepts and insights to get through the body in service of the transformation of those default settings.

Three somewhat differing questionnaires are used during the term. The repetitiveness of some of the questions is a key element of their power to direct and discipline attention, to reveal blind spots, and to create opportunities for relentless confrontation with old habits and new possibilities.

Three additional forms of this reflective discipline also appear in the course. These are: written study questionnaires related to one or two assigned films, each serving as a case; an assignment asking students to reflect on their ambitions and aspirations (see chapter 5); and a final paper.[2] One of the TA's central roles is to read, evaluate, and give timely, written responses to the questionnaires and papers, tracking the work of each individual and the small group as a whole.

The first weekly questionnaire begins as follows:

> The purpose of this questionnaire is to help you analyze the work process of the consultation group sessions. We suggest that you fill it out within one day of the session and that you spend no more than two hours completing it.[3] Please limit your response to three pages. [Note that people are asked both to reflect and also to respond fairly rapidly as they must in the actual practice of leadership.]

The first of nine questions reads,

What was the purpose and what was the task of the consultation group session?

It is remarkable how difficult it is for people to actually recognize and name the deep purpose of why they have convened—in this case, to learn the art and practice of leadership—that is, how to mobilize people to make progress on tough challenges. Throughout the course, people are reminded that in unprecedented conditions vision is problematic, but clarity of purpose is essential—the North Star—in the practice of adaptive leadership. Clarity of purpose depends on the capacity to discern the values that make risk taking meaningful. As in the practice of adaptive leadership everywhere, it takes some—even very bright—people weeks to recognize the deep purpose of the group. In the meantime, the experience of the consultation group can be quite a ride!

The questions proceed, directing attention to predictable patterns:

What was the initial event of the group session (i.e., what happened in the first few minutes)?

What was the primary hidden issue of your consultation group session?

Did the initial event provide a clue for identifying the primary hidden issue of the group session? If so, what was the connection?

Not surprisingly, most people are initially puzzled by the notion that paying attention to an initial event might be helpful in interpreting the remainder of the session. They are also uncertain about the presence of hidden issues. But, again, one of the convictions of this approach is that more often than not, in most human groups, there are unspoken issues that have considerable power to thwart progress if they remain unaddressed. Learning to surface hidden issues, make connections among seemingly disparate events, and thus become alert to predictable patterns is essential to adaptive leadership. Indeed, as week after week the questions repeatedly draw attention to the actual events within the small group and the underlying currents that shape them, people discover more of what is really going on. They gain practice in analyzing what is happening within the social system, and they can test the adequacy of their own perceptions and choices of action or non-action.

Orientation to the Small Group
Consultation Process

The potential value of this kind of consultation process is not immediately evident to most participants. The teaching staff, therefore, spends a good deal of time orienting the class to the work of the small groups. Describing the questionnaires, Heifetz reveals the seamless linkage between the work of the large and small groups when he says, "Hopefully, you'll get good at getting on the balcony and seeing the patterns. Typically you won't see them at first—like looking at any new terrain. But over time you will recognize patterns within political-organizational-social systems." He suggests that the response of the TAs will "help you figure out what you did and didn't see, and they will help you make connections among things."

Students inevitably ask what kind of experience they should present as a case of leadership failure. The course is intended to assist in their professional development, so by implication, the case they choose most appropriately comes from their professional experience, even though the course may be useful in their personal life as well.

Students and potential instructors alike may wonder whether dwelling on failure can turn into a therapy session and whether this is appropriate in a leadership course. There is a difference between therapy and this case analysis. Although they can never be mutually exclusive, in therapy the focus is on the individual person, whereas in this work the focus is on the system within which people find themselves having to act. Heifetz uses the metaphor of harp strings as those features of personality that are apt to be plucked by various forces in the social system in the process of trying to exercise leadership. "Your own 'tuning,'" he says, "may play a part in what is going on and be worthy of reflection, but it is not the whole story. It is only a part of a larger system or pattern of interactions."

When students begin scanning the first questionnaire, it evokes curiosity—and some anxiety. A student asks, "What do you mean by the question, 'What was the primary hidden issue of your consultation group session?'" Heifetz responds, "Well, let's use our own large group session last Monday. The hidden issue there seemed to be that the class wanted to discuss 'Who will get into the class?' whereas I wanted to invite you to think about how you gain informal authority when you only have formal authority. You see," he continues, "grappling with the questionnaire is designed to have you operate on both the dance floor and the balcony in the small group. You have to get good at going back and forth several times within a brief time frame. You have to track both the specific content of the case and the work of the group as it holds and shapes the content."

As the time commitment of this work begins to loom into view, not unexpectedly someone asks also about the readings for the course, and whether it is important to read all of them. "The class will be more valuable to you," replies Heifetz without sarcasm, "if you do the reading." [4]

Then, reminding the students that attendance in the small group is essential, Heifetz says, "People will lose sleep when trying to prepare a case of their own failure. You have to be there." This call for consistent, engaged presence to the work is a part of creating a strong enough crucible for the formation and practice of adaptive leadership. [5]

This approach, however, does not create a fail-safe environment. The course is a part of the real world, and some people may get hurt because, as Heifetz says, "I cannot fully protect you from the ways you are prepared to hurt each other. But there will be lots of opportunities to learn from your wound if it happens. For example, if you volunteer for being a scapegoat, we will not protect you, but we will help you reflect on it afterwards. I will not keep you from doing what you do already in your workplaces. There are risks to taking this course as there are risks in the practice of leadership."

Becoming more aware of the perils of engagement, a student asks, "Can you be trusted? Will you intervene?" Heifetz responds enigmatically, "If you expect me to be the only one to intervene [to protect you], we are going to learn a lot about dependency."

Though students often want to change groups, unless there is a very compelling reason, they may not. One of the intended challenges is to learn how to make use of the people who are in your small group—whom you may or may not like—which is similar to most situations in which one exercises leadership. Indeed, it is precisely in relationship to this particular point that a good deal of learning takes place because bringing one's practice of leadership to the scrutiny of very diverse perspectives can significantly enlarge the range of insight. For example, a forty-three year old National Security fellow told us:

> I remember thinking as I looked around the table and we introduced ourselves to each other, "Oh, gosh. Here's a woman who's in theater. What in the world is she going to know about leadership in the Army?" I had picked a military case because it was the only thing I knew. But [after I presented my case]—when I got up from that table, I could truthfully say that everyone had said something to me that was significant. And I thought, "Gosh, there might be a little bit more to this than I had thought."

Similarly, a man from India, presenting a case relating to his failure to avert a strike at a bank where he was the chief executive, was equally dubious about the value of the diverse perspectives in his small group:

> I started off with the apprehension that the American students in my small group would not appreciate the context, they wouldn't get the nuances, and so it would be only a general discussion. But surprisingly they caught on to all the

leads in the case. They were able to make very valuable points. We had one trade union organizer who really cottoned on to the case and who made me see points of view that had escaped me.

He added that it had been his habit to discount gender and ethnicity as categories of analysis, preferring what he called "a structural point of view." But after being "lambasted" by the group for this stance, he began to feel that maybe those categories of analysis were also important—a part of the structure. A multiplicity of points of view can enrich the perception of what is at play in the field of engagement, and can take people across the borders of their habitual assumptions, illuminating new patterns of interpretation and potential acts of leadership.

In other words, a small consultation group is a good space for the kind of reflection and practice that adaptive leadership requires—work on the edge of discomfort and curiosity, the familiar and the unknown.

Blind Spots Become New Vistas

Blind spots are characteristic ways of behaving (and their consequences) that one is unaware of. Working cases of leadership failure with other people uncovers and helps one to adjust these default settings—opening new vistas of insight and alternative, more effective action.[6]

Knight on the White Charger—The Lone Ranger

A student in his late thirties, working in the FBI, doubted that the small group would contribute any insights to his experience of leadership failure beyond those he had already gleaned from the course early on. To his surprise, midway through the term, when he presented his case in his small group, there was a woman—a journalist—"who was sort of the spark plug . . . who started to unpack it, and the others quickly joined in and helped her develop it."

The consultation helped to reveal a characteristic behavior, a default setting, that he used unthinkingly and repeatedly: a knight charging in on a white horse in defense of the downtrodden. The essence of the case was that he had learned that two women in another department were receiving poor treatment from their manager. He intervened on their behalf. Taking on the challenge alone, he acted in a way that "did not give either of the women any part in the fight." Though he believes that the fight would have been lost in any case, the failure in his own eyes is that neither of the two women is still with the agency. He now wonders if the resignation of one of them, a particularly strong and competent colleague, might have been averted if he had been able to choose to stay off his white charger. "If she could have had a part in the fight, she would probably still be there."

Interestingly, further along in the course, even though he had already presented his case in the small group and understood his knight on a white charger pattern of behavior, he repeated the same pattern (his default setting) in the large group, championing the younger students (one faction) in the face of criticism they were receiving from mid-career students (another faction). It was very powerful for him to watch himself repeating the same behavior (including the failure to create his intended result), and it deepened his respect for how hard it is to change established, sometimes lifelong patterns. Yet further along in the course, when a similar situation arose, he told us afterward that he literally bit his tongue so he would not recreate the same defeating dynamic. It took three rounds: two rounds to see the pattern and a third to begin to be able to make a conscious, alternative choice about how he wanted to respond.

The Knight Finds a Partner

This approach to teaching the art of leadership underscores repeatedly that, in complex systems, it is rarely appropriate to go it alone. Forming *partnerships* within the faction one is working in, creating *allies* across the boundaries between factions, and finding *confidants* who are outside the field of action altogether is critical to the art of adaptive leadership.

The biggest take-away for the knight on the white charger was learning how to find good partners and use them well. The woman in the small group who had been most helpful was significantly different from himself. In his words, "She is a reporter. I'm a spy. I'm a conservative. She's very liberal—in fact, she's gay." During the term, however, she became a good partner in thinking through cases, and a friend of his family, and he began to realize that the differences between them were part of what enabled her to help him see his blind spots. After the course had concluded, he was actively planning how he could find and use partners more effectively on his return to his agency. Changing behavior at the level of default settings requires new insight and ongoing practice, practice, practice.

Lightning Rod

Note that in the previous example, having more than one context within the learning milieu in which to practice (both large and small group) was useful in learning to recognize and transform a repeated and defeating pattern of behavior. The same is true also in the following example.

A college chaplain in his early thirties presented a case in which he felt he had quite unfairly become a lightning rod for people's resistance, anger, and frustration. Becoming a lightning rod is a particularly dangerous and usually ineffectual role because it is the very opposite of developing other people's responsibility, that is, giving the work back to the group. This occurred when he was attempting to provide leadership on an issue of economic justice on his campus. As a consequence, he had eventually been eased out of that position—that is, killed off.

But, as it happened, when he presented the case in his small group, he received much the same response, again becoming a lightning rod for strong feelings and a distraction from the consultative work of the group and the justice issue in the case. Undaunted, he volunteered to present his case in the large group. To his considerable bewilderment, he again became a lightning rod, evoking irritation, anger, and criticism. As he slowly realized that the response to his own behavior was replicated across three social systems (the college, the small group, the large group), he began to be able to see it. It dawned on him that his own behavior was a blind spot in his rather self-righteous analysis, contributing to the defeat of his own best purposes and hopes. As I left the campus at the close of the day, I saw him sitting alone on a bench, seemingly staring into space—while looking inside.

Distinguishing Role from Self

Becoming a lightning rod is one danger in exercising leadership, and confusing self and role is another. The capacity to distinguish role from self is one of the gifts of developing a critical, systemic perspective and can yield a useful analysis of what is really going on. It is often vitally important to be able to recognize that what is happening to you is *not* about *you*. It is often much more about the issue you represent and the role you are playing in the drama. Roles are formed in the social systems we inhabit. They never perfectly correspond with the fullness of one's humanity. As Heifetz has stated it, "Confusing role with self is a trap. Even though you may put all of yourself into your role—your passion, values, and artistry—the people in your setting will be reacting to you, not primarily as a person, but as the role you take in their lives. Even when their responses to you *seem* very personal, you need to read them primarily as reactions to how well you are meeting their expectations. In fact, it is vital to your own stability and peace of mind that you understand this, so that you can interpret and decipher people's criticism before internalizing it."[7]

A city budget director, for example, knows that there is considerable frustration when budgets are being redrawn. As she is being verbally attacked, she imagines that she is not sitting in her chair but simply watching how "her chair" is serving as the target of considerable angst, sometimes expressed in outrageous forms. Distinguishing self from role in this way, she can remain both calm and respectful. She also remains in charge of how much her own self-worth is and is not at stake. She is clear that she is a part of a system in which she has taken up a particular role. In not letting systemic issues become merely personal, she is able to hold steady in a complex, political, and emotional process.[8]

Discovering Roles Within the Group

In the small group, students are encouraged to become mindful of the roles they do and do not take up, the issues they may represent, and how their own personal tuning or default settings may affect the roles they are inclined to play. The first questionnaire, for example, poses the question: Has there been any difference between your capacity to contribute in the consultation group and in the large class?

A thirty-four-year-old woman, who had been working in state government as the governor's chief of staff, had always felt that she had to prove to people that she was competent. She discovered that her small group perceived her to be not only competent but intimidating. Reflecting on her participation in the course as a whole, she became aware of two contrasting participation styles. In the large group, she found she was too reticent (holding back), but in the small group she was perceived as somewhat overbearing. Having two different contexts in which to practice helped reveal that the binary default settings from which she offered or withheld her interventions were defeating her effectiveness in ways that she could potentially modify.

The interplay of the large group and the small group in this instance and in the other cases are examples of how several coordinated studio–labs can create a single ecology for learning. In varying combinations, they can provide constellations of usable experience from which students can discover their multiple roles within the social system. The second questionnaire, for example, asks,

How were you used by the [small] group? Were you used well or poorly?

How was the chairperson (DA) used by the group?

To whom did the group give informal authority and why?

Grappling with these sorts of questions provides practice in becoming more mindful of the roles being played in the present by oneself and others. The third form of the questionnaire deepens the inquiry, beginning with the question:

By now each member of the group has probably begun to take on a particular role for the group. In terms of those roles, what perspective on the case did each member of your group represent?

As one international student began to sort it out, he wrote,

Fernando: He is a scientific conciliator. Hearing the conflict among our comments, he often introduces his ideas about the case by weighing several possibilities out loud and then saying "maybe it's" and constructing a third view framed as a compromise theory.

Emilio: He believes in our own inner knowledge, and with his enigmatic questions, expressed in short bursts . . . he urges us to be more open so that we will see the hidden issues.

Rachel: She understands and uses shock value . . . She holds herself on the edge of our engagement, telling us not to go too far. From that safe edge, she blurts out . . . some of the hard and shocking things going on in the case.

Carl: He has come here to learn how to understand the disenfranchised, and he seems to be experimenting with what can be seen from the perimeter.

Liz: She changes the channel a lot. She could be the mother, but she withholds her warmth and keeps herself contrary and a little disobedient somehow. She knows the fear of being hurt by loved ones, so scrambles it up if we are too lovey.

Meg: She is gentle but authoritative. She is looking for the right kind of authority . . . She often puts our work in order from an outside place . . . I feel it provides welcome protection . . .

Bridgit: She wants us to see some relationship between our particular cases and the wider world.

This structured reflection helps students to recognize varying roles within the system as a whole—and reveals the potential tensions and conflicts among them. Students have opportunity to test their perceptions with each other, as each term one of the small group consultations is devoted exclusively to this conversation.

From Analysis to Intervention

As people become more skilled in reading the patterns of the social system, in both the large and small groups they begin to consciously experiment with making interventions in a complex system. In the questionnaires, they are encouraged to observe and learn from the effects of their own and others' attempts to intervene, tracing and evaluating whether or not the intervention assisted in making progress on the adaptive work of the group. Questions such as "Identify the most productive intervention of the meeting. What made it so?" and "Can you identify a moment when you thought you had something worthwhile to say and you held yourself back?" are invitations to yet further reflection, analysis, experimentation, and practice. A twenty-seven-year-old woman told us,

> I went through a couple of classes where I thought, "I'm not learning anything—what am I learning here that I don't already know?" And then they changed the questionnaire to more of a strategic kind of question: "What advice are you going to give?" And it was very helpful because I stepped back and said, maybe I have heard some of this stuff, but how are you going to use it in a group setting? . . . Giving advice is a lot harder than analyzing a problem. You analyze it, and that's good. But then you've got to give a solution and that's much harder.

Work Avoidance Activity

As observed earlier, adaptive leadership is difficult because the system will always seek to maintain the current equilibrium (even though it may be highly dysfunctional) rather than undergo the distress of the disequilibrium needed to move to a more adequate equilibrium. The arena of the small group is not exempt from work avoidance activity, and sometimes apparent engagement in the field of action does not mean an absence of work avoidance, which can take the form of sterile conflict or proxy fights. A former student recalled, "The course swallowed me up in a way—it wasn't just an intellectual exercise alone. It touched one's entire being—a visceral, emotional engagement in which I sometimes found myself in quite heated debate. And then I would step back and realize that something else was going on." Referring to a relationship within his small group, he said, "The person I was debating was not a mere fool as I wanted to believe. He was bright, intelligent, and capable—but I discovered that we used our sparring to avoid doing a lot of the work that we really needed to do, and I had to figure out what that was about."

Thus, as Heifetz has put it, "a key question in the practice of leadership becomes: How can one recognize and counteract the expected forms of work avoidance and help people learn despite resistance?" A question asked early on is

Did the group use any work avoidance mechanisms to maintain equilibrium? Did the people in the case use any work avoidance mechanisms to maintain equilibrium? If so, what were they? Was there any similarity?

This facet of the work is deepened in the third questionnaire, which presses for awareness of yet more complex patterns:

Sometimes, work avoidance mechanisms are easier to identify than the issues being avoided. The timing and nature of the work avoidance mechanisms often provide a clue to a hidden issue. What issue was being discussed at the time when the group generated a work avoidance mechanism? What was the work avoidance mechanism? Did anyone intervene to redirect the group's attention to the issue?

Though the cost of work avoidance can be significant, nevertheless, coming to terms with it can take a long time. A journalist, for example, reflecting on his small group experience a year later, wrote:

> It took me several months to realize the value of my small group. In many ways, it was atypical, and I found it quite annoying until the very end of the term. I have no idea if this is the norm, but in my class, many of the small groups became incredibly close. They would emerge from the sessions with warm smiles and congenial laughter, and in many instances, they continued to socialize throughout the remainder of the year.
>
> Our group was fairly dysfunctional. One member of the group pouted most of the time, and as the semester progressed, she said little more than that she thought our group was wasting its time and that the whole idea was stupid. She was close pals with several other members of the group, and they would sometimes whisper or pass notes to each other while someone was talking. Several members of the group, myself included, tried to persuade our obstinate colleague to explain in more detail why she was frustrated by the group or how we might perform better. Those efforts were unsuccessful.
>
> None of us, however, addressed the uncomfortable dynamic [the hidden issue] that was created by the social friendships. We were, to borrow Heifetz's phrase, "avoiding the work."
>
> Nonetheless, I came to realize at the end of the semester that what happened in our small group in many ways was perhaps more realistic than in the congenial groups. After all, nearly every workplace is full of cliques and social relationships

that impact one's ability to perform adaptive work. And nearly every workplace has at least one difficult employee who needs to be persuaded, coddled, or threatened in order to participate in the task at hand.

I regret that I didn't come to understand the parallels between our group and a work environment until the end of the term. Still, I found it incredibly useful to realize my own culpability in the group's stunted progress. Instead of raising the issue in our group, a task that surely would have been uncomfortable and created significant tension, I chose instead to grumble about it to my wife and to my Teaching Assistant in the questionnaire I submitted each week about our small group sessions. This idea of "getting on the balcony," as Heifetz puts it, and watching how you interact with others can be humbling, but it's extremely useful.

Reflection as a Discipline

In sum, the small group and questionnaire process leads students into critical domains of inquiry and asks them to tie their feelings, assumptions, and perceptions to particular evidence in their own immediate experience. If they find that the evidence is missing or could be interpreted in more adequate ways, they are then faced with the need to modify their perception of reality so they can see what is really going on and to respond more effectively. This ongoing practice yields a new framework for analysis, interpretation, and action. One person summed it up this way:

It's been shocking to me. When I sat down to do the first questionnaire, I thought, "These are stupid questions: Do we really have to go through this every week?" I thought I already had it all worked out. Then, when I actually went to write it out, I realized how much further I could take the

95

analysis than I had originally . . . I think I can read things quite well, but the questionnaires are making me think in a way where I'm seeing things I hadn't seen.

Similarly, another said,

I'll be honest with you. I was learning more, a ton more, in the small group because the questionnaires were forcing me . . . I spent loads of time on the questionnaires. I got really involved, really engrossed in them. They were very productive. The first one in particular was very difficult for me to answer . . . but once you got into the third questionnaire, you zipped through it.

Another reflected,

I think that the kind of introspection this process promotes is good for anybody because busy people—students, professionals—don't really have time (at least I never found the time) to sit back and contemplate . . . But the weekly questionnaires force you to stop and think about what went on and how it could be of use in one's approach to attempting to lead. After the first few, I kind of got into it, and I would tend to get up very early in the morning, maybe three or four, when things are quiet, and it seems like the night belongs to you, and you can really get into your thoughts. And I found it to be a very personally rewarding thing to do.

Not all students approached the rigors of the questionnaires with equal enthusiasm. The TAs play a critical role in maintaining discipline: one student confessed, "Honestly, sometimes I skipped out of the questionnaires. I'd make up issues because I was not in the mood to sit there and analyze. I just made up analyses. I did get caught. The TA wrote on my paper, 'What happened to you this week?' So the TAs spend a lot of time on the questionnaires. And the comments they write back are really important."

Grist for the Learning Mill

This approach to teaching and learning leadership is designed to reduce the chances of leaders being seduced, sabotaged, "assassinated," or otherwise defeated by their own naïveté or arrogance—products of various forms of ignorance, blind spots, insufficient analysis, and inadequate skill. But it is intriguing to watch how often the small groups resist using the framework offered by the course until they have suffered the defeat of their other instinctive responses—the defeat of their efforts to be insightful and to help that are rooted in their default settings. This tendency to repeat what is familiar and to resist the authority and leadership of the teaching staff (typically subtle) becomes itself more grist for the learning mill. But as the theoretical framework is repeatedly offered and discovered to be useful in one's own experience, it begins to take hold and serve the formation of a new practice of leadership.

Learning from Failure in Public

It must be underscored that it is the reflection on one's own experience of leadership failure that is the essential, vital feature of this leadership formation process. Further, some evidence indicates that presenting one's own failure in a semi-public, professional setting contributes to a greater sense of confidence and freedom. The discovery appears to be this: if I can survive having failed in the eyes of these peers—and if everyone here also suffers failure—then I have a greater degree of freedom to act. I am no longer as distracted by my need to inappropriately avoid the risks of failure that are inherent in the art of leadership. As one person expressed it:

> It was very difficult to sit in public and talk about failure—
> mine—and what the cost of it had been. It was also very

revealing. It had been internally painful. But presenting it in public put it in a different light. It also helped me break a myth of leadership—about perfection and that leaders don't make mistakes. In this course your first public act is not to come forward with your strength but from where you really messed up and what's eating at you. And I learned a great deal. I learned a lot about what I was blind to . . . Some of the information I most wanted not to hear was some of the most valuable information I got.

At the conclusion of his first book, *Leadership Without Easy Answers*, Heifetz wrote, "Leadership . . . requires a learning strategy. A leader has to engage people in facing the challenge, adjusting their values, changing perspectives, and developing new habits of behavior . . . The adaptive demands of our societies require leadership that takes responsibility without waiting for revelation or request. One may lead perhaps with no more than a question in hand."[9] The small group consultation and question process distills an approach to teaching and learning the art of leadership that is congruent with what adaptive leadership requires. With questions and questionnaires in hand, Heifetz and his colleagues give the work back to the group, inviting them to face the learning embedded in their own experiences of leadership failure, adjust their perceptions and values, and develop new habits of behavior—a praxis of teaching and learning that takes teachers and students together to places they didn't plan to go.

Students soon discover that this journey requires a measure of courage that is anchored in a quality of person that can be described as a capacity for presence. The development of this capacity is the focus of the next chapter.

CHAPTER FIVE

Listening to the Music Beneath the Words

The Practice of Presence

MOST PEOPLE have experienced what it feels like to be "held" by someone who might be described as a powerful speaker, whether a political leader, a musical performer, or a great teacher. At such times, we sense a kind of inner strength, public poise, and a quality of connection that is difficult to describe and unmistakable when experienced. We might call this a capacity for *presence*.

In the imagination of oneself as a leader, it is often presumed that what is needed are innate or acculturated traits of personality—including the capacity to secure an easy celebrity and the illusions of control. The discovery that the activity of courageous, adaptive leadership inevitably must take place within a field of complex systems requires a shift in perception. In the practice of adaptive leadership, what really matters is the capacity for effective participation—ways of being present that foster the building of a collective strength. That is, even if one is standing in the spotlight, it is more useful to envision oneself as a resonant and responsive node in a dynamic network or field of energy and an agent of emergent possibility and progress, rather than imagining oneself as simply gifted and entitled to be on top and in charge.

This elusive quality of presence affects one's ability to attract and hold attention, to convey trustworthiness and credibility, to inspire and call forth the best in others, to intervene effectively in complex systems, and to be a conduit of creative change.[1] The depth and strength of one's capacity to be present enhances the ability to read the patterns, especially the nonverbal clues that reveal a group's level of readiness for work. It can significantly determine one's capacity to conduct the energy in ways that keep the temperature (the heat of the conflict) within a range that motivates change without unleashing immobilizing anxiety.

The ability to hold steady and to improvise in the midst of the conflict and tumult of adaptive work depends on cultivating an inner consciousness of the connectivity of which one is a part—especially when there is a high degree of voltage on the wires. It requires the ability to recognize and intelligently manage strong feelings—one's own emotions and the emotions in others (as individuals, as factions within the group, and within the group as a whole). It requires an understanding of one's self in relationship to audience, the ability to pay close attention, to listen, to feel, and to bring one's own heart-mind into the present in a way that responsively holds both the self and the group in the work. It combines mindfulness and centeredness in the right proportion. The practice of presence is integral to the capacity to be a creative agent in the moment—poised on the edge between the known reality and the emergent possibility. *Presence* is the meeting place between the inner life of a person and the outer life of action in the world.

The Artistry of Good Coaching

This quality of presence is a vital element in the practice of the art of adaptive leadership. It calls for a centered, responsive, and committed self, and levels of consciousness and competence that cannot be cultivated by mere techniques such as those offered in media briefings. The development of this quality within an interdependent social system arises from a powerful mix of awareness, humility, and courage that over time can deepen into wisdom. Once again, the question is this: Can this seemingly elusive quality be taught and learned, or is it something one just has?

When leadership is recognized as an activity rather than simply the product of genetically endowed talent or cultural socialization, it does not mean that talent or other natural gifts are irrelevant. To use a musical example, as Heifetz sometimes does, one may have a natural gift for playing the violin. This natural gift can be crippled by poor teaching or it can become extraordinary through the artistry of good teaching and coaching. On the other hand, a person with a lesser degree of talent with outstanding teaching may become a very fine musician. Similarly, in the formation of leadership, the features of personality given by genetic endowment and socialization may lend themselves to the activity of leadership, but these can be strengthened and additional competencies may be cultivated through good teaching. In combination, they may be brought to a level of refinement that is manifest as the quality of presence—effectively attuned and engaged expressions of one's personhood, enhancing the capacity to assist in mobilizing people to make progress on the toughest challenges.

This perspective sets a brake on the assumption that to lead one must either have the right stuff as a natural talent or defer to waiting for those who do. Rather, through the art and practice of good teaching, people representing differing gifts and talents may become capable of offering acts of leadership within the social system.

Heifetz and his colleagues sponsor the development of the qualities of person that we are describing as presence in several ways. First, the enhanced mindfulness that is a part of the deep transformation of consciousness (described in chapter 3) from an Authority-bound, dependent mode of knowing to a systemic, critically aware, and more inner-dependent mode enlarges one's capacity for developing this quality of presence because it makes it possible to take more into account. This developmental shift also makes possible the capacity for critical thought that is required to distinguish role from self (described in chapter 4), and sponsors the discovery that one can use oneself as a barometer of what is happening in the group (chapter 3). Each of these capacities contributes to becoming more effectively present within the group. But there is also a yet more explicit process by which Heifetz and his colleagues initiate students into the formation of presence.

As with the many other dimensions of this approach to teaching and learning, this capacity for presence cannot be taught by telling. Yet, again through the artistry of good coaching, it is possible for people to begin to see what they most need to see—and in this instance, to be. The process can work within either a large or small group. In the course described here, it occurs primarily in the context of three required evening singing sessions, each involving the large class as a whole. As in chapter 2, let's step into the classroom to see how this works.

Listening to the Song Beneath the Words

It is mid-November. Barely a week remains before Thanksgiving break. Soon classes will conclude for the holidays, and in January after final papers are written, read, graded, and returned, the course will be over. A cold rain is falling softly but steadily. The night is already dark when the big classroom begins to fill again a little before 6 p.m. There is a lively buzz as umbrellas and parkas are stashed and sandwiches appear out of backpacks. Everyone in the course left this same classroom only three and a half hours earlier. A few people can be heard to comment that three more hours is going to seem like a long time.

The students have been instructed to come prepared to read a piece of prose or poetry that is meaningful to them. It does not need to be something they have written themselves, though it can be. Further, since typically thirty countries are represented in the class, students are encouraged to bring something in their own language, along with a translation.

Heifetz stands in the pit, and after finishing a number of brief exchanges with TAs and students, he looks out at the class and waits. The room settles into a comfortable but wondering silence. "We are going to have three evenings in this series," he announces. "Tonight we will focus on listening."

"We begin with silence. There is more than one kind of silence. For example, there is silence that is full of presence and there is silence that is absence. I'd like all of you just where you are to become absent." He pauses for a long moment. "Now become present. Bring yourself into this moment." He pauses again. "Now absent." Pause. "Now present." Somewhat surprisingly, the contrast between silence-as-absence and silence-as-presence is palpable, and the class gets its first glimpse of the power of presence and their power as an audience.

He then suggests that as the evening unfolds it will look as though the person in front is doing the work. "But the challenge for the rest is to listen—and to explore what it takes to listen." (A central part of what he is up to here is helping people to learn to recognize the dynamic interdependence between the group and the leader—in this case, the person given the authority to speak.)

"So," he continues. "Who would like to volunteer?" Out of a group of approximately a hundred students, only two hands go up. In the ensuing hesitant silence, a student voice asks, "To do what?" Heifetz responds, "You are all volunteering for working on a range of capacities to hear music beneath the words of what is being said."

"The person who volunteers to stand here in the front will read their prose or poetry. And then we might ask them to make up a song." The part about singing gives rise to a ripple of uneasy laughter across the class. "Without words," Heifetz adds, reducing the quiet laughter to something close to low-grade terror in some, fascination in a few. "Because," he continues, "leadership is about improvisation."

There is another long pause—then one more volunteer.

Nodding toward one of the first volunteers, Heifetz says, "I saw you first. Do you still want to go?" The student nods.

As the student takes his place in the front of the room, Heifetz stands at the student's side and says to him and to the class, "We are trying to demonstrate two things in how to be a holding environment: how to hold people's aspirations, energies, the fears of the community, and also your own fears. There are three instructions that you are going to hear over and over."

"First, stay with your audience. There's no use in speaking if no one is listening."

"Second, make each word count. Each sound, like a song, has an ancient history that you are bringing here—all the variety of meanings and resonances that it has taken on."[2]

"Third, allow for silence. Let the beginning emerge from silence, and hold the silence at the end."

Then Heifetz turns directly to the student, who is about to read the piece he has chosen, and tells him to hold the microphone close. The student resists using the microphone at all, but Heifetz prevails: "It helps you to hear yourself out there in the room."

The student holds the mike close, looking down at the desk and not looking at the class. Heifetz prompts, "Hold everybody. There is a lot of nervousness in this room."

"I'm nervous too," the student responds.

"Use yourself as data," Heifetz reminds him. "You are picking up their nervousness too. Speak through the terror. Take your time. Give the words to them. Don't read into the desk. You've got to hold steady."

After another moment, the student, a young man in his early thirties, begins to read: "I, [name], will uphold the Constitution . . . " He is a military officer, and he has chosen to read the oath of military office. He is wearing civilian dress, but at the end of the oath he raises his right hand in a smart salute.

After a brief pause, he looks to Heifetz. Heifetz says simply and respectfully, "You have to know that this is a very disturbing statement to a lot of people in this class. You have to get behind it if you are going to disturb them, or they won't let it in." Heifetz steps again to the side of the student, and looking at the student while gesturing toward the class, he says, "Say it to them—hold the people you are challenging." (The class is once again serving as a case-in-point, and the young officer is having an opportunity to practice—and practice again.)

The student repeats the oath and the salute—this time with more eye contact, strength, and a bit more connection to the audience.

Then Heifetz says in a low-key manner, "Now make up a song. Make it up, and if you find yourself singing something familiar, move off into the void. Also, don't take the first exit. Don't stop the first time you are inclined to. And hold steady at the end. Then pointing to one of the students sitting near the center of the class, he says, "Sing to Roy a heroic song. Let Roy draw it out. You have to hold everyone, and Roy has to hold you."

There is a long pause. Then, singing without words, using only the vowel sound "ah," the student begins. The song is hesitant and soft—but there. He has taken a small step in using his own creative capacity to improvise his way across that edge between the familiar and the unknown.

When he has finished, the class begins to break into applause, partly in admiration and partly to release the tension. But Heifetz holds up his hand and asks them to hold their applause so that the silence is not broken. He suggests that they can find other ways of conveying their response. He is asking them to stay fully present to the tension of the moment.

Then he invites the class to comment on what they have just seen, heard, thought, and felt. Comments are made about risk, improvisation, and the experience of holding a group even with all of the electricity going through it. One person remarks on the significance of just holding steady, being there, standing firm, and having the courage not to run away. Initially the comments are essentially generous, but then some acknowledge that it was hard for them to receive the words of the oath. It was easier to identify with the student when he was singing. "It is hard to listen to the 'music' of the oath and the old loyalties that some still cherish," Heifetz remarks. "It is hard for some to hear the need to prepare for war, combat, enemies, and the need for protection. Can you sing a duet with that music that does not take away your own virtues—*your* song? You have to listen to be listened to. Everyone brings their own experiences to this moment, and without the conflict, there is no room for creativity." (*Creativity* is the key word here. In adaptive leadership, conflicting perspectives and factions must be brought together to create a workable harmonic.)

A student comments, "Every single face in this room was filled with emotion of one kind or another." More comments flow in this vein, and collectively the group is learning yet another way to pay close attention to what is happening in the social system.

Then there is a renewed invitation to volunteer, and a woman comes to the front of the room. She reads her passage only once before she, too, is asked to sing. Later a student comments, "Hearing it only once, you don't hear as much." Heifetz responds, "Sometimes you don't get another chance to hear." (Once again, he is disappointing their expectations and at the same time awakening the group to an important piece of reality.)

Another student observes that if one person says something negative about the "performance," it makes it easier for others to be more critical, a comment that reflects the ability to trace the effect of a particular kind of intervention. The students also observe that it is more difficult for a student reader who appears to be a skilled performer to convey authenticity—a paradoxical challenge in the practice of presence. You need to be good, even skilled at it, but you also have to convey the integrity of an authentic, congruent self.

In this fashion the evening proceeds, and to the surprise of many, it does not seem long. In the two singing sessions that follow, the pattern will be similar, but with additions and variations. The three singing sessions coincide with three regular large group sessions, each devoted in turn to Listening, Inspiration, and Partners and Boundaries. In the third singing session, for instance, everyone in the class is asked to form a pair with one of the people sitting next to them. Then, remaining seated, they are asked to carry on a dialogue or duet, singing without words. This provides another experience in partnership, conflict, negotiation of power, reflection on roles, improvisation, and creativity.

What Do Singing Sessions Yield?

The opportunity to practice presence in the singing sessions meets people in differing places in their own readiness to learn. A few essentially don't get it because it just doesn't meet them on their learning edge. But for most, it enlarges their awareness of the scope and depth of the work of adaptive leadership and what it takes to become an instrument of creative change. Students begin to learn some of what it takes to effectively hold a group's attention and anxiety and how to speak powerfully and meaningfully—which even low-profile people must do from time to time in the process of exercising leadership. Students begin to see the ways in which they and others are moved, and rediscover the power of underlying emotions and nonverbal as well as verbal communication to convey deep feeling. They gain access to the awareness that the field of action includes the inner life of everyone in the group as well as the inner life of the one who attempts to offer acts of leadership.

As one person put it,

> The sessions where we were singing and reading poetry were fascinating, wonderful. I found a part of me that maybe I hadn't realized was there or maybe I hadn't taken advantage of. I mean, it's that holistic approach again. There's a lot to be said for the tone in people's voices, the look in their eyes, and for getting a feeling for how the group is—the stillness or the fidgeting. Getting more deeply in touch with people's real feelings, in contrast to how you think they may feel.

Another was grateful to have been given a space in which the value of practice becomes so obvious:

> I found the notion of practice incredibly valuable. We have this fantasy, I think, that if you're actually thinking about getting up and inspiring and moving a group of people, there are people who can just do it. Whereas the idea of practice, and working at it, and that there are skills involved, and there's a technique—I found that a really valuable, good lesson.

Again, the notion of practice, so critical to the art of leadership is made visible, viable, and rewarding. A part of what is happening here is that yet another environment—a studio-lab—is created in which, as one person put it, "fumbling around" is encouraged, and people discover that at least some aspects of charisma can be learned.

Discovering the Power of Your Own Affective Life

The singing sessions help some students discover the power and role of their own emotions (their own *tuning*) in the practice of the art of leadership. The FBI administrator we met in chapter 4 described his learning this way.

> That nighttime singing bit—again I said, "Okay, I'm putting my seatbelt on," because I'm thinking, "this is really fruity." And then when one of the other men in the class read one evening—I cried. And I was like, "Damn, now I get what he [Heifetz] is doing. He's getting to those basic feelings that grow up into your leadership model." I never would have thought in those terms. Is the singing itself a tool I'll be able to use? Probably not. But do I have greater self-awareness now? Yeah, I think I know that's there now. So when I talk about my desires and ambitions, I realize that there are roots that are real basic there. I have to admit that being exposed to that made me think in a different way. I now think it's a part of your operating instructions—the things that make you tick, the things that mean you get a button pushed and you fire off about something—why are you that way? Why is that such a hot button for you? There are things that you feel strongly about.

He has become conscious of how very deeply rooted emotions are woven through one's practice of leadership and that if they remain unrecognized and unexamined, they can blindside and sabotage you.

If they are made conscious and examined, the same emotions may positively inform the activity of leadership.

This focus on the emotional realm and on the intangibles of "interiority" is one more way in which this approach addresses the issues of purpose and meaning that nourish the practice of leadership. One student, for example, talked about finding in the singing sessions the missing link in her understanding of her own failure. She said that she had always valued keeping things at a rational level. But in her own case of leadership failure, she felt she had been unclear about purpose. Then she discovered in the singing sessions, that purpose is anchored in "the things that move us." She realized that competence in the practice of leadership requires the recognition that the rational and the emotional are fused.

Finding Authenticity and Integrity

As students watch each other being coached on this quality of presence, they gain awareness of specific practical skills such as: being with the audience, making words count, and using silence. It is important, however, to note that these skills are not offered alone as mere technique. Rather, they are linked with insight into the power of one's internal reality. As a result, students begin to see how the strength of their inner resources, their sense of purpose, and knowing themselves more deeply all contribute to their ability to be present on behalf of the common good of the group. They discover what it means to have the authenticity and integrity to sing your own song, not just the song assigned to you in some predetermined score. For example, one thirty-four-year-old man recalled,

> I did learn from it. The speaking part was helpful, since as a practical matter leaders need to learn how to motivate people and speak. That was more of an external thing, I thought.

But the singing part was internal—that was the part I was uncomfortable with. What I learned from the singing about the internal thing was (and maybe it was different for everybody else), but for me it was finding harmony within yourself. If people could jump out of the actual act of singing and realize that it's symbolic—the singing part is nothing, it's a zero, unless you realize that it's part of being who you are. And it's very hard to do. You've just got to let yourself go and figure out who you are.

Others also spoke about the singing as a scary call to step across the edge of the assumed self into a deeper integrity—and capacity for creativity. For example, one person reflected on how her experience of the singing sessions moved her toward an unaccustomed mode of internal improvisation:

The reading part wasn't so hard. But then the songs . . . What I was struggling with partly in the course was feeling that it's easy for me to be analytical, and I want to do an organizational analysis as deeply as I can. But it's more difficult to deal with the emotional aspects of being a leader—and even being creative. I think I'm a fairly creative person, but it's orchestrated creativity, and theirs was completely unbridled, and that was frightening. But it was also inspiring.

Inspiring a Sense of Commonality Amidst Diversity

A particularly powerful lesson that comes from the singing sessions is that presence can be inspiring. *Conducting energy* understood from another angle of vision is the capacity to embody spirit and to "in-spirit" the field of action. Inspiration may be understood in spiritual, religious, or secular terms—but its force and role cannot be ignored in the work of adaptive leadership. People must be drawn together into difficult work and find the strength, energy, and commitment to sustain the work across the long haul.

The singing sessions often create a positive turning point in the course. It appears that in seeing more of the deep feeling and, thus, the humanity and vulnerability of their classmates, new alliances are formed, and for some, the class becomes closer and more fully engaged with each other. Many people came away from these sessions impressed with the power of activating layers of humanity previously kept hidden or simply unconscious. As one student observed, "After the first evening session, it was like a quantum leap in the way people related to the class." "What shifted?" I asked. "I think the sense of trust and compassion . . . There was a coming together of the group and a trust finally established there that seemed to make a really big difference."[3]

The experience of compassion and respect plays a vital role in inspiring trust and building bridges across difference.[4] Given that factions of various kinds inevitably develop within the class as within any human group, the singing sessions appear to foster a new basis for common ground and even healing as students gain more insight into the context from which others come. For example, though there are often significant tensions between older (mid-career) and younger students, a forty-two-year-old woman who is Hispanic-American discovered that she could learn from the presence of a much younger woman from Mexico:

> She had a heavy Spanish accent, and she read a poem that starts out with a recipe. She was incredibly powerful for me because she had never said a word in the large class. Yet she came down [to read] very calmly with this serene-looking look—sort of a non-look—nothing about her particularly jumped out. She started reading this recipe, and I thought, "Where are we going with this thing?" But I didn't dare leave. I could feel the lead in her shoes—like she was just so

solid. And that was a new kind of leadership for me. She was young, she was female, she was not American, she was not speaking the language of the larger group—and she was solid.

I asked, "That suggested to you that it was possible to lead beyond the assumed forms of authorization?" She responded,

Yes. It's possible. And I shared that with her. In fact, when she went to Mexico for Christmas, she bought me a copy of the book she had read from, because she knew that I was really moved by it. Not just what she was saying—her whole presence. And the reason that she could carry it was because she just held steady.

Holding steady is a key metaphor at the core of this approach because it captures the recognition that in the process of adaptive leadership there are always powerful forces at play. Leaders who can be fully present and resist being buffeted about in the wind and chop of adaptive work help to provide the ballast that is critical to making progress.

Modeling the Behavior

In this approach to the art of adaptive leadership, one of the aspects of thinking politically is the importance of modeling the behavior that you want to encourage in others. In reference to learning presence, people have to be able to see in embodied form that it is possible to bear the voltage that they are experiencing and that human beings can act from a place of depth and an examined integrity rather than superficial reactivity. Thus, an important feature of the coaching in the singing sessions is that the instructor is modeling the behavior that is being taught. There is nervousness in the room and the instructor is not exempt. But as the instructor holds steady, listens, stays with the audience, makes every word count, and uses silence, students are given an opportunity to see what they most need to see in their own experience. In this way presence is caught as well as taught.

More Grist for the Mill

The recognition that these sessions do evoke the good stuff of compassion, trust, and inspiration should not mask the fact that as in the other studio-labs of the course, everything that happens in these sessions is grist for the mill. In the give-and-take of the inter-action, there remains the real possibility of conflict and contro-versy—the difficult stuff—as responses are varied, opinions diverge, and end-of-the-term stress and fatigue come into play.

Even attendance at the evening sessions may become a subject for case-in-point learning about presence. When several students were notably absent from one of the singing sessions, Heifetz challenged the class, reminding them of the importance of attending all sessions and asking, "Why didn't you let those who aren't here know how important they are?" This is another way of awakening people to a reconsideration of the scope of their personal contribution in a complex system and the significance of the work of the group as a whole. It is also yet another way of giving the work back to the group.

Listening Musically to the Dynamics of Adaptive Work

These sessions demonstrate an unusual approach to teaching the art of leadership in a large group context (especially within the academy and other professional settings). This creative deviance fosters learning that moves what was formerly background—the power of mood/tone, emotion, listening, inspiration, silence, and the relationship between the leader and the group—into the foreground of awareness in revelatory ways. People discover that they have opportunity to exercise various aspects of leadership from wherever they sit. People have an opportunity to learn how to listen musically—that is, to listen to the music beneath the words, tuning into the patterns, themes, conflicts, and hopes that are inevitably a feature of any group and a part of the orchestration of its evolving, potential wholeness. Though often hidden beneath the surface, these deep currents provide vital clues to what can happen next.

Particularly important to detect are those clues that reveal stress in the system. Listening musically, deeply, to one's self and to others, is a central pathway to the kind of intelligence and compassion that are critical to adaptive leadership. In her final paper analyzing her own leadership failure, a woman reconsidered the difference it might have made if she had listened better, especially to the various voices of stress—fear, pain, confusion, and resistance. She wrote:

The class on "listening" was the most powerful of the entire semester for me. Listening musically, as I understand it, is essential to hearing the underlying meanings and voices of others. I tend to listen "literally," to the words that are said—because I find words so powerful, or perhaps because it is all I can do to respond to the words. But I have learned this term that I need to listen for *the song beneath the words*. If I had done that, I would have heard more of the pain and confusion that I was generating in my efforts to encourage change. I would have heard the pressures and worries in the voices of my supervisor and the union president, rather than just hearing their formal response to my reports. I might have heard the anger from the local union not just as a defensive resistance to change, but as their fear that they did not know how to face the disempowerment of their union and their members.

I recognize now that my own tuning makes it both easy and hard for me to listen. I am very sensitive to the distress of others and to power and authority. Yet I also operate in a very analytic mode much of the time, which makes it hard to listen for feeling. As a woman whose voice often was not heard when I was a child, and in a union dominated by men, I sometimes fear that my silence, or not talking, will be taken for not having any existence. So I learned to speak up and speak out—at times anyway. But I know now I have the option of silence. I know that I also need to create conditions for real listening to take place. So, I realize I might have listened more musically and allowed for more silence.

Permission to Operate in Uncertainty and Silence

A key value of the singing sessions is that they cultivate an inner sense of permission to operate in uncertainty. This dimension of strength is nourished in large measure by the capacity to be comfortable with silence. Joan Chittester, both a contemplative and a public voice, observes, "Silence is the lost art in a society made of noise . . . But until we are quiet and listen, we can never, ever know what is really going on—even in ourselves."[5] Silence can feel awkward and even frighten us because silence brings us face to face with ourselves individually and collectively. It is often filled with tension because it amplifies what we have not resolved within ourselves. Silence is one of life's greatest teachers. It reveals what we have not yet become and "teaches the public self in us what to speak."[6]

When the instructor coaches people to wait until they are ready and to use silence, students are being invited to become more comfortable in the zone of uncertainty and possibility. And as the audience learns that silence can be full of presence or absence, an openness to a greater depth of discovery and learning in relationship to others and the capacity for "presencing" is being cultivated. A shared silence full of presence can create a common bond and the ground of a common hope.[7]

Creative people give themselves permission to operate in uncertainty. There is a necessary back and forth between acting and reflecting, articulating and listening, forming and dissolving, sound and silence. It is not solely one nor the other but, rather, the pairings that resolve into presence and create a new horizon of possibility.[8]

Trustworthy Inspiration

This way of being present on the edge of the unknown is finally sacred work. Practiced with authenticity, it has the power to give people hope for constructive progress and to awaken a shared confidence that it is possible to wade into the complexity and challenges of the new commons. Yet, as Heifetz cautions, working at this depth and especially seeking to draw others into it, carries certain responsibilities and requires an earned trust. Heifetz reflects,

> I want people to learn that inspiration is a profoundly powerful way of engaging people in the process of evaluating their values—questions about what matters most. Inspiration takes you beyond simply bargaining about stable preferences and a static set of stakes. It is important in adaptive work to engage the questions that sort out what is precious and what is expendable at a very deep level.

On the other hand, inspiration is dangerous. To teach a politician or a business manager how to be inspiring without also trying to teach them the importance of being trustworthy with the power they will gain because of their inspirational capacity is negligent, even immoral. In an inspired state, people are vulnerable to being sold a set of vehicles to realize their values—vehicles that are bankrupt, such as scapegoating the enemy and other work avoidance mechanisms. You can sell a particular action plan to people that is dangerous to them by playing to longings that are deeply anchored in their spirit, thereby garnering moral authority when you are actually exploiting them. In the practice of leadership, whether you are going to disturb people or inspire people, first, you have to be trustworthy.

It might be asked how one can model trustworthiness while disappointing people's expectations in the way that adaptive leadership often requires. The deeper practice of trust that becomes apparent over time is located in being consistent in the values that one holds for oneself and the group and also in the competency one demonstrates in acting on behalf of those values.

As a way of developing a consciousness of the values one has or may want to develop, students are asked to write an essay on how or if their ambitions differ from their aspirations. *Ambitions* are those things we want for ourselves, and *aspirations* are those things we want to be and do on behalf of others. It is an opportunity to set up an inner dialogue and find ways to mesh or distinguish one's yearnings for recognition, wealth, and power with one's aspirations to care, to love, to contribute, and to make a difference. The ambitions and aspirations paper sets up further dialogue with the teaching assistants, who read and respond to the papers. This is another of the ways in which the course creates opportunities to teach elements of presence, by bringing to consciousness those dimensions of the self that must be in sync with one's capacity to inspire and to offer other acts of leadership.

The evening singing sessions are intended to be a trustworthy space in which the power of presence, the necessity of stepping into the creative void, and the inspiration it evokes may be glimpsed experientially. Even for those who feel they get it immediately, it will take years of practice—a lifetime—to perfect the creative pairings of sound and silence, balcony and dance floor, or to listen to complexity in a way that is simultaneously musical and analytical. What will keep them at it? Do the lessons from the singing sessions and the other insights that arise from this mode of teaching and learning endure over time? This is the question we take up in the next chapter.

CHAPTER SIX

What Endures?

The Power of Language, Image, and Metaphor

ANY COURSE, program, seminar, training, workshop, or coach-client relationship may be experienced as valuable at the time and incorporated into what one knows. But in the long term, it may have little effect on ongoing thought and action. Leadership education is intended to affect significantly the actual practice of professional life however, so the critical question is, "What endures?"

It is enormously difficult to trace reliably the direct cause-and-effect relationship between professional education and subsequent practice. So it is rare that leadership educators can claim more than anecdotal evidence for the value of their enterprise—often drawn from comments made during or shortly following the course or training. Here, however, we have made a modest attempt to assess the long-term affects of this approach to teaching and learning the art of leadership.

I formally interviewed fifteen people who had participated in the course three to ten years earlier. In all but two instances, I met them in their professional context.[1] For purposes of corroboration, in ten of the primary interview settings, I conducted an additional, separate interview with a supervisor or coworker—someone who was in a position to observe and assess the former student's leadership activity in the present.[2] The former students represented a broad range of organizations and roles including: a banker specializing in international markets, the director of a federal agency, a campaign consultant, a second-term city council member, a school administrator, a speaker pro tem in a state legislature, a protestant minister, a General Counsel for a large urban county, a lobbyist for Native Peoples, a university professor, and the head of a police precinct in a major city. I subsequently interviewed more informally a county executive and a man working in international business. The interviewees were identified by various members of the teaching staff and by me. They do not represent a random sample, but they do represent the demographic makeup of the typical class.

Default Settings Reset by Conscious Choice

There is compelling evidence that all of the people I interviewed, with one exception, have been significantly affected in positive ways by their work in this leadership course.[3] They have gained a greater ability to use a critical, systemic perspective and to understand and deploy themselves in more strategic ways; they also convey a greater sense of choice and confidence. They appear to be somewhat less vulnerable to earlier default settings, enlarging their capacity to lead. This is not to say that each person learned and applied precisely the same concepts but, rather, that in one or more dimensions their analytic awareness and apparent competence had been strengthened. They appear to be able both to manage themselves and to work with their constituencies more effectively.

A study of this size can only be suggestive and lay the ground for further evaluative study. But the findings are informing. Consider, for example, a thirty-six-year-old doctoral graduate working in a federal environmental agency who told us that if he had not taken the course, he would have made more frontal attacks. Now he says,

> everything I'm doing is about changing the culture of environmental protection in this country, and I recognize it as such. I've learned about each division—their way of thinking and enough of their language that I can pass for any one of them. I've taught myself the languages of air, water, and waste, so I'm a polyglot and "religious studies major" in the sense that there's an "air religion," a "water religion," and a "waste religion." And when I work, I recognize that I have to first pay tribute to their gods in order to show them the larger truth, and I have to speak their language, or else they'll think I'm speaking in Swahili. Or, they'll think that I'm just an amusing fool from the outside.
>
> When I was in the course, I challenged Ron in class. Ron pointed out that a quarter of the people couldn't hear me and didn't care enough to ask me to speak up. Here I thought I was leading the charge, and everybody was sort of rallying around me and watching this wonderful battle. The fact is that probably 95 percent of the people didn't give a goddamn about what we were saying. They were shut off . . . And that was a lesson that I have taken to every meeting, every conference call. That was my own personal learning of what he always says: "Make an intervention, sit back, see what happens. Go up to the balcony, go down to the dance floor." I

try to make an intervention, go up to the balcony, and hope people dance around the intervention.

Heifetz drew these stupid pictures on the board [little wavy lines progressing along] that were just perfect, and there was the ritual of his saying—and I would think, "Oh, God, here's the time for us to hear again about moving the group." I remember everything around that—the words, his movement, the deliberateness of his pace.

I asked, "And do you feel that is what you are doing now—moving the group, the culture?" He replied, "I'm definitely trying to do that."

The Power of Language

Though people may take influential courses that become a part of their mental architecture over time, if asked years later to describe what they learned, typically few would use much, if any, of the specific language of the course. A completely unexpected finding in this case, therefore, was how regularly and fluently people used language and images drawn directly from the course, as they described changes in their practice of leadership. To a striking degree, even those who had been in the course nine or ten years earlier naturally and without prompting used explicit language from the course to describe how they think and work in the present.

Upon reflection, this should not be surprising. A part of the art of leadership is the ability to pay attention to multiple dynamics and hold in one's mind fitting and efficient ways of naming what is going on and needs to happen. People who practice leadership must be able to link their perceptions with effective strategies. They must develop powerful modes of understanding and mapping the complexity of strategy itself. *Images used as metaphors help to hold complex and disparate elements.* Conflict and chaos are clarified, simplified, and unified with fitting metaphors, and thus, we should expect to find a distillation of useful metaphors at the core of the practice of the art of adaptive leadership.

I have come, therefore, to an unanticipated respect for the way in which this approach to the formation of leadership gives access to a practical and powerful set of metaphors—a language that names key features of the landscape that those who practice adaptive leadership must learn to read and operate within. This metaphorical language enables new insights to remain alive in the imagination, and to take root in the life of the practitioner.

In the perception of outsiders, metaphorical language initially parades as jargon. But a good deal of the language used in this approach is accessible to most people, with minimal or no interpretation. *Work avoidance activity, the hidden issue, giving the work back to the group, knowing the history of an issue, pacing the work,* the distinction between formal and informal authority, and *assassination* or *being killed off*—all are phrases that an uninitiated audience can reasonably understand with minimal explanation.

But some of the metaphors, such as *personal tuning, getting on the balcony, using yourself as a barometer, you can't answer a tuba with a piccolo, walking the razor's edge, orchestrating the conflict, and creative deviance from the front line,* require a bit more interpretation to be usefully understood. If a person who has taken the course is heard to remark, for example, that they developed their strategy in part by "doing the pizza," we have a clear instance of in-house jargon—no matter how useful it may be to the initiated.

Icons

The phenomenon that gives rise to the pizza is, however, a central part of the framework for analyzing adaptive challenges, and it is an example of how images become icons in the process of teaching and learning this approach. The "pizza" is simply a drawing on the board that emerges repeatedly in the process of analyzing the students' own cases of leadership failure. An "X" is written on the board, signifying the purpose at the heart of the adaptive challenge in the case and the importance of putting the work in the middle. Then multiple small circles (the size of pepperoni) are added, each representing differing individuals, departments, stakeholders, or points of view. Lines drawn among them delineate factions (slices of the pizza) and additional lines link various ones of them together revealing partnerships, alliances, interactions, and the forces at play—all within a large circle that represents the whole field of action within which leadership is being practiced. When the discussion and analysis is over, what is left on the board looks, indeed, something like a pepperoni pizza. This becomes a central icon in the course—an image that subtly but steadily takes on power and meaning during the term because it holds together and distills several elements of the analytic framework being taught.

Other icons are also at play in this approach. A *pressure cooker* represents the crucible or container that is required to hold the process of adaptive work and the regulation of heat required to manage the stress. A *harp* represents an individual's personal tuning—meaning that unless one is conscious of how one's strings might be plucked, one is less able to use one's own self as an effective instrument.

These and other icons appear spontaneously over and over again as quick, symbolic drawings on the board, naming elements of the theory as they appear in the flow of case-in-point teaching. As their meaning becomes established, they may appear simply as words in the flow of conversation—conveying concepts anchored in these visual images.

Repetition

The repeated use of key phrases and icons and their evolution into metaphorical language appears to be a significant strength of this approach. Many teaching designs function on the principle that after a concept is introduced, often at a high level of abstraction, the course moves on with the assumption that the material is now in hand—or will be after the final exam or paper. In contrast, when Heifetz and his colleagues introduce a key concept, it is captured with a visual image or a short phrase (a kind of metaphorical shorthand) that simplifies the concept and provides a cognitive anchor for it. Then without apology or embarrassment, it is used again and again and again in what becomes, as the student quoted earlier described, a kind of ritual. As this language is repeated in multiple contexts throughout the course (large group, small group, questionnaires, singing sessions, and informal conversations), key concepts have a greater likelihood of becoming deeply etched into the core of the learner's imagination. A new and more complex apprehension of reality becomes dependably available along with an enlarged repertoire of possible responses.

A central dynamic in this process is that though this language and the patterns of behavior to which it points may initially seem obscure, it gains power as it names and interprets one's own experience in the past and in the present more adequately than would otherwise be the case. Access to new language offered within case-in-point teaching and learning provides a vehicle for conveying into one's own awareness aspects of reality that were previously unrecognized—embedded in the unconscious or present only in peripheral awareness—where, unnamed, they are close to invisible. One former student put it this way:

> One of the things that I've found about the language [of the course] is that it gave me a way to explain things to myself . . . Heifetz provided a language, or words, that I could use to tell me what was going on so that I better understood what the possibilities were, and the opportunities, or what I was caught up in: "The dance floor," "work

avoidance," "everybody's part of the group." Now I had words—I wasn't just feeling things—I had words for things that were happening.

As students subsequently make their way into the ongoing life of their professional work, it appears that the new language endures because it faces little competition. There is not yet enough language in conventional discourse by which to grasp the features of what is needed for the practice of adaptive leadership in today's commons. Thus, though all but poets and advertisers in our society have largely lost the practice of metaphorical thought, Heifetz and his colleagues direct attention to the strategic work of crafting worthy images and language by which people can learn, live, and lead in more adequate ways. If adaptive leadership is the work of helping to create new realities on behalf of the larger good, we may say that this approach appears itself to be creating important elements of a vital imagination and an emergent language for the work of leadership in a changing world.

We heard specific instances of this linkage between the consciousness that the language evokes and the competence it yields in relationship to, for example, self and role, the hidden issue, and silence.

Self and Role

The first woman to head one of the U.S. federal agencies told us in considerable detail how significant it had been for her to learn to distinguish role from self. Once when she was testifying before a congressional committee, one of the congressmen responded in a highly inappropriate manner for which he later apologized. Less dramatic but not dissimilar things had happened when she had served earlier in state government. But after taking the course, she had a way of understanding and managing it. She recalled,

The kind of cautions that we were taught in the course such as, "Remember that most of what's directed to you is about your role, it's not about you." That helps fend off some pretty vicious attacks. I am aware, keenly aware, that my very presence in a position of power will set off a certain type . . .

The other side of that caution is that even when your successes start happening, or when you sense appreciation or followership coming at you, that's also about your role, and it's about what people project onto you. It's not about you. And that's the biggest pitfall that people make, and it's real important. Not to say that you don't enjoy your successes. But that it's real important to know that's very fragile—it can change tomorrow. It's really about them. It's not about you. Just keep that all in perspective.

Referring again to the incident in the congressional committee, she told us,

It bothered me, sure, and I went home a little shaky that night. [But I understand that] the reaction I get is often not about me, it's about the chair I'm sitting in. That's been so freeing . . . I don't spend six weeks wondering what in God's name I did to bring this on, and was I too this or that. So that's been very helpful.

The Hidden Issue

We heard evidence that the hidden issue—the matters that are alive and powerful within the group but are not directly articulated or addressed—remained a particularly potent feature of analysis for some. One former student offered "It was important to learn that what is being talked about in the group is not what is going on." Another put it this way:

To me the most important things in the class were what happened in the large group because you could see some of the lessons of corporate culture and all that kind of stuff more vividly in the large group . . . So what's the overt agenda? What's the hidden agenda? What are the themes as betrayed by the language?

Silence—the White Space

Silence, understood as a complement of language and a communicator in its own right, also endured as a powerful element in the ongoing practice of leadership. A campaign consultant we interviewed had previously been a journalist. At the time of our conversation, she had just come through a campaign season in which she worked with thirty candidates, of whom sixteen had been in trouble. She had figured out a strategy for each of them, and although cause and effect are difficult to determine in any campaign, she could report that ultimately each of the campaigns had been successful. When I asked her about the singing sessions in the course, she responded,

> I thought it was honest. For those of us who deal with communication that sometimes is more than just words (which is what the role of political communication is all about), it was probably one of the best experiences in figuring out that you don't need words to convey what is most powerful to people in the world of communication. I mean, I do it all the time.

Somewhat surprised, I responded, "You came from a background in journalism. Didn't you already know that before—?" She interrupted,

> Just the facts, ma'am—I was into the facts. I hadn't even graduated to a picture's worth a thousand words, hadn't

even graduated to that yet. It was like I discovered there are other ways to communicate with music, with voice, with visuals, with the most powerful of all, the silence—white space as we call it in the business.

Some contend that 80 percent of all communication is nonverbal, so the lessons around silence, holding steady, and modeling the behavior you want to encourage appear to be particularly vital pieces of enduring learning.[4]

Make Each Word Count

The artful practice of language, so critical to the activity of leadership, appears as more than an implicit element of this approach. It is also taught explicitly. As described in chapter 5, in the singing sessions students are coached to make every word count, and to recognize that 'each sound, like a song, has an ancient history that you are bringing here—all the variety of meanings and resonances that it has taken on."

The ability to pay attention to the power of language and to use language effectively is cultivated also in the small group work through the study questionnaires. After each meeting of the small group, students are asked to identify a key word that appeared in the group's discussion, to look up the Indo-European root, and thus, to explore the etymology of the word to see if it casts light on the issue at hand. When Heifetz first introduces this task, he points out, for example, how the word *experiment* has embedded in it the root, "peri" which is also the root of "peril." He suggests that when we choose words, we often fail to pay attention to the ancient memory that a word bears. When a person in a position of formal authority says, "this is just going to be an experiment" (in an effort to be reassuring), there is some sense in which the group knows that to experiment is to put oneself (or the organization) in peril.

This respect for the hidden depth of meanings that words may carry and the practice of exploring that depth to interpret and inform the social system is a practice that is apparently sustained for some. One former student, a minister, now regularly uses this etymology practice in sermon preparation. Another former student who became a legislator told us that for a full year after taking the course, when the legislature was in session, each morning he placed on every desk the etymology of a word that had been used in a dominant way in the previous day's debate. Not surprisingly, he received flack from some of his colleagues. But others, he told us, were intrigued.

Authority as a Resource

Because the distinction between authority and leadership is one of the defining features of this approach, it was useful to look at this particular aspect of people's ongoing practice. Most of those we interviewed were in some position of formal authority. There is a common pattern among them: they believe that without the benefit of the course, they would have tried to address issues primarily by imposing that authority. Following the course, they are conscious of using their authority as an important but limited resource, and they work in ways that take more elements within the field of action into account, recognize greater complexity, and involve the active engagement and learning of more people. They believe that their work is, therefore, more effective.

The captain of a police precinct in New York City, for example, reflected on how he now exercises his formal authority and has come to understand the importance of giving the work back to the group. Describing how he dealt with a recent personnel issue, he said,

> In the past, I would have called in the two cops, one male and one female, and I probably would have said, "You two

are not doing the job. I'm getting rid of you." Because that's what I wanted to do—get rid of them. After taking the course, I involved more of the organization, and it became an organizational issue. It allowed them options. It also allowed me to share some of the responsibility for that action, so I'm not perceived as just cutting their legs off, which would create problems for me within the organization. It also allowed me to exert more authority and independence in relationship to the higher command—"This is my command, and this is what I'm going to do. I have to live with it. I have to pass the mirror test. Not you, I do. I want to give them an opportunity. I want to do it my way"—which I did, and which so far has worked.

Similarly, a man who had taken the course after he had a well-established career as a successful lawyer and legislator described the course as "a very useful, humbling experience." When I asked, "How was it useful?" He responded,

I think it's been useful in the group work in the legislature. But it's a constant challenge. Two years ago, I decided I knew enough. I could just pick up the "Health Care Decisions Act" and run it through as an amendment, and I did. But I missed participating with the Senate and with the senior citizens. When the Senate came to the Conference Committee, I lost the bill. And I said to myself afterwards, "You dummy, you were failing to recognize the others who were stakeholders in this whole thing, and you were just an Authority. You were not trying to get the [adaptive] work done on a very tough piece of legislation." I had to back off and let the Bar Association Committee over here, and some seniors over here, and some senators over there put the bill together. And then I still end up walking it through the process the next year. Fine. But they all had their fingerprints on it, and it ended up practically the same as it was before, but it got passed. And the reason why it failed the first time was that I had failed to learn to apply the lessons.

"But you had a way, when it failed, of thinking about that?" I asked.

That's right, I could say, "What happened?" and I could see why. My own allies, the seniors, who were stakeholders, "assassinated" me in the Conference Committee. They didn't trust that I was doing something *with* them.

Maturing Leadership: Confidence, Choice, and Courage

These examples provide glimpses of enduring learning. But how does such learning play out in a bigger picture of ongoing practice? What follows are two vignettes that locate enduring learning within a larger frame.

Each of these stories, one about Andres Alvarez and another about Jolene Jamieson, provides an account of someone working in a complex system over time, using this approach to adaptive leadership, understood in part as the management of a learning process. Both are working out of a critical, systemic consciousness that informs their sense of purpose and responsibility, and the scope of their field of action. Each one is working on an issue that is vital to the life of the commons—Andres on public health and Jolene on environmental protection.

As we meet Andres, we will see that since taking the course he believes that he deploys himself differently—listening to the emotional tone of the group, his thinking no longer confined within static organizational models, and less dependent on the imposition of his own authority as a primary means of action. He strategically recognizes that everyone represents a different issue, and he is able to facilitate adaptive learning in the group. He is more attentive to issues of timing and is intelligently alert to his own vulnerability within the system.

When we meet Jolene, we will see how she has been able to move the work of a state agency and its several constituencies by creating strategic partnerships and alliances, giving the work to those who have to change and adapt, taking risks, significantly turning up the heat, investing herself in a learning process, and holding steady over the long haul.

Now I Know That Truths Have to Be Negotiated

It is early dawn over the Andes as the plane approaches La Paz and the glow of an orange-red sky reveals the silhouette of a dramatic mountain range presided over by an enormous peak named Illimani—The Bright One or The Wise One. Then the plane descends into the dark, the tarmac takes hold, and when I emerge from the plane a few minutes later, I am greeted by Andres Alvarez, a tall man in his forties who speaks English as well as Spanish, who was a mid-career student at the Kennedy School three years earlier. I am to be a guest in his home, where his family encourages me to spend at least a few hours adjusting to the altitude.

Later in the day, I visit Andres's office, located in the new United States Agency for International Development (US/AID) building. There I meet and interview the head of US/AID in Bolivia to hear her perspective on Andres's work in health and related community development projects. She has known Andres since before the time he participated in the leadership course. He had always done good work, which is why he had been recommended for the program. She tells me that now, however, he seems to be both more analytical and more confident.

The following day, as it happens, the head of US/AID for South America is visiting from Washington, D.C., and he is sent on a tour of the work Andres has played a primary role in establishing and the project he loves most—a whole constellation of health care clinics that are effectively delivering health care to very-low-income families. I'm invited to go along.

We first visit a clinic and later the administrative offices. Most of the conversation between Andres and the visitor from Washington is in Spanish, but it is my perception that though his questions are many and probing, the visitor from Washington is impressed. My perception is confirmed in our conversation later in the car, and in subsequent correspondence he writes that the project we visited is "possibly the best health services program in our portfolio, and one I would hope to have emulated in other parts." This is, in part, because in this instance US/AID money has provided the start-up capital for what has proven to be a self-sustaining program.

I am curious about what effect the approach to leadership that Andres experienced at the Kennedy School may have had in this work, primarily because I remember the case of leadership failure Andres had presented in his small group. As he described it, he had been responsible for the administration of a large grant designated for the building of sewers. A significant amount of work was accomplished, but because Andres had focused on the political power dynamics above him at the expense of paying attention to the whole system (including the legitimate needs of the head engineer), the head engineer eventually resigned, and after the special grant money was spent, fewer sewers were being installed than was the case prior to the grant. I remembered that an American in his small group (in an apparent attempt to comfort rather than to consult) had naively suggested that the number of sewers that had been installed seemed significant, and "maybe there are enough." Andres— a strong man with deep commitments, accustomed to having the authority to act on them, and keenly aware of the role of sewers in the development of public health—was obviously moved and quietly replied, "There will never be enough sewers in my country in my lifetime."

As I invited him to reflect on how the leadership course may have informed his ways of working he tells me,

Normally, I have . . . to have my organizational diagrams and say, "this is the square that this activity fits into." Not in Heifetz's class . . . [Now] I think I'm more responsive to the situation. One of the things that I believe has changed, and I believe that it changed to a great degree because of the class, is that now I am more conscious about the emotional aspects that are involved in any task. I trust more in my hunches about what's going on . . . Perhaps the strongest improvement is that I allow myself time to understand what's the emotional atmosphere within our team and in the other team—that we're either competing, we are going to collaborate, or we are in conflict.

I'm frequently working with groups. [He works, for example, with all of the regional managers.] Now I allow them more time. I'm less—how can I say—less stubborn on the technical aspects. I allow more time for the group to develop their own processes. Before that, as you probably remember, one of the things that I didn't have was listening skills. I don't know if I have more now, but at least I try to give more time to understand what's happening and to listen. And perhaps . . . I learned to understand and to approach conflict with a more informed attitude, or a more tolerant attitude toward what the causes of conflict are. Before, I would say, "Well, take it or leave it. I'm right. I know I'm right." And leave. Now I know that truths need to be negotiated. There is no such thing as this is *the* technical solution.

As an example, he tells us about supervising a young man with exceptional promise who was being trained in La Paz to supervise physicians working in the clinics. When the young man returned to his assigned region, he had trouble being accepted by his colleagues. Using the language and concepts of the course, Andres told us that the young manager "represented the issue" of regionalism. That is, one of the regions felt keenly that it (where the program originated) should dominate the training process, but as the program evolved from a local/regional to a national program, this was no longer appropriate. Andres described how he had been able to intervene constructively. By recognizing the various factions and their differing perspectives, he had been able to bring them together, create an occasion where this hidden issue could be surfaced, and then build acceptance for the new manager. He did this not only by bringing the hidden issue into open discussion, but also by reminding the group of their primary purpose: delivering good health care. Andres was subsequently invited by each of the regional managers to conduct a similar event again.

Andres also spoke of his own vulnerability to "assassination," and the skill required to do the work and "not get killed off," in this case, when he was in a position of limited authority:

> In my position (you can imagine?), I'm a Bolivian working for a U.S. government agency. I work with Bolivians a lot of the time. Sometimes a lot of ideological aspects are involved—not in reality but in the perception of reality. "Imperialism . . . [T]hey are trying to mingle in our internal affairs." Or, "You're telling us what to do, who do you think you are?"—all those things. So those aspects are present every single day, sometimes overtly expressed, sometimes covertly manipulated. So it's important. It's very important for a project in which I don't have a direct line of authority. I have to work around . . . the edges and periphery—contacts, making

linkages, building agendas here, convincing them about the agendas, including people, excluding people. It's very important to me.

Less Authority-bound, and knowing now that truths have to be negotiated, Andres has become keenly aware of the importance of being analytical in a way that considers fewer organizational boxes and more systems, factions, and strategy—especially building partnerships and alliances and respecting the power of hidden issues held within the complex emotional tone of the social systems within which he works. He exercises more compassion and patience—the "more time"—that adaptive learning requires.

I Had to Learn by Watching

Two weeks later, I am in a midwestern U.S. city and make my way to a rectangular grid of impressive government buildings not far from the state capital building. I walk up the broad steps, past classic pillars, through a long, wide corridor, and take the elevator to the fifth floor to interview a woman who took the leadership course a decade earlier. An administrative assistant offers me a comfortable chair in a corner office where large windows open to a wide-angle view of the city. I am a bit surprised when a few moments later a woman somewhat younger than I had imagined enters her office. Jolene Jamieson is the head of the state's environmental agency.

Over the next three hours, I interview her, and then I speak separately and confidentially with one of her associates. I begin to understand how Jolene has addressed the challenge of securing adequate funding for the work of the state's environmental agency in a heavily industrialized state where the business community strongly resisted change, specifically the possibility that environmental regulation might be beneficial. Now, several years into the process, adequate funding and, hence, more adequate staff levels have been achieved for the agency. More, there is greater understanding of the issues within the political and business communities throughout the state. Recounting the lengthy process, Jolene drew repeatedly on course concepts.

> Initially (it's understandable why this didn't quite succeed) we tried to move from $150 for an industrial waste fee to $80,000 in the highest case—a petroleum company. So that was maybe "moving the group," as Heifetz would say, a little too quickly—even though "too quickly" in this case was two years of public hearings around the state to get people educated about why we were doing this.

When this typical approach was unsuccessful, Jamieson and her staff took the risk of creating a crisis and turning up the heat, thus fostering more disequilibrium in the service of promoting the adaptive work. They went to the legislature saying, "We can't continue. We need to have these funds, or we really can't continue operating. Therefore, we may have to return some of the programs to the federal government."

No state had ever done that. No governor had ever done that. This threat was made only after building a consensus among the governor's senior staff that included the sober recognition that the threat would have to be carried through if the legislature did not approve the funding plan. All involved knew that these were very high stakes.

Jamieson told us that amid the brouhaha that followed, she determined that it would be strategic to meet with all the legislators in their districts and "tell our story, because we had a good story." During the ensuing four-month road trip, she also went to the executives of the major corporations, the heads of medium and small businesses, and directly to editorial boards of newspapers throughout the state. She told the story, and she also listened. The consequences were dramatic. She learned that people knew very little about environmental protection, and that she had underestimated the need to make clear what the responsibilities of her agency were and the costs. Responding to requests for independent proof of costs, she hired a nationally known accounting firm to assess the costs in an open, public process. "When they came out with this number of $30.2 million just to run waste and water, I can't tell you the shock among the regulated community."

She also learned that the legislature wasn't getting adequate input from industry. So at her request, the governor created a task force of fifty people to work on permit fees, with the lieutenant governor as the Chair. It included prominent people in the business community as well as mayors and legislators. "Since the problem was going to be getting it through the state Senate, we also made sure we had the environmental leaders in the Senate on the task force. Knowing where your allies are, where to go to get that support, and to keep the thing moving along is critical."

As we have seen, Heifetz describes adaptive leadership, in part, as the management of a learning process that includes "giving the work back to the group." This is reflected in Jamieson's account as she continues:

> Then we began to educate them. What we did basically was engage them in making it their work, so that it was no longer my agency and my issue. It was now their problem and their responsibility to solve. So shifting that was pivotal. Instead of my making recommendations on what municipalities should pay, the heat was all deflected to . . . the people who were going to actually pay it. In the meantime, we had been talking also on the national level about the federal mandates and the oversight issues and had formed a national organization for all of the environmental directors . . . So suddenly we have quite a bit of leverage with the EPA.

Jamieson was very gratified by what had been achieved and by the recognition she had received from her coworkers. She seemed to accept as part of the work that skeptics remain in the mix and would still need to be convinced. I then asked her, "Do you think that you have done all of this any differently or thought about it differently because of the work that you did in the leadership course?" She responded,

> Absolutely. Absolutely. There is not a day that goes by that I don't use the course somewhere . . . "Getting on the balcony and getting on the dance floor"—that is such an important concept, to be able to remove yourself, particularly in the middle of the heat, but in the middle of anything, to be able to pull back and say, "What is going on here?"

She also told us,

> Heifetz's ability to hold steady when everybody was looking at him . . . Every week you watched, and you learned through his example how hard that must be and yet how powerful it is. And it's something that I use here all the time. With my staff in particular—I'll ask a question, and they'll all look at me, and I'll just sit there. And I'll sit there for forty or fifty seconds if need be, and I'll finally say, "I've got all day, so I'll just wait until you're comfortable." So that is very important. And I'll say to them, "I don't have the answer. I asked the question, so I'd like to know what you think." And they get uncomfortable. And being able to hold the silence and hold steady is a very important tool, particularly for someone who's an extrovert, which I am, managing a group of introverted engineers, which I do.

"It would be easier to just keep talking?" I asked.

> Yes. And get sucked into trying to give the answers, rather than holding steady while these introverts process and analyze.

And it takes minutes sometimes, and it seems like years. So watching him do that week after week was a very powerful tool that could only be learned, for me, through his example. I had to learn by watching.

What Jolene also appears to have learned by watching, and through her own experience, was how to engage others in the work, even and especially those most resistant to her objectives.

What can be observed in the both Jolene's and Andres's accounts, beyond the importance of giving the work back to the group, is the ongoing maturing of leadership through the development of stronger analytical capacity and skills, a deepened appreciation for the reality that truths must be negotiated, and greater patience for the often long-haul nature of adaptive work.

Less Control, More Confidence

This approach contends that those who practice leadership are not in control in the way that heroic leadership and organizational charts imply, so it is interesting to observe that though people learn a way of seeing and acting that opens into greater complexity and takes them beyond their comfort zones, their sense of confidence is not diminished but rather enhanced. Surely no single course alone can take credit for the enhanced confidence observed in former students who have experienced also at least several other courses in the school as well as other influences. It does appear, however, that surviving the public disclosure of their own experiences of failure, and gaining access to analytical concepts anchored by powerful metaphors and linked to their own experience does give people new powers. They are enabled to develop modes of conscious leverage in relationship to things that were formerly either invisible or presumed to be impossible. To have words—language—for what is happening can enable people to be more confident and competent because they are less victims of circumstance, less simply awash in the swirl of events. They are less apt to be blindsided and consequently disempowered. In other words, though the course brings about a deepened consciousness of the ways in which one is not in control, there is the companion discovery that one can achieve a greater understanding of what is happening in the field of action and intervene in potentially more effective ways.

The Courage to Practice an Art Never Fully Mastered

Seeking answers to the question, "What endures?" and interviewing former students and their supervisors or other colleagues, I found substantial correspondence between self-report and the observations of others. Not surprisingly, there was also evidence that the art of adaptive leadership cannot be mastered in a single course. Again, every student learns on his or her own horizon of readiness. Thus, though those we interviewed provided considerable evidence (again, with one exception) that they had gleaned new ways of seeing and new modes of response, their learning did not necessarily include vital companion elements. Since these other elements were not, therefore, a part of their repertoire of leadership practice, former students remained vulnerable to blind spots of varying kinds—a reminder that leadership understood as an art is always a matter of some courage in the face of never knowing everything. The former students themselves tended to be aware of this in principle—a consequence perhaps of the strengthening of their critical awareness and a deepened respect for what adaptive leadership requires.

Significantly, I discovered a group of former students who had found the small group consultations and their reflection on failure using the framework of this approach so valuable that after completing the course and returning to their home region, they met regularly for more than a year and continued to work cases of leadership failure together. Given the demands of their professional commitments, I asked how they found the time to do this. One responded, "Why wouldn't you want to keep sharpening your blade?"

Courage and Costs

Discovering How to Teach the Unteachable

L EARNING is forged in an alchemy of relationships—among a student, a teacher, and the subject matter.[1] Though the approach to learning leadership described here weaves a far tighter and more seamless fabric from these three elements than most forms of teaching and learning, we have focused primarily on the experience of students. What about the formation a teacher? How did case-in-point teaching in the service of adaptive leadership develop? How does it feel to teach in this way? What does the approach ask of the instructor-coach-teacher?*

Acts of adaptive leadership depend on a capacity for self-knowledge as well as an understanding of the systems that need

---

*This chapter is composed of material from three extensive interviews across a period of several years. One was conducted by Karen Thorkilsen and the others by Sharon Daloz Parks.

to be mobilized to address tough problems. This practice of leadership calls for a willingness to be radically honest with oneself in relationship to the reality at hand. It requires self-observation within a complex field of action—and the capacity to improvise. Teaching adaptive leadership using case-in-point requires similar capacities, and it offers considerable rewards and satisfactions. But just as there are dangers in the practice of adaptive leadership, there are dangers inherent in teaching. Teaching case-in-point requires a kind of courage, and it does exact certain costs. In dialogue with Ronald Heifetz, I explored what this teaching method asks of the teacher and key influences in the process by which this teacher has come to teach what is often regarded as unteachable—leadership.

Ron, you have developed a practice of teaching leadership that is distinctive and departs from the way most people think about teaching. As a teacher, how do you experience and understand this approach?

This way of teaching isn't safe in the sense that I do feel exposed and sometimes I feel embarrassed. It is also intense. In the early years, I would teach from 4 to 6 p.m. Then I'd go back to my office and spend an hour taking notes on what had happened. I would try to identify the primary themes so that I would know where to pick up the threads the next week and manage the process in a way that could be productive. Then I would go home and by 8:00 p.m. I'd go to bed—I just felt totally exhausted.

You see, this kind of teaching requires continual analysis, searching for patterns beneath the surface of what is happening in the class. It requires taking risks in naming what may be uncomfortable but useful to learning.

Listening is the key to it, and I have to try to listen and act at the same time. If I get it right, then I've named an issue or dynamic that at once makes sense to people but also surfaces a hidden or resisted topic. For example, just after President Bush's reelection in 2004, I suggested that the unusual quiet in the class was symptomatic

of the foreign students' frustration with the United States, and
their difficulty, for a variety of reasons, in engaging in productive
dialogue with their U.S. colleagues. That interpretation made
sense, and it surfaced the suppressed conflict. Because the theme
of the week was "orchestrating the conflict" this became a useful
case-in-point. On the other hand, when my interpretation is
wrong, I have to face that, acknowledge the obvious, and figure
out where to go next from my public mistake. I believe this kind
of "listening in action" is an essential skill in the exercise of leadership—particularly when we're facing adaptive challenges rather
than technical problems.

Teaching case-in-point also requires a kind of "moving into
the void" as Buddhists might describe it. Freudians would call it
tapping into wellsprings of the unconscious. Jungians would call
it tapping into a collective unconscious. You are working on an
edge, and in that space you feel confused. That's a symptom of
being in the void. Often, I don't know what to make of what's
happening. I don't see the shapes in the fog, and yet I've got to.
I have to give myself permission to stay with the confusion until
I begin to see the outline of something in a way that begins to
make sense. Usually, if I stay with the confusion long enough, I
will begin to see a shape, a pattern in the classroom dynamic or in
the student's case. Then I can point out that pattern. The class can
work with it to see if it makes sense to them and if they can use it
as they learn how to provide leadership within a group that is trying to make progress on a tough issue.

I want them to learn how to take somebody's poorly formu-
lated story, be curious about it, and help them make sense out of
it. That kind of diagnostic work has to be done in professional life
every single day—taking a messy situation, trying to make sense of
it when you only have one fragment to begin with, and maintaining your curiosity so that you don't jump too readily to conclusions.
To exercise leadership, you need to build a systemic framework

that will yield a bigger picture and give you access to a larger field of understanding and action. So what I'm trying to do in the way I teach, and what I am inviting students to do in the class, is akin to what they have to do in their practice of leadership in the wider world.

> *This kind of teaching requires you to sift through issues relating to the presentation and flow of course content while discerning issues of students' readiness and resistance—all on the fly. Doesn't that mean that there is a sense in which you are not exactly in control of your class?*

It isn't easy to describe. It's not that you are out of control, or that you don't care about outcomes, or that there isn't any discipline, but somehow these commitments are deployed differently. Teaching in this way is fundamentally about improvising. For children, improvisation comes naturally. For many adults (including many traditionally formed teachers), it may take prodding and encouragement to recapture that mode. But it can be done. It does entail a kind of letting go of a mind-set that is attached to a single plan and pathway. In an improvisational mode, I have to be ready for whatever is pitched at me. I still have an agenda, but there is a lot of flexibility within our structure to meet the agenda in ways that turn out to be unique to each group.

This course in leadership has a lot of structure—weekly themes, large class sessions, small group meetings, readings, case presentations, singing sessions, study questionnaires and other written assignments—but within that structure (which we try to maintain fairly fastidiously so that there is clarity about those boundaries), there is a great deal of room to improvise. It's a matter of learning to contain periods of confusion and uncertainty without feeling compelled to take action, and at the same time to keep inventing, discovering, probing, experimenting, trying this and that. Our class, then, provides a model for adaptive processes, which are by nature experimental and cumulative.

When, for example, students stand before the class and present their own cases of leadership failure, the way they frame the problem is often part of the problem. Frequently, they would not have gotten themselves into trouble had they understood the problem differently early on. But even after many years of teaching this way, I often sit confused in the front of the class for forty-five minutes or so while the students discuss the case, before I begin to have some diagnostic ideas.

> *This way of teaching is obviously demanding, but when you look at it from another angle of vision, in some ways it appears easier or safer. You can make mistakes and you can even be lost—a luxury compared with the expectations in most teaching contexts. As you become more practiced, does it become less stressful?*

As I have become more experienced in teaching this way, it has become less exhausting. I'm not as anxious about it as I was. I am better at training the teaching staff so that they carry more weight, and I don't have to carry as much of it.

My experience still varies from class to class. There are classes after which I feel elated because it just sings. And there are other classes that are troubled, and I go home feeling spent and troubled. I've learned not to draw too many conclusions from either of those experiences but to view my emotional responses as data. Sometimes the best classes are where I feel awful afterwards, and the awfulness is because I've connected with the confusion of the students and their dilemma, and I have taken on board some of their own emotional experience. And sometimes when I'm elated, I'm misleading myself. I may think I've done something great, but it doesn't mean anything great actually happened. So I'm wary of over-reading my experience. It provides clues. But the teaching staff is really crucial in helping me test out the clues.

The teaching staff is essential also in preparing for class so that I understand what dynamics I'm walking into: What is going on with the students? What do the teaching assistants perceive from having read the weekly group study questionnaires? What were the events of the previous week?—all of which informs what might unfold. It is not about planning what will actually happen. It is preparation for knowing what some of the possibilities and themes might be, and how we might connect those themes to the theme of the current week.

I have come to regard this way of teaching as both harder and easier. It is harder because of the unpredictability of much of the classroom process, though I am now more at ease when it takes time to find the threads. It is hard to offer myself up for scrutiny, but I'm not as worried now about making mistakes, and it has become easier to acknowledge them. In other words, this is where it gets easier. You don't have to be a clean machine. You can use your mistakes in class rather than being afraid of making any. Correcting your stance becomes feasible. If I lose credibility, I can also regain it. The mistakes I make, the misinterpretations I make, the times when I misunderstand people, or when somebody catches an edge of my personality, or I get short-tempered with someone—all of that becomes available for people to scrutinize as illustrations of what are both sloppy and elegant tactics of interaction. Students can learn from my errors as well as my skill.

What do you mean when you say, "someone may catch the edge of my personality"?

There are easy moments and there are hard moments. The easy moments are when people project onto me issues that are not terribly provocative to me personally. So they can project them onto me, I can see it as a projection, but it doesn't hook much of myself and my own personal history, and I don't get drawn into my own personal quagmire. I can find an appropriate response, maybe immediately or maybe later, and comment on it: "Look what you're asking me to do, or look what you expect me to do. What would happen if I disappointed your expectation right now?"

At the very beginning of the class, for example, people want to know the structure of the course, and I will tell them it is in the syllabus, and then I question the function of my answering their question [see chapter 2]. This upsets people because students normally expect their teachers to answer questions. If I suggest that answering would alleviate their anxiety and that it may not be in the interest of their learning for me to do so (because a part of the formation of leadership is learning to take risks and to generate a stomach for disorder), I am exposing and violating an implicit part of our social contract, which understandably disturbs people. But I am comfortable enough with this way of teaching to comment on that without getting personally hooked.

The hard moments, in contrast, are when somebody will say to me, "Well, I think what you said to so-and-so was really unfair." That may be harder for me to process, because I have to think, "What did I say, what was behind it, where was I coming from, is this something in my own blind spot?" Then if I don't think that it is, how do I respond in a way that doesn't sound like I'm just defending myself? At the same time, how do I draw attention to issues such as how the comments of an authority figure might sound stronger or more harsh than if the same comment had come from a peer, or that the student may have had their own investment in hearing me a certain way?

If, on the other hand, I did make a mistake, perhaps a prejudicial remark, then it would probably take me a while to figure it out. I would have to debrief it with the teaching staff and maybe lose some sleep over it in order to figure out what's me and what's them. If a piece of it is me, I have to acknowledge that in the classroom. This is what we describe in the practice of leadership with the sophisticated phrase: "owning your piece of the mess." I have to do this because the trust that enables me to work with the class is contingent on my willingness to be honest in the same way that I'm asking them to be honest about themselves as cases-in-point. So in this approach to teaching, I can be myself with my own edges—as long as I'm willing to have those be grist for the mill as students learn about the deployment of their own selves in positions of authority or in the exercise of leadership. I can restore my credibility only if I allow my mistakes to become useful teaching moments in the classroom.

I have to do this, however, without being self-serving, manipulative, ingratiating, or asking anything in return—which are all temptations. In other words, the basic contract is that they have authorized me to serve their learning, and that contract must remain intact. I'm in the role of serving their education, though part of their learning comes from my learning out loud in front of them. But I'm still holding them and not asking them to hold me, forgive me, or take care of me—and that's a hard line to draw.

The development of any approach to teaching emerges through the particular life experience and imagination of the one who aspires to teach. What are some of the primary features of your experience that have shaped the development of this approach to teaching leadership?

Well, life rarely unfolds in a linear fashion. But let me see if I can put this in some kind of sequence and trace key influences in a way that will give you a reasonable take on a complex story.

First, I know that I've had some great teachers who intentionally and unintentionally modeled important lessons for me about teaching and learning. When I was at Columbia, for example, I sat in on a Philosophy of Law seminar taught by Ernst Nagel. He was a brilliant man, a beautiful man, and a good man—but sometimes boring for some of us to listen to. Occasionally, there would be a student or two who would nod off and go to sleep. And Professor

Nagel would then begin to talk in a quieter voice, as if not to disturb them. That was perhaps the most important thing I learned from him, not the philosophy, but that level of humility and thoughtfulness, a kind of reverence, a respect for students and their experience. It moved me quite a lot.

Though I feel I am light-years away from attaining that kind of humility, that experience does help me to be more compassionate toward students and more mindful of the courage and costs of learning. If someone is not paying attention, I can get irritated. Or I can see that unconsciously they may be making a decision to tune out because there's a difficult lesson for them on the table, and they are opting out of a conversation that is too confusing or too disturbing to them. Then I see that it is my responsibility to find a way, if I can, to draw their attention back to the questions on the table, but in a way that they can manage.

In terms of the intellectual history of these ideas and this approach to teaching, the concept of adaptation intrigued me from my background in evolutionary biology, a topic that interested me in college and later in medical school. In terms of method, I was surely influenced by my medical school experience, which was anchored in experiential learning through an apprenticeship model and clinical work.

Then, when I made the shift from surgery to psychiatry, it was clear that psychiatrists had a different mode of approaching problems than surgeons. Surgeons exercise their authoritative expertise by diagnosing the problems and then treating them, and often they do a magnificent and artful job of addressing problems amenable to surgical treatment. Psychiatrists have quite a different mode of working. When a person comes to you with a problem, it is your job as a psychiatrist *not* to own the problem. Obviously you do diagnostic work to try to understand and treat. But the treatment is often directed toward developing the person's own capacity to solve their own problem—and that is a very different mode of operating. This difference between surgeons and psychiatrists contributed to the development of the subsequent distinction we made between technical problems and adaptive challenges.

Another primary influence in the development of this approach to leadership and teaching is my relationship with Riley Sinder and the early development of our music seminars. I met Riley in 1971 when we were both at UCLA. He was a doctoral student in physical chemistry teaching the organic chemistry laboratory course, and I was a pre-med student. I had taken a leave of absence from Columbia for a year to study the cello with Gregor Piatigorsky at USC, and went also to UCLA part-time to continue my pre-medical studies. Riley was interested in models of sudden transition, as in phase changes, and was working with the mathematical modeling of chemical systems. I was interested in creativity. We were both musicians. Together we experimented with small groups of friends, frequently just playing music, but sometimes trying to help them discover that they were creative and could make music too. As we continued on our separate paths, he went to Washington D.C., I went to Harvard Medical School, but we continued to think and experiment together.

About seven years after we first met, I had decided that psychiatry was my exit route from medicine, and I was going to pursue thinking about the problems of leadership, conflict resolution, and public policy. I had come to realize that I wanted to work not only with individuals, but also with the systems they live in.

About that time, Riley and I developed a seminar in music and creativity that we called simply "The Music Seminar." For five years, while I was going through my psychiatry residency and transition out of medicine, Riley and I went around the country giving intensive two-day workshops, working with ten or twelve people at a time. Those seminars became our laboratory for experimenting with how to teach the unteachable, and how to hold people through what looked terrifying to them—for example, making up a song without words from scratch in the intimate setting of someone's living room.

In this same early period, one of my most significant teachers was Edward Shapiro, who directs the Austin Riggs Psychiatric Hospital in Stockbridge, Massachusetts. I spent a year as a resident working with Ed in the adolescent and family treatment center he designed and ran at McLean Hospital, treating adolescent kids in the context of the family—a whole systems perspective. This exploration of a systemic perspective moved beyond the focus on the individual alone, and it was one of the ways in which I was mining psychiatry for tools that I could apply to politics and organizational life.

Ed suggested that we take a look at the work of the A. K. Rice Institute and their Tavistock workshops. One of the key concepts they focus on is authority and the nature of authorization. So Riley and I started thinking pretty hard about the nature of authority and authority relationships. Tavistock was important also because it developed a social systems perspective based on a psychological approach that complemented the systemic paradigms coming out of engineering and biology, and it was a further step along the spectrum of experiential teaching in which the workshop dynamics themselves became "a case."

The Music Seminar continued to evolve as we began to think about using it as a vehicle for teaching leadership, inspiration, productivity, authority relationships, and group process. This little laboratory gave us a lot of opportunity to experiment because these were very intense workshops, involving twenty-five hours over the course of a single weekend. Because we did this workshop fifty times over five years, we learned a lot from our successes and failures.

During this same early period, we looked at the Erhard Seminar Training. That was an important experience because we saw two hundred people in a room over two weekends go through a powerful curriculum and have a learning experience that seemed to change many of their lives. It was also important because it was largely experiential. With both Tavistock and the Erhard Seminars we did a great deal of pretty rigorous sifting through what was valuable and what we thought was counterproductive or misleading.

Then, when I came to the Kennedy School for the mid-career program, I learned from the traditional case study method and particularly from the outstanding teaching of Mark Moore how you might weave together a string of cases to illustrate a set of ideas. These cases did not provide direct experiences, but students would vicariously have an experience by reading and then discussing in some depth someone else's experience as distilled by the case. I have chosen to focus on using the class itself as a case and student cases as extensions of the formal case method. I do not believe that the traditional case method has the power of the methods we have developed, but they are an important adjunct, particularly in some contexts. These pedagogical techniques can be integrated. Whatever technique is chosen must fit the context, the audience, the length of time you have to work with them, the level of trust they have in you, and the content that you want to make accessible.

How did you move from being a student at the Kennedy School to being an instructor?

When I was a student, the work of several members of the faculty became important in the intellectual development of this approach. For example, I wrote a paper on U.S.–Soviet relations for a course with Joe Nye and Graham Allison. I drew in part on the writings of Robert J. Langs, a psychotherapist who had done seminal work on the concepts of the adaptive context and the adaptive work of patients. Joe and Graham challenged me to develop a framework that would take into account the complexity of large systems, and not just small groups, dyadic relationships, and individuals. Dick Neustadt, Mark Moore, and Marty Linsky challenged me to think politically and organizationally, and they influenced our thinking about formal and informal authority, the distinction between leadership and these forms of authority, and about the normative dimensions of both sets of activities. Dutch Leonard challenged us to think empirically and more rigorously about the underlying assumptions of the emerging framework.

In their start-up phase, institutions are often particularly hospitable to long-shot gambles. In 1982–1983, my student year, the school was relatively young, and it was a distinctively creative, risk-taking, and experimental milieu in which to work. The school's stated mission was "to train leaders for government." The faculty, however, had not yet focused on developing a curriculum in leadership. At just that time, Riley and I had been encouraged by two business executives and alumni of The Music Seminar, Joe Goodnough and Sue Williamson, to develop a workshop on leadership, and we had begun to design a leadership curriculum. I told Tom Schelling, a creative thinker and one of the founders of the Kennedy School, about our experiences with teaching and our ideas about leadership education. He invited us to offer our newly designed leadership workshop to faculty in the hope that it might be useful to them in their efforts to generate more creativity among students. Tom sponsored a luncheon seminar in which I presented the idea of giving a faculty workshop. Twenty or so faculty members attended, and though many said they were interested, no one signed up for the weekend workshop. So over the next several days I went to talk with each professor individually. In the end, nine adventurous members of the faculty participated. The response was sufficiently encouraging that Dean Graham Allison offered me a one-year contract to experiment with developing courses in leadership.

The leadership and authority distinction began to emerge in the discussions that Riley and I had while designing the workshop for the faculty. We were joined by a team that included John Lopker, Alan Silverstein, Joan Singer, Nan Trent, Virginia Thorndike, and others. I recall toward the end of our design weekend arguing late into the night with Riley about theory, and I finally fell asleep. In the morning, I discovered that Riley had completed the manual for the workshop, and he had written on the title page: "The Management of Leadership and Authority." I said to him, "What do you mean? This is crazy! There are no such distinctions!" And then we heatedly argued and debated some more about his intuitive leap. And that was very, very exciting.

The full development of the idea, however, took another ten years to clarify—in ongoing collaboration with a number of colleagues, including my wife, Sousan, during my first decade of teaching at the Kennedy School. Richard Neustadt had distinguished the formal powers of authority from informal influence, inspiration, and persuasion, in his book *Presidential Power*. Other scholars had distinguished headship and leadership, or as Robert Tucker of Princeton analyzed it in *Politics as Leadership*, the difference between a constituted leader and a nonconstituted leader. We came to view this insight primarily as a distinction between formal and informal authority, anchored within a concern for the nature and sources of *power* in human relationships. Critically useful to practice, we use it every day in our teaching. Yet we also found from working with the case dilemmas of our students the need to make a further distinction. We saw that many people were exercising leadership without much authority of either kind, and many people with a great deal of authority, even of both kinds, were not exercising much leadership.

By distinguishing leadership from both formal and informal authority, we have used a different anchor for the study and practice of leadership. Rather than using social or political transactions as the central unit of analysis, we have used *progress* as our basic unit of analysis—the activities by which work is mobilized to achieve progress on difficult challenges—particularly adaptive challenges.

How did "assassination" and the importance of "staying alive through the dangers of leading" become a central feature of your perspective?

I grew up in California, and I was coming of age during the time when President Kennedy was assassinated. Later, at the age of seventeen, I was working for Robert Kennedy's presidential campaign in Los Angeles, and I was at the Ambassador Hotel the night he was assassinated—two months after Martin Luther King was assassinated. Assassinations were real events in my own development. I learned early on to respect that taking up a role that represents change and loss to some people can be costly. Sometimes the assassination is physical—but usually people go after your character, your competence, or your family, and you can be scapegoated, marginalized, seduced, or otherwise neutralized. If you are going to make progress on tough issues, you need to learn how you can "walk the razor's edge"—challenging people at a rate they can stand to make hard choices and adjustments in some of their ways of life and work—yet staying alive to assist your group, organization, or society in making progress on adaptive work.

The use of silence is a feature of your approach that some experience as distinctive, useful—and powerful. How did silence become a part of your practice?

Again, back to the music seminars. When someone found that they could sing in front of a group in a way that revealed a measure of their authenticity, often an extraordinary silence would follow— a pregnant, prayerful silence. We began to experiment with silence. Riley may have noticed the power of the silence because he has some Quaker heritage. Perhaps I was ready to notice this because I can remember that when I was a boy my father, who loves the arts, asked us once at the dinner table what in sculpture would be the analogy to silence in music? The four of us kids around the table began to guess, and someone in the family guessed "space." Whatever the prompts were, we began to see in those seminars that sometimes you need to pause to give people the time and space to catch up with you and with their own thinking. There is a kind of cadence that carries you along together.

I have learned that I need the silence too. Most of my use of silence is giving myself permission to think on my feet, and I'm willing to pause, sometimes for an extended period of time, because I give myself a lot of permission to operate in uncertainty. If the pause goes on too long, of course, that doesn't work either. So in my teaching, I'm working musically and analytically at the same time.

Over time, you have woven more stories into your case-in-point teaching. Like images and metaphors, good stories take up residence in us below the neck. How has this aspect of your teaching evolved?

When I began teaching leadership in shorter forms in one or two-day sessions, for example, rather than in a full-term course, I learned that carefully selected stories can serve as a mini-case that can become alive in the moment. A story can distill and anchor a key concept you are trying to get across. You choose a story that you hope is resonant with people's experience and especially their experience in the immediate moment.

I mentioned that as an undergraduate, I took a leave from Columbia to go to USC where I had the honor of studying the cello in the master class of Gregor Piatigorsky. Two days a week, five hours a day, he would teach primarily through storytelling. Each of the seven or eight of us in the class on any given day would play a piece of music. In the middle of a phrase of Brahms or Bach or Beethoven, Piatigorsky would stop and launch off into a story. I was enormously intrigued by this great, animated storyteller with his deep voice and Russian accent. Not only did he tell fabulous stories, I was also really fascinated by how he was trying to teach musicianship and interpretation. He wasn't much interested in teaching the techniques of cello playing, which he left to the more senior students to give us in private coaching. Piatigorsky was interested in teaching matters of heart, interpretation, elegance, refinement, and nuance. Well, how do you do that? Occasionally he would pick up his own cello and he would play a phrase. But more frequently he would sit behind his desk in a classic European style, telling stories. Initially the stories would be confusing, and it seemed to me that he had launched way out in right field, and it was not at all clear what he was talking about. But slowly, kind of like a hawk circling in the air, he would land on his object and the import of the story would become clear. And I saw results. I saw people's hearts open, and I saw people playing the cello differently. That was a big experience for me.

In case-in-point teaching you have to draw a line between the value of presenting ideas illustrated with good stories and simply getting swept up in lecturing. What are the lures toward the latter?

I still don't feel, even after more than twenty years of teaching this way, that I get this right consistently. I intentionally give mini-lectures—ten to twenty minute lectures in the midst of the conversation in the class or in a case analysis—in order to illustrate and clarify a set of ideas. I usually do so only after I've seen that the students have grappled with a set of ideas sufficiently that I feel that when I present the mini-lecture it's more likely to fall on curious and fertile soil because they've achieved confusion by having struggled with these questions.

Occasionally, I will provide a ten- or fifteen-minute mini-lecture at the beginning of a class session in order to orient them to a difficult set of questions—themes like "assassination," the uses of conflict, or the need to be able to receive anger with grace, or how to handle one's own hungers and appetites in the practice of leadership. To engage people in conversations on such powerful and sensitive issues, I will begin at times by setting the context and establishing not only a conceptual frame, but also a tone that authorizes or validates a conversation at a deeper level of meaning and import. I also make myself sufficiently present to the process right from the beginning that the class is going to feel more tightly held, which hopefully increases their ability to take risks and go into fearful terrain. I do that, for example, at the beginning of the singing sessions [see chapter 5]. I provide conceptual material so that the students can be oriented to what kind of lessons they might learn from the experience, and I also set a tone to validate the kind of risk-taking they're about to engage in.

But I have to check myself, and I give my teaching assistants permission to interrupt me if I go past the point where the "mini-lecture" is really serving the learning of the students. So a TA might interrupt me and say to the class: "Look what's happening here, Heifetz is talking on and on, and the class is going into a state of delightful complacency and calm comfort. Are we calling forth this behavior as a form of our own work avoidance?" Sometimes I appreciate this interruption. And sometimes I am annoyed because I am really on a roll. I'm really enjoying hearing myself talk. I've got six more ideas I want to get across. At those moments I have done two different things. Sometimes I've blown through my TA and continued my talk, which usually is a mistake. More often, I stop. I let the class deliberate on the question, analyzing the dynamics in which I've gotten swept up in letting the class depend on me in an unproductive way.

I can also put a check on the lure to lecture by noticing that a part of the class is tuned in and a part of the class is tuned out. That is usually a sign that I'm off the mark, and I'm losing the aliveness in the class. I am losing the thread that might bring the whole class together in terms of its collective experience and learning. If I fall into being a talking head, I'm not giving students the opportunity to learn how to speak and how to listen to each other, how to generate a climate in which they can be heard, how to ask for consultation, raise questions, and make use of the air time that they take, and the effects of what happens when they squander that air time. I have to practice what I teach and "give the work back to the group."

In other words, I believe that if you want to teach leadership, the design and practice of the course must embody the model of leadership you want. You must model by style and course organization. Students will almost inevitably model themselves to varying degrees after those with authority in the classroom. Particularly in courses about practice, I think we have an obligation to ask ourselves, "If people model themselves after me, will they be acting according to the principles I want to teach them?"

What is the biggest challenge or demand in case-in-point teaching?

The biggest emotional demand is that I have to make it through the interim period of disturbance and distress that is generated when I challenge students deeply by going against the grain of the cultural norms they expect me to conform to as an educator. As teachers, we understandably want to protect ourselves from students disliking us, being confused, being angry at us, and talking badly about us behind our back, especially to our colleagues—all of which happens to some degree for four to six weeks in the first half of this course. It is hard to tolerate that and maintain some faith that in the end students will appreciate having been challenged.

But this demand is actually secondary to the central challenge of case-in-point teaching, the pressure to stay alert in a conversation that's often like popcorn—popping along among a hundred or so students. I can occasionally acknowledge that I don't see the connections between what is going on and the theme of the week and then ask if anyone else can. But primarily I have to have myself well enough versed in the theory, the conceptual structure of the course, and the currents of the class that I can make strong and useful connections that will serve the learning process. This means that sometimes I have to be willing to skip two weeks ahead in the syllabus because that's what is being illustrated in the moment. I have to be grounded in the course design without being overly attached to it.

> *That capacity to be alert and flexible while holding steady and taking the heat in the middle of a learning process with all of its bewilderment is precisely what is asked of adaptive leadership, so it appears that this kind of teaching requires more than simply a willingness to experiment—some deeper sense of purpose and passion. What fuels your commitment to this approach?*

This approach to teaching leadership is one way to enable people to enlarge their capacity to take action in their own lives that will contribute also to the well being of others at an individual level, a communal level, and at a large structural level. The world is full of unnecessary pain. I think there is a sense in which I'm still being a doctor. I am trying to make people's lives better—healing wounds, wanting people to have the capacity to generate healthier patterns of life. Leadership is a way to describe the activity of persons engaging in the mobilization of people around them to make progress on the important challenges of their place and their time. I want to help create a better world through the formation of better leadership. The world is so full of wasteful pain.

When Heifetz speaks of "wasteful pain," it suggests that the criteria for identifying adaptive work and assessing *progress* include attention to levels of unnecessary pain—whether one is attempting to lead within a corporation, a community, or a society as a whole. In a world full of wasteful pain, there is no shortage of the need for persons—across all sectors—who will cast their role in relationship to the common good and who are equipped to make progress toward it.[2] This approach appears to be a particularly effective means of cultivating this quality of leadership. But the important question of transferability remains. Can people in addition to Ron Heifetz learn to use this approach to teaching leadership? This is the question to which we now turn.

CHAPTER EIGHT

The Same Approach—
Other Teachers

The Question of Transferability

TRANSFERABILITY is one of the big questions that has surrounded the bold, practice-oriented, case-in-point approach to teaching adaptive leadership that Heifetz and his colleagues have developed. There are two dimensions to this question. The first, explored in chapter 6, concerns whether the learning is readily translated into professional practice. Here, we turn to the second dimension: Can the approach itself be used effectively by anyone other than Ronald Heifetz?

After all, goes the haunting question, isn't it the case that Heifetz has a very distinctive background that has played a critical role in the development of this approach and the way he teaches it? He was trained in science, medicine, psychiatry, and group and family therapy. He is a classically trained musician. He has had an intellectual partnership with Riley Sinder and others with whom, over time, he has been able to build and practice a theory of leadership and a mode of teaching it that are integral to each other. Thus, isn't the work likely to be a one-of-a-kind, personal, and personality-dependent approach? Can anyone else adopt this approach, use it with integrity, and achieve comparable results? Further, can this approach be used in quite different contexts, or is it best suited to a major professional school and primarily mid-career professionals—presented in a large class format?

There is now clear and strong evidence that others can and do teach using the essence of this approach—the framework of ideas and the case-in-point methodology—in the same and in other formats and contexts. No one is, nor should be, a Heifetz clone, but now there are many—five of whom we will meet in this chapter— who are significantly informed by this approach and use it effectively as teachers, consultants, and coaches, adapting it to their own styles, contexts, and commitments.

As a group, they demonstrate that this approach can be adopted by educators who are not trained in either psychiatry or music. Instead, they represent a broad range of backgrounds, interests, and concerns. Each brings a different style and set of talents to the work. What does seem important is that they share in common (1) a curiosity about how to practice a quality of leadership education that can more adequately address systemic change on behalf of the common good, (2) an informed respect for the process of human growth and development, and (3) a willingness to take on a mode of working that challenges both their own and others' assumptions about how teaching and learning take place. They each adopt this approach, however, in ways that harmonize with their own particular tuning, and they have all carried it into other contexts representing different challenges and opportunities, losses and gains.

Some of the questions of transferability that they help to illumine are these: Can anyone else teach essentially the same course with similar effect? Does this approach to teaching transfer across the differences of gender? Can this approach be used within different time frames—including the significantly shorter time-frame in many consulting situations? Can this approach be used with younger people—particularly with undergraduates in college, university, or other leadership development programs?

Climbing Everest

Dean Williams, author of *Real Leadership: Helping People and Organizations Face Their Toughest Challenges*, is among those who along with Heifetz teach PAL-101 at the Kennedy School on a rotating basis.[1] He teaches in the same classroom, using essentially the same course design and the same conceptual framework mediated by case-in-point teaching. He also receives the same outstanding course evaluations. He demonstrates specifically that the approach is not an idiosyncratic, personality-dependent methodology but has an integrity and strength that can be replicated by others. In so doing, however, he brings his own talent and perspectives to the work and its ongoing evolution. For example, he places an additional importance on the TA sessions as a focused, intensified arena in the ecology of the course—both for the TAs and for himself. And one of the primary lenses through which he interprets the work of teaching and learning is the apparent paradox of courage and humility. In another course, he has experimented with a different format and time-frame. He also brings a very different background to the work.

Dean grew up in Australia and later lived and studied in Hawaii and Japan. After two years of organizational change work in a large coal mine back in Australia, he became the director of leadership and organizational development for the National Productivity Board for the Government of Singapore. The search for a theoretical perspective that would be relevant to leadership development in the Asian context brought him to doctoral studies in Harvard's Graduate School of Education. What drew him to this approach was the sense that it was a way to engage critical realities that were otherwise unaddressed.

Dean remembers,

> My first day here, someone said, "There's a new program at the Kennedy School. It's a crazy class, but you ought to look at it." So I signed up. On the first day of the class, I knew this was something important—reality was clearly present in the classroom, and real issues had to be engaged, dealt with, and worked through. In my previous experience, on the one hand, there was too much in the realm of leadership and change that was touchy-feely, human relations stuff. On the other hand, there was a very American, "think positive, get the team on board, and roll ahead" approach. Both offered a bunch of strategies, but nothing that ever dealt with the full reality in a way that could interpret a complex social system—for example, the nature of Singapore, its history, its factional in-fighting, why there were riots in the streets in the fifties and sixties, and why Lee Kwan Yu was so tough in some ways and so free and laissez-faire in others.[2]

> I began to see ways of understanding the power and nature of groups—small, large, families, organizations, countries—and the unconscious forces that are always swirling below the surface of any group whenever people come together to try to get something done. The essence of resistance to work and the dynamics of assassination, subversion, and marginalization are all shadow aspects of human behavior that no one seemed to deal with adequately. I said, "Yes, let's look at that. That's what I'm here for. This is important stuff."

After completing his doctoral work, Dean taught in Hawaii and several years later returned to take a course offered in the Kennedy

School's executive program, "The Art and Practice of Leadership Development"—a master's class for consultants, educators, and training professionals. He was subsequently invited to teach PAL-101 and is now a member of the faculty, based in the Center for Public Leadership.

Dean holds a fierce and unadorned respect for the humility and courage that the formation of leadership demands. This comes through in his interactions in class. For example, it is a few weeks into the fall term, Margo has raised her hand, and Dean has given her a nod.

"I don't want to change the subject," she begins, and immediately Dean interrupts her: "You'll have to speak up, Margo, so the people in the back of the room can hear."

"It's all very nice that we all agree on the importance of good listening," Margo continues, "but in this class we have a serious problem with interrupting people. I think that's how a lot of people feel they're silenced. And usually it is the same few people who are doing the interrupting. Maybe they can't help themselves, but they keep doing that. When the group tries to invite the speaker who was cut off back into the conversation, they often just quietly refuse."

Dean responds:

"Yes. It's all very volatile. We're dealing with a whole mix of emotions. People are pretty fragile. So part of your challenge here is to develop greater strength to be in that environment. Don't even think about leadership if you are going to be worried about people cutting you off. Don't even think of making an intervention. I mean, go out and talk to the stars if it is all about you and expressing your opinions. That doesn't move anything. Put your self in the belly of the beast, or as someone many years ago said, "Yea, though I walk through the valley of the shadow of death, I will fear no evil." Well, it can be a terrifying place. But that's often what you've got to do to walk people through tough adaptive challenges. And your feelings are going to get hurt every second. It's not a nice place."

Margo persists,

"But how, if you are a leader and you are leading a group, can you insure the"—again Dean interrupts and remarks, "If you are a leader and you're leading the group, the group's about to kill you."

"Yeah," Margo responds, "but how do you insure the minority whose voice is to be heard is—it's not like we want to protect them, but at the same time, the other factions are trying to silence them by interrupting them."

"Yes," Dean affirms. "So who are your partners in this room? It is always too much to do alone. Who is going to help protect that perspective and insure that it stays on the table? Even if you get opposition, when someone engages you from a totally different perspective, don't think for a moment that they're not actually a partner. The fact they are engaging you is valuable. There are a lot of people here who speak, and then they feel terrible—they feel like 'No one hears me, no one listens to me.' They feel pretty invisible. And that's hurtful, because no one knows how to pick up their comment—their intervention—and give it voice, give it wings. The opportunities for partnering are everywhere—and it is too easy to partner with people of our own faction. That's playground stuff."

Gaylin asks,

"Is the idea that you should speak your heart and speak what you really think? I can think of a few things that I know would hurt quite a few people here."

"There are a lot of things that you probably would not want to say because the group is not ready for it," Dean suggests. "So part of the challenge is how do you actually ripen an issue? There are ways to nurse, to provoke, to build the readiness. See, if it's all about just speaking what you think, then we've lost it again. Then we know it's just going to fall into a ping-pong match. You need to be a little more strategic than that."

After class, Dean reflects further on humility and courage in this teaching and learning process:

The power of the course is in its encouragement of reflection and writing (the study questionnaires and the papers), where you really have to dig deep to understand what's going on in a group, in the class, in yourself. It forces you to look at things with a degree of humility that is unusual. Having now taught the course for a number of years, I see that those who are humble in a kind of vulnerable way—not groveling but rather becoming humble in the face of challenge—are the ones who learn.

At the same time, it requires enormous courage for students to ask a real question, to present their point of view, to engage the professor. I have students come to me at the end of the term and say, "I came in three, four, five times throughout the term, saw you in your office, but I didn't knock." For many students, you become an intimidating figure because you embody all that they disdain or admire about Authority, and they don't know how to engage you as an ordinary human being. So you begin to appreciate the courage it takes for people to transcend whatever barrier there is for them that distances them from engagement. But those who can finally "knock on the door," get a breakthrough experience, and they can begin to act in new ways.

It also, however, takes courage as a teacher to really challenge a group. Ninety percent of what you have to offer to a group probably isn't going to be useful to them. The work is to get into that other 10 percent and see if it can matter. If it does matter, is it because of me, or is it this model of learning leadership? Probably it is a combination. But the model is profound, so who I am is just the spice in the model. If I can keep clear about that, I can resist succumbing to the hero syndrome.

To keep clear about that temptation, Dean counts on his partnership with the teaching assistants. He continues,

To teach in this way, you need assistance—like Ulysses and the Sirens. The Sirens are trying to tempt him, so he's asked his crew to tie him to the mast of the boat so he can hear their song, but not be destroyed. Everyone attempting to practice leadership that addresses adaptive challenges needs someone who "ties you to the mast."

Of course, the TAs have to move through their own process of learning how to take up their authority and use it responsibly. I coach them in the same way that I do the large class. We talk about what happened in class, and I ask them why they didn't do this or that, when it would have been really helpful. They begin to see that if they don't engage me, engage the class, and provide perspective, I'm not going to be clear about what is going on, and I'm going to get killed off, and the group will be avoiding the work of learning leadership—learning how to make progress on tough problems. Once they get that, wow!

The TAs can be really tough with me, and then it becomes an extraordinary learning experience for them and for me. It is a whole other realm of the teaching. I have twenty or thirty meetings with the TAs over a term, so maybe by the twelfth or fifteenth meeting we get to that space. But that first third of the term is a rough journey.

When I ask Dean to reflect further on the most challenging aspects of this kind of teaching, he echoes Heifetz and points to another form of courage. He talks about feeling the stress himself when, usually early on in the course, there are students who go to complain to their adviser or to other professors about the course:

> If these other colleagues are new, they'll say, "Yeah, that's stupid stuff." If they go to one of the seasoned program directors, they'll say, "Yes, that's a rough class isn't it? Get back in the game." But it isn't always easy to bear those dynamics among your professional peers.

Then, taking another turn into the core of his own experience of teaching, he reflects,

> I often feel inadequate to the task, given the profound nature of what we are dealing with. There are students who are going to go out there and try to do things in the world to make a positive difference—in schools, countries, or local government. These mighty challenges are always there for me. I don't know how to transform the world. I don't know how to exercise leadership and win all of the time. There are always pieces I'm missing and discover only as we keep working the framework, grappling with issues, week after week. My confidence is simply in my capacity to wrestle with what's there. Throw out that big mighty problem—the treacherous conflict and the hope—I'll explore it with you.

For three years, Dean has also taught a shorter, six-week form of the course required in the Master of Public Policy program that typically serves somewhat younger graduate students. Though the course "works well" and gets very good reviews, he finds it less satisfying because there is less time, there is no TA staff, and therefore, the holding environment just isn't as strong. "In the longer course you are trying to get people to climb Everest and come back down safely. In the shorter course you just want to get them to the base camp and back. I like being on Everest."

"Climbing Everest" is symbolic of what this approach in its fullest expression aspires to and can potentially yield. Dean Williams demonstrates that other teachers can join and make that climb. The conceptual framework, course design, and case-in-point method can be transferred with integrity and effectiveness through the life and practice of another teacher—who inevitably and often masterfully informs the ongoing experimentation and development of this approach.

Another Kind of Strength

For Win O'Toole, the initial attraction to this approach arose from her search for a way to teach that could deepen the integrity and authenticity she aspired to within herself as a teacher. Her story focuses on three key challenges of transferability: how to use the framework and practice the art of improvisation; how to adapt to differing contexts and populations; and how to take into account differences in gender and ethnicity.

After having taught for several years at both primary and secondary levels, with expertise in special education, Win chose to pursue doctoral work because she wanted to effect change in the educational system as a whole. She hadn't been in school as a student herself for a long time, and she had three small children.

> I was scared because you can sense the level of involvement you need to bring to this approach. But I was captivated right off the bat. It felt like, "this is something that I've

thought about, but I've never had words to describe it, and I've never had people with whom to talk about it." For me it felt like I underwent a change of heart—something like the heart surgery I had as a child.

When I asked Win about that change of heart, she described the discovery of a way into an inner authenticity

I suppose it's the experience of reaching your full power and authority—though even "authority" doesn't quite capture it. It's being able to be you, and at the same time interacting with people in a way that you can get things done, that works for people. It is a way of holding the group and all the functions of authority and at the same time having mutually respectful relationships, rather than the conceit of the leader and the led. I had never seen that happen, which was probably why I was so hungry for it. I thought that to meet the hard challenges I needed to toughen—in the sense of closing my heart in order to get things done. I discovered that you meet the challenges better if you keep open and you are compassionate. I didn't know how to be effective and open at the same time.

Win confesses,

When I became a TA, I had a false sense of pride because it really meant something—at least to my peers. It was a big opportunity to try out what I was learning about authority and role, and how to stay within role but not mix myself up with it. But I knew I couldn't make interventions in the class in the way Ron could. One day when we were walking to class, I asked him, "How do you do it?" And he said, "It's an experiment. I make an intervention, try something out, as a kind of test, see what happens, and then use what happens to inform me the next time." I felt a huge sense of relief. I began to see the work of leading and teaching as

more of a process, and it was the trying—the practicing—
that was important.

Having decided that leadership education was a path she wanted
to follow, and while still completing her doctoral work, Win came
to a point where she decided to jump into using this approach on
her own. Her first opportunity was at Clark College in a summer
program for eighty mid-career students from Israel, including two
Palestinian students with Israeli citizenship. Some people were her
age, with sons in the Army, and they were survivors of very difficult
challenges. "And it was just me," she says, "no teaching assistants—
one class meeting including small group time, four days a week, from
9 a.m. to 1 p.m., for six weeks. You can imagine how nervous I felt
on the first day. Sure enough, almost immediately somebody says, 'I
can't hear you.' I said, 'Well, then you're going to have to listen very
hard.' Of course, I also adjusted myself, and I was able to speak
louder as I became more comfortable."

The first case presenter had been in the Army and then had become a principal in a school. His case was about one of his students
who, ten years earlier, had committed suicide on the playground.
He had never been able to reflect on this event without concluding
that he had been totally responsible. Using the framework of this
approach to leadership, however, and working it in both his small
group and the large group, he began to see it in a more complex
light. "So I thought," says Win, "All right. I've got to be here for
this group. I can't be wallowing in my own worries." (This is an example of how clarity of purpose, the orienting center of adaptive
leadership, is also the orienting center of adaptive teaching.)

Respecting the challenges this approach poses to someone newly
practicing case-in-point teaching, I asked whether it demanded a
lot of energy. She responded immediately: "Absolutely—though
a different kind of energy as the years have gone by." In earlier
years, she had thought more about learning the framework and

teaching accurately and thinks she has probably read Heifetz's *Leadership Without Easy Answers* about ten times. "I had to keep reading and reading to integrate all the concepts":

> In the beginning, in order to teach the concepts, I had all these note cards with me when I was teaching. Then one day the cards slipped, began to fall, and as I grabbed them, they got out of order. It was clear this wasn't going to work. They were my crutch. So then I had to start to wing it. The more I winged it, the more I realized, "This is working better, and it's the way it really should be in this approach." The framework really had to be embodied.

Then, reflecting a consciousness of the relationship between the inner life and outer action—the quality of "presence" that this kind of teaching and learning requires—she continued, "Now my energy flows in two dimensions: one is internal (I have to keep growing and deepening in my knowledge of who I am) and the other is external (course, model, or theory related). The integration of these—being and doing, giving and receiving, thinking and acting—is a continual process."

Later, she took this approach into another context and format. For six years at the University of Massachusetts, Boston, she taught the course, Leadership Workshop. The course met once a week for three hours for a full semester. The class was typically a group of twenty people who were already practicing leadership in the schools in their communities. They sat together at a large table, with Win sitting at the head of the table. Though the context was significantly different from the Kennedy School, nevertheless, almost invariably, early in the term, one of the students would challenge the authority of the instructor, in this case by attempting to sit at the head of the table in Win's place. As a case-in-point, it would provide good grist for reflecting on the role and functions of authority in the practice of leadership. Win observed:

It is, however, very different working with twenty than it is working with a larger group. It's easier to hold the group, and I find that I can be more inventive and experimental. We learn to know each other better. If you're observant and the students are observant, there is nothing that they can't see sitting around a small table. They can't hide. I used humor a lot to hold the group, and I didn't introduce a lot of fear because there was already a lot of fear on the table. I tried to uncover that.

She did not divide them into small groups (a decision she still questions). She made only three study questionnaire assignments throughout the term, in part because she did not have teaching assistants to help read them, but also because the students were mid-career, beginning doctoral students. She was mindful that the concerns they often carry about getting back into the skill of academic writing, sharing it, and how it is being judged could become a distraction that would eclipse the work itself (which calls for reflective writing, not "academic writing" per se).

As would be expected, though ranging in age from twenty-five to fifty-five, many were not experienced in systemic thinking and analysis. But they began to learn to think more systemically as they worked with the framework to address their own cases of leadership failure.

Some who are familiar with this approach and who hold only traditional images of gendered roles have argued that this approach to leadership education is more difficult for a woman to use because it requires a significant measure of energy, strength, and willingness to deal with competitive dynamics. I asked Win what she thought about this. She was unambiguous in her response:

I learned two things from this approach to leadership. One is to be aware of the perceptions that people have of you (and the issues you represent) because of your gender, ethnicity, status, and so forth, and the other is to know how to use your different identities strategically. There are trade-offs in being male or female—you just have to be in your own gender in the best possible way. The kind of "force," if you will, that it takes to hold a group and to respond to varying individuals and factions is not a muscular strength in the ways we often differentiate males and females. It is more a quality of calm, a certainty along with all the uncertainty that is something like the Buddhist notion of being in the present. Anyone can learn to be that kind of strength. Men and women are working and managing different sets of fears from different experiences.

Win has taken this approach also into other cultures—teaching and doing related research in the Gaza Strip and the West Bank—and as Win is an American of Irish descent, Ireland lays a special claim on her imagination and commitments. Among those she has interviewed in Ireland is a city councillor, a man who remains dedicated (even after taking a bullet in the back) to the resolution of conflict in Northern Ireland. She is moved by his conviction that a central piece of the practice of leadership is "helping people to see the contradictions in such a way that they can discover what is in everybody's best interest"—what Heifetz describes as "recognizing the gap that signals adaptive work." Working with this councillor and others, she realized that her interviewing itself, similar to the small group process, was meeting a need for people to talk about and reflect on their own experiences of practicing leadership in regard to whatever "relationships they see in disrepair." She wrote to one of her doctoral colleagues at Harvard, Hugh O'Doherty, "You've got to get back over here."

Leadership for What?

"Here" is familiar turf for Hugh O'Doherty, who was born in Coleraine in Northern Ireland. He came to Harvard hungry—

"ravenous for anything that would give me a handle on life in Northern Ireland." Hugh also demonstrates the integrity and transferability of the approach as he, too, has successfully taught PAL-101 at the Kennedy School. And just as Dean brings his particular lens of courage and humility to the work, and Win the quest for effective authenticity, Hugh brings a particular focus on purpose. He has also taken the approach into the field as a learning process within a living case.

This approach to learning leadership initially attracted him because both the systems perspective and the very interactive methodology were new to him. "It was very helpful to begin to think, not only about my system in Northern Ireland, but also my own role as part of one of the factions in that system. It took me a while to actually plumb the concepts of the framework, but I understood it intuitively early on."

Serving as a TA while he pursued his doctoral work, "I was able," he says, "to see patterns over a period of three years—each group learning its way over time, from initial nervousness, to rage, to despair, to the light starting to dawn." But it was the way the approach uncovered the dynamics of authority that caused a shift in his own default settings:

> One of the most important aspects for me—a hidden aspect of my life—was my own inability to work with a person in authority. Coming out of Northern Ireland, all I knew was to be utterly intimidated by authority or to secretly try to kill it off. So for me, learning to partner with authority (as a TA working with the instructor) was a profoundly difficult, challenging experience. Once I began to see it, I began to shift my behavior around it. But I had no idea how crippled I was on that issue.
>
> There was a moment in class that was a big turning point for me. In my second year as a TA, there was a guy who sat

up in the back row at the beginning of the course. He was pretty aggressive, regularly taking verbal potshots at the instructor, and each week he would move closer to the front where the instructor was. Then one day he walks towards Heifetz and he gives him a hug. But when he first stood up, I was all the way at the back of the classroom, and I felt a nervous twitch in my stomach. Later, I woke up in the night and realized that it could have gone either way. He could have stuck a knife in the instructor as easily as he hugged him. And the people who would have been least able to do anything were the TAs, because we were all perched up on the back row. It was a profound moment for me. I realized, "Here's this instructor who's hired me, and he's entrusted me to partner with him in this course." Not that I'll support blindly anything he does—but a light went on. The next class session I sat in the front row, and I could tell that gesture had a profound impact on the class, on the instructor, and on me. It was a commitment that I had never made before: "I'm going to partner with this person in authority and I am going to protect this man." That was the first time in my life I had ever done anything like that in relationship to someone in authority.

While still pursuing his doctoral studies, Hugh carried this new capacity into the field of action that most concerned him, partnering with people holding or preparing to hold positions of authority in Northern Ireland, a context perceived by many as one of intractable conflict. He created the Northern Ireland Inter-Group Relations Project. Along with three other colleagues, he pulled together seven people from the Nationalist background and seven people from the Unionist background. He talked with each one of the participants in advance, and framing the adaptive work as a compelling question, he asked, "Can we learn our way out?"

Everyone agreed to meet for six weekends at four- to six- week intervals. The facilitators did not all come from the same theoretical orientation, but the basic frame they agreed to was (1) How do we define the problem? (What is the adaptive work?); (2) What are the needs, concerns, and fears of each group that must be addressed? (How do we get on the balcony and read the factions and the system?); (3) What options can we generate for resolution that would take into account the various needs, concerns, and fears? (What interventions can be made that will dislodge the current assumptions and foster learning?); and (4) What interventions are this group willing to make into the political decision-making processes in Northern Ireland? (Can these people help others move beyond default settings and discover new, constructive forms of response and action?)

Because everything was taped, they were able to re-hear and reflect on pieces of dialogue when things got tough and examine how each participant had construed "reality." "That helped us," Hugh recalls, "see how our small group was mirroring the larger system."

During the process, Hugh introduced key principles from this approach, including the recognition that they were grappling with an adaptive challenge, and the distinction between authority and leadership. "This was important," says Hugh, "because most were or soon would be in positions of authority in their political party or in the new Assembly." Other features of the framework that were vital were "tolerating the heat" to simply stay in the same room with each other and then, if they could do that, discover what else they could do; "distinguishing self from the role or the issue you represented," because each person represented to someone else in the room a long-standing adversary; and "giving the work back to the group," which was critical in a place like Northern Ireland where there was a need to create learning experiences in which people could devise their own way out of the problems rather than depending on third parties coming in from the outside. "That," says Hugh, "was a primary purpose of mine."

Later, back at the Kennedy School, when Hugh was invited to teach PAL-101, he recalls that though he made the dean's list for outstanding teaching as have Heifetz and Williams, "initially it was pretty terrifying because of the reputation of the course and the fact that I was an unknown." When I press him regarding ways in which his teaching of the course may be different from Heifetz and others, he says that he doesn't know for sure, but he has a hunch that one variation may be that whereas Heifetz works particularly hard on the notion of authority, Hugh works particularly hard on the notion of purpose. "For me, overall, the fourteen-week class is very much couched in the questions, 'Why are you here? Leadership for what?'"

Explaining further, he says,

Right after the terrorist attacks, in class discussion some of the students were giving the students from the military a hard time. Then a woman spoke up and risked naming a hidden issue: "I think what's going on in here and why we're attacking the military is that perhaps we're ashamed that we don't have a clear sense of purpose like they do." I have learned if you take people to that edge in the practice of leadership, you come up against the purpose of life itself—a spiritual realm that is inherently a scary place. At one level this set of ideas might just help someone be a better manager or whatever. But when you work the framework in a way that keeps deepening that central question of purpose, you keep asking: "What do you want to accomplish? What do you really want to make progress on? What is your life about?" As you do this, you start out with a kind of pseudo-community in the class, and then you move through some conflict and chaos, and it spills you out into a desert where you really have to ask, "Why are we here and what do we really want to do?"

Hugh tells us that once on the last day of the course a guy came up to the front of the room and said, "The class and I want to give you something." Hugh was bewildered as he found himself looking at a stuffed toy, and it took him a moment to recognize that it was a porpoise. Then the student said, "It's something you've been looking for all semester—it's your porpoise!" "And it was a wonderful moment," says Hugh, "because it symbolized exactly the heart of it all, and I knew that in some way they had come to see what they most needed to see."

Undergraduates—Beyond Achieving to Leading

Fluent in Spanish, Alma Blount was engaged in human rights work in Central America for several years, eventually becoming director of an interfaith organization. When six Jesuit priests (two of whom she had known) and their housekeepers were murdered in El Salvador, she came to a turning point. She knew that she was burned out and needed time to grieve and gain perspective, so she returned to the United States and entered a master's degree program at Harvard Divinity School. Her struggle to make sense of her own efforts to practice leadership led her to PAL-101, and after completing the course she became a TA.

Now she is back in her own home region at Duke University, where she is Director of the Hart Leadership Program at the Terry Sanford Institute of Public Policy. There, still grounded in what she describes as the service and social justice tradition, she demonstrates that this approach, with modifications, can be used also with college students. Her purpose is to help undergraduates cultivate a strong sense of public commitment and the capacity for political engagement and leadership in democratic societies. The students Alma and her colleagues work with are typically eighteen to twenty-one years old. Many are public policy majors, but the classes also attract pre-med, English, comparative studies, and other majors. "Colleges and universities are hugely important, and in a sense they are sacred institutions because they are so influential in students' lives," she says. Alma knows that these students are developmentally ripe for thinking about their relationship to authority and their role within a group. They are ready to develop critical thought, a public identity, and a sense of meaningful purpose—and their emerging adult voice. She has adapted the approach to the undergraduate years, using both the conceptual framework and case-in-point teaching.

A course she has taught several times, "Leading from Within," uses case-in-point teaching throughout and most closely mirrors the course design at the Kennedy School. The program that she has subsequently developed, however, Service Opportunities in Leadership (SOL) involving an internship framed by two courses, uses a modified form of case-in-point teaching. The similarities and differences are instructive.

Her classes are smaller, sometimes limited to fifteen or twenty, because she believes undergraduates need a different quality of attention. She has them work in small groups (usually five students in a group) that meet independently once a week to work on assignments that relate to the theme that is designated for that week. She does not have them work with their own experience of failure in practicing leadership "because they just aren't old enough. They have been busy achieving and thinking that leadership is being a student body president, holding a position. They haven't had much practice in trying to make progress on a difficult issue." If, however, there is a student who is trying to address a campus issue, she incorporates it into the class discussion and it provides grist for the learning mill, such as when one student worked to address binge drinking and another worked on sweatshop labor issues related to university insignia clothing.

More typically, Alma has students learn in relationship to their own experience in several other forms, and in class, she does use a modified form of case-in-point. That is, having assigned preparatory reading and writing, Alma presents material in class and then invites students into discussion by evocative and challenging questions. But she also asks them to pay attention to the underlying currents of what is going on and to move past merely trying to perform. "Don't try to pose the perfect question," she challenges them. "Don't try to be the star performer who wows the class. This is going to be hard for you, but just notice how the conversation unfolds. Don't be so invested in your own little position in this conversation, because if you do, you're going to miss the conversation. Just get into the conversation."

Alma reports that a few start to get it, and then others catch on, and by the end of the course almost all of them "get it," meaning they begin to sense what adaptive work is. They discover that it requires skill to use what is unfolding in a group and to understand what the resistance or the blockage is in getting the work done. They begin to see that there are ways of collaboratively turning your attention to the work and giving the work to the people who need to do it. They discover, as Alma puts it, that "leadership is a property of the group." She adds with a sigh, "Of course, along the way the students are bewildered, and I wonder why I'm doing this. But by the end, the course gets off-the-chart evaluations."

She knows this kind of learning takes time, so she has created the SOL program as a twelve-month cycle, beginning with a course for twenty-five students in the spring. The students do their internship in community service in the summer (in sites as geographically dispersed as Pittsburgh and Namibia, all representing a range of complex, tough issues), and then they take a follow-up research course in the fall. In other words, with students who have limited experience in the practice of leadership, she creates experiences that will yield significant opportunities for the kind of reflection and analysis that is needed if they are going to learn to practice adaptive leadership. At the same time, the students gain access to the framework of adaptive leadership through an extensive research project, reading assignments, class presentations and discussion, and case-in-point learning. The final section of the research project includes an analysis of a social issue using the adaptive leadership framework.

Alma has "whittled the framework to four key questions": (1) What is the adaptive challenge?; (2) What is your strategy for focusing attention on the issues that need to be addressed? (Here they are encouraged, for example, to think about where the conflict is ripe and how they could use that as a way to focus attention.); (3) How do you regulate the stresses of the learning process? (Is there a holding environment? How do you pace the work? How do you use the resources of authority?); and (4) What is your approach for giving the work back to the people?

Alma tells us,

The students often come in thinking that they are superstars. They think they can do anything, and they think this fancy language is ludicrous, and they make jokes about it. But then they get into it, and they use it. I keep working at how to make it work for them. I found that before they could figure out the adaptive challenge, for example, I had to ask them first, "What is the problem?" They got too frustrated without first seeing the difference between the presenting problem and the adaptive challenge. It takes a lot of thought on their part. They'll quickly say, "There isn't one adaptive challenge, there are many adaptive challenges, layer upon layer. How do we frame which one we're going to look at?" I respond, "I don't know, but that's your job. You have to figure out what's the most important thing we should be looking at right now."

So they go off to their small groups and spend way more than the required time, because they know they are going to present in front of their peers.

In this way, Alma is both giving the work back to the students and she is leveraging her awareness that where these students are developmentally, their peer group has enormous power.

One of the elements of the framework the students grasp most easily is the metaphor of the balcony and the dance floor, which she uses as a primary means of encouraging the development of critical-systemic thought and helping them move from Authority-bound knowing to a more inner-dependent awareness:

I introduce it early in the course, and at first when they hear that metaphor they assume it means distancing. They think, "Okay, you're on the dance floor and then you go up to the balcony, so you remove yourself." And I say, "Mmm, it's not distancing. You're in the midst of what is unfolding, but you develop a psychological space that makes it possible while you're in the midst of the action to see the larger shape of what is unfolding, to start to see the patterns within what is going on. So it is not at all about removing yourself, it's a different way of thinking about it. It is a way of seeing clearly in the midst of the fray." They scratch their heads, and they don't really understand at first, but then they begin to see it, and they tell me that they find it enormously useful—not just in the class but in their wider life.

Developing this capacity for critical reflection on their own experience in the midst of the action is encouraged by an assignment during their summer internships called Letters Home. Instructions include the following: "Look hard at what you like. Look harder at what you don't like." They are encouraged not simply to tell, but to show by writing specific, clear, and vivid stories about people and events. They learn to write from a place of strong emotion, while at the same time they develop a reflective stance in the midst of the action and begin to think about their own patterns of thinking and communicating. They discover how to unleash their own authentic voice and to write from the truth of what they see. Alma describes this assignment as "private work that points to a public purpose, which is a basic part of the leadership development process."

In the course that follows in the fall term, students write five-hundred-word weekly essays designed to help them (1) develop a public viewpoint from their own reading and thinking on the political theme of the week, and (2) write in an informing and evocative way that can stir a public discussion in class. Alma chooses one essay each week to begin the class discussion. The students begin to learn how to develop their own point of view, and then how to cultivate provocative discussions with others who may have opposing viewpoints and values. The class becomes the case-in-point for the learning process.

In this modified form of case-in-point teaching, Alma goes into class knowing there are topics she wants to discuss, and at the same time she is prepared to respond to what appears in the group. Alma describes this kind of teaching as something like being the conductor of an orchestra and one of the players at the same time. For a period of time during the class, she will have her hands up pointing first to one student and then another as the discussion proceeds. Then she goes solo for a while—and then the student orchestra starts playing again. This often involves asking difficult questions that meet with resistance and require her to respond to that resistance constructively—"shaking things up in a way that often makes students uneasy," while holding the group in a trustworthy way.

One female student, for example, who was interested in labor issues as her major research topic, resisted the notion of leadership, saying in a fairly shrill way, "I never thought of myself as a leader or in an authority position, so this is irrelevant to me." Alma responded, "Well, you've read the first part of Heifetz's book, so you should recognize by now that in relationship to the issues you care about you already are 'leading without authority,' and notice that I am not using the word 'leader,' I'm talking about the activity of 'exercising leadership' and what it takes to be effective." This student tended to go off on tangents when she was talking about issues, and Alma would interrupt: "You aren't being effective." The student complained, but over the course of the semester, she began to listen more, pontificate less, and experiment with different ways of contributing to the group conversation. Alma is committed to finding ways by which her students can learn that "passion has to be married to strategic wisdom."[3]

At the end of the fall term, students draft a policy memo about their social issue and research topic. This assignment assists them in developing problem framing skills and policy judgment. Accompanying the policy memo is a summary analysis of a leadership strategy for changing the system or structure in question. Using the framework of adaptive leadership, students are challenged to see the issue in systemic terms, to identify what needs to change (the adaptive challenge), and to recommend who needs to do what to make progress.

Students are required to present their work to the class, "holding the group" for thirty minutes. Alma wants them to learn what she learned in the singing sessions at the Kennedy School, that holding the group is not simply about public speaking or even facilitation. It is not about how to make a flashy PowerPoint presentation. "I want them to learn about a quality of presence, and how they conduct energy, and how you engage people on a profound level." One of her students remembers, "It was much harder to do than I thought it would be—I learned that when I was nervous I rocked back and forth, and it distracted people from what I was trying to say." In the end, students often echo one of their number who said, "The follow-up class is so hard, and you have to do a lot of work, and there is hard grading—but I learned so much." [4]

They Have Already Tried Everything

Al Preble never took PAL-101 at the Kennedy School. He was an entrepreneur who had created several businesses in Hawaii, and had made some money. He was looking for something that would give further meaning to his life, and that took him to a course with Dean Williams, who at that time was in Hawaii teaching adaptive leadership using case-in-point. Both Williams and Preble were surfers, and during a break, they met on the beach. Though Al subsequently went to study at Columbia, he stayed in touch with Dean and did some work with him after Dean had returned to Cambridge. Meanwhile, Al gained greater familiarity with the approach by observing Heifetz when he was doing some consulting at AT&T.

Now a successful organizational consultant and executive coach, Al Preble works primarily with mid-level managers to vice presidents in *Fortune* 500 companies. Though he is informed by several theoretical perspectives, he draws in a primary way on key concepts from the framework and mode of teaching he learned with Williams and Heifetz. The concepts he finds himself turning to most often are (as he names them):

Technical problem equals quick fix versus adaptive challenge equals change,

- stakeholder analysis ("the pizza"),

- ripening the issue—getting attention around it,

- constraints and conflicts,

- work avoidance mechanisms,

- distinguishing self from role,

- and getting on the balcony.

Then, reflecting on the corporate scene from his own balcony perch he adds, "Too many people are dancing themselves to death."

As with other consultants and coaches who value this approach, Al has the challenge of working with people for only a relatively brief time—a few days and sometimes less. He has to discern how this approach that he believes is both powerful and meaningful can be translated into a time-compressed context.

As others who do such work have also expressed, "the ideas are intuitively powerful." But changing default settings is another matter, and Al confirms, "It is when people learn through their own *experience* that the concepts and language really come alive for them. They begin to have a way of naming previously unnamed features of their experience and seeing new possibilities for action." Thus, once again we hear the conviction that the framework is best learned when it is learned through experiential, case-in-point teaching.

Al often casts his work in three phases: (1) Trips and Traps (head trips and ineffective, repeated behavioral patterns); (2) Case Study (one of their own work situations); and (3) Monday Morning (what are you going to do when you go back to your everyday context?). In each of these phases he uses both the framework and case-in-point. This is most evident in phase two—Case Study.

Working with groups of five to fifteen people, he invites them to identify a challenging work situation that is alive for them in the present and then to clarify what is at stake. Then he asks each person to imagine and articulate an intervention that he or she thinks will help to make progress in the situation. As each one offers his or her contribution, Al encourages a great deal of role-play as a means of helping people experience how the intervention would work. The last one to offer his or her contribution is the person in the actual situation, the one who will have to make the intervention. As they explore the possibilities, Al offers relevant elements of the framework as ways of analyzing and interpreting the situation and their responses to it.

When I ask Al what gives him satisfaction in this aspect of his work, he says that he loves to see people come in with a case in which they have already tried everything. Then in the course of working the case in the group with access to this framework for analysis and intervention, they begin to find new ways to move. He observes that the process yields an increased confidence that arises from seeing more of what is going on, discovering more leverage points, and developing and testing a larger repertoire of potential responses.

When he works as a coach with individuals, the process is similar. But instead of a case, he may ask the person, "Tell me your story about why you aren't listened to and why you are ineffective." After hearing the response, he may follow up, for example, with the challenge: "Tell me a *true* story about your work—versus the one bad story that you remember." Here he is destabilizing their habitual patterns and working to help them see for themselves what they most need to see. He reflects that though the process of analysis, interpretation, and experimentation is similar to his work with groups and does lead to new behavior, he does not believe that it is as powerful without the group. "The work in the group that more closely approximates case-in-point teaching," he says, "provides a more generative field of action, reflection, and crossover learning."

Beginning with Small Steps and a Light Touch

Dean, Win, Hugh, Alma, and Al all use this approach, including case-in-point teaching in both full and modified forms, and provide further insight into the practice and potential of this approach. As we have seen, most who experience this pedagogy and then use it in their own work as a teacher, coach, or consultant take on an adaptive challenge of their own—learning to think and to teach in a new way. Inevitably, all adaptive work is a creative act. Every modification or further development of the approach has consequences pro and con and affects learning differently. If, for example, the approach is used with less discipline (for instance, without the study questionnaires or their equivalent) and over a shorter period of time, there is less opportunity for discovery and practice, less opportunity to transform those default settings. Must those who would teach leadership using this approach either embrace every element or step aside?

When Heifetz is asked this question, he responds,

One can enter into this mode of teaching with small steps. You could begin with a course or a workshop that is designed to use whatever pedagogy is most comfortable. And then you could occasionally make observations about what is taking place in the group. Raising a question, for example, if the students seem to be asking a host of questions about grading or about some structural matter, or if a small group of students has monopolized the conversation and is pulling you off on a tangent and you notice that two-thirds of the students have their eyes glazing over and they are disconnecting. You could stop the action, and you could say, "If we were to use ourselves as a case for a moment, what would you observe is happening here? Or what do you think I ought to do about this dynamic?" So one could begin with a fairly light touch. Just every few weeks or days, raising a question when you happen to notice something that doesn't seem to you to be terribly productive, but is also illustrative of the kinds of unproductive behavior that you'd like people to learn about and to become more mindful of in their own practice of leadership.

Further, if you are working with teaching assistants or other colleagues, you could debrief what happened with them, and you could ask if anything happened in class that would illustrate the content that will be coming up in class next week. You could also ask them to reflect with you about what you did in class that was strong and what you did that was sloppy and what could be done differently.

The transferability of this approach into one's own practice may also begin by inviting people to work with their own cases of leadership failure in small and large groups, using the concepts from this approach as tools for reflection and insight, and depending on the context, inviting them to write about their case using the framework. In these ways, one may take small steps into the art—the creative process—of learning, practicing, and teaching adaptive leadership.

The recognition that leadership and teaching is, indeed, art and calls forth the imagination and courage of the artist in each of us, invites a consideration of a revised myth of leadership. A reconsideration of our prevailing leadership myths is perhaps the most critical adaptive challenge this approach serves—and is the subject to which we turn in the next chapter.

CHAPTER NINE

Toward a More Adequate Myth

The Art of Leadership

L IKE MOST of our ways of life, acts of leadership are in-formed by tacit metaphors and unexamined myths. Mak-ing these more visible can be a first step toward enlarging our range of possibility and choice. In chapter 6, we observed that the practice of adaptive leadership as Heifetz and his colleagues have developed it can shift perception and behavior and has enduring use-fulness, in part, because it is distilled in a compelling set of metaphors. It is my growing conviction that these metaphors are mere stepping-stones to a yet more significant shift—the transformation of the pre-vailing myth of leadership from hero to artist.

It has become almost a cliché among leadership theorists to dis-avow a heroic command-and-control model of leadership. But the heroic image of leadership that prevails in the conventional mind is more than a model. It is a deep and abiding myth.

Myth cannot be dismissed as mere fiction. Myths are epic, powerful stories that arise from, pervade, and shape the cultures we breathe. They are formed from our collective capacity to understand, interpret, and shape our world. The potency of myths is that they provide ways for us to make sense of our experience, to make meaning we can count on and share with others. Myths give us anchoring images and stories, and they seed the assumptions by which we understand who we are, what is true and untrue, right and wrong. Myths interpret the past, locate us in the present, and shape our expectations of the future. Myths define reality—especially when they catch us unawares and we are swept up within a great myth that presents itself as simply the way things are. Myths are not easily swept away. The transformation of myth is always an adaptive challenge.

The images of leaders that prevail in society today—the one in charge, the chief (CEO, CFO), president, governor, general, captain, dean, director, head, chair, or simply the boss—all draw on the mythic power of more ancient and still resonant images of shepherds, warriors, and kings. In the more contemporary and popular imagination, these heroic roles of power and authority are distilled in the myth of the Lone Ranger and his equivalents (the Army Rangers, Batman, Superman, Agent 007, Indiana Jones, Braveheart, Spiderman, the Terminator). These images stir the blood. They are powerful and attractive in the American psyche—exported through the media to the global commons.

Though the Lone Ranger is not used explicitly as an image of managerial authority, in the culture of American individualism it holds sway as a background motif in our conception of leadership across most business and professional sectors. This image suggests that a leader should be powerful, male, effective, and able to use force (or at least the threat of it). He is a heroic figure, needed especially in times of crises, appearing just in time to save the day. He is always on the right side and those who oppose him are on the evil side.

Above all, he is independent and conveys a confident, self-sufficient identity—with just a touch of mystery![1]

Those who look to others for leadership and those who aspire to be leaders themselves are vulnerable to a deep belief that leaders are most recognizable when they ride tall in the saddle with an unquestioned, clear, and steady purpose, taking decisive, unambiguous action. Whether male or female, most who carry leadership responsibility know something of what it is to experience the expectations of a heroic–Lone Ranger model of professional and organizational leadership—a model of authority that provides enormous reassurance in the personal and social psyche, especially in times of stress and fear.

The images of shepherd and sheep, hero and rescued victims, find their analogue in the relationship of leaders and followers as generally conceived. Shepherds, warriors, and kings wisely and powerfully preside over flocks of others who depend on the leader for their well-being (and ultimate fate). The power and protection arrangements of these heroic command-and-control images retain their strong mythic pull because, as Heifetz has put it, "they are comforting."[2]

The most potent expression of this imagination in recent times has been what Joseph C. Rost has described as the twentieth century's myth of leadership: "leadership as good management." In this conception, good management is the apex of industrial organizations and an industrial economy is unthinkable without it. In this frame, Rost observes, "leadership is rational, management-oriented, technocratic, quantitative, goal-dominated, cost-benefit driven, personalistic, hierarchical, short-term, pragmatic, and materialistic."[3] This is a stark and bald account. But it conveys central assumptions about the practice of managerial leadership in which dominance, efficiency, and material productivity (and therefore a kind of security) are central values.

Now, however, we have moved into a postindustrial, nuclear, information-rich, and ecologically informed age in which an intensified connectivity and complexity are primary features of the land-scape—the new commons. In every domain, externalities break in on even the most heroic attempts to lead and protect. These include not only fast-moving technological developments and the shocks of terrorism, but also a growing awareness of social and humanitarian claims and the unintended consequences of human action upon the more-than-human (natural) world. Even seemingly unassailable commanders are vulnerable to finding themselves tangled, bogged down, or blindsided. The mythic power of heroic command-and-control leadership has not become irrelevant, but it does appear to be increasingly inadequate.

What is at stake is not simply whether myth and metaphor drawn from an agrarian age and central to an industrial age can be translated into contemporary life. Rather, growing numbers of people intuitively recognize that although these metaphors have positive features within certain contexts, they are limited and even dangerous in the conditions of our present life. Many leaders, whether chief executive, mayor, head of agency, or even leaders of religious congregations, experience a growing resistance to the shepherd-warrior-king image or its command-and-control offspring.[4] As societal stress mounts, however, others embrace the heroic leadership myth more fiercely than ever, as, for example, the imagery of empire gains renewed currency. In either case, few would deny that the heroic myth remains a dominant player in the commercial, social, and political psyche.[5] Whether we are dealing with fame or blame, we continue to prize and promote the myth of the individual person as autonomous and in control in our assumptions about leadership.[6]

The heroic myth of leadership is resonant with Heifetz's understanding of the role of authority. The big questions center in how to practice the functions of authority that maintain equilibrium and at the same time recognize their limitations in a time of profound change. We need a more spacious myth of leadership, grounded in more adequate metaphors that can embrace the complexity of systemic, adaptive work and the full range of perception, understanding, and skill that the practice of courageous and creative leadership now demands. Acts of adaptive leadership are acts of imagination and commitment. Practices of authority and technical mastery alone are insufficient. Adaptive leadership is necessarily the practice of creating new realities. Bennis and Thomas have described the adaptive capacity characteristic of effective leaders as applied creativity.[7] Thus, a practice of leadership for today's world is rightly informed by the practice of artists.

The poet David Whyte has written,

> The inherited language of the corporate workplace is far too small for us now. It has too little poetry, too little humanity, and too little good business sense for the world that lies before us. We only have to look at the most important word in the lexicon of the present workplace—*manager*—to understand its inherent weakness. *Manager* is derived from the old Italian and French words *maneggio* and *manege*, meaning the training, handling and riding of a horse . . . images of domination . . . and the taming of potentially wild energy. It also implies a basic unwillingness on the part of the people to be managed, a force to be corralled and reined in . . . most people don't respond very passionately or very creatively to being ridden . . . Sometime over the next fifty years or so, the word *manager* will disappear from our understanding of leadership . . . It is the artist in each of us we must now encourage into the world, whether we have worked for the Getty Foundation or for Getty Oil.[8]

The call to acts of leadership, which can be practiced from wherever we sit, is also an invitation to reclaim the creative capacity within every human being—especially those who are willing to engage the complex, adaptive challenges of our time.

This invitation to a greater awareness of the self as an artist does not thrust another demand upon the already burdened back of those who would lead. Rather, as we shall see, it is a pathway toward releasing constraints that heroic models imply, liberating the capacity to move in more limber and authentic modes, honoring the creativity dwells that at the core of what it means to be human.

A More Complex Myth

Whether or not the power to exercise leadership has ever been as simple and forthright as the image of command and control implies, clearly a seismic shift has been under way for some time for what leadership may now mean. Titles such as *Complexity* by M. Mitchell Waldrop; *Leadership and the New Science* by Margaret Wheatley; *Force for Change* by John Kotter; *The Fifth Discipline* by Peter M. Senge; *Getting Things Done When You Are Not in Charge* by Geoffrey Bellman; *The Connective Edge* by Jean Lipman-Blumen; *Birth of the Chaordic Age* by Dee Hock; and *Tempered Radicals* by Debra E. Meyerson—all have signaled new understandings of cosmology and organization coming from physicists, mathematicians, economists, engineers, biologists, computer scientists—and leadership theorists.[9]

Insights from the new science and the metaphors to which they give rise find a pocket in the contemporary imagination because they are the stuff of new, more adequate and satisfying myths. They convey an emergent story that we experience as more truthful. They are resonant with our growing experience of complexity, diversity, and overwhelm. Nonlinear interconnectedness, field theory, self-organizing systems, ecological perspectives, strange attractors, and information-rich reality yield significantly new sets of images that point toward a fundamental reordering of our understanding of how life works and catalyze a cultural, mythic shift—not instantaneously, but relentlessly.

Alternative images of leadership that are more congruent with this new reality have begun to emerge—for example, "flattening the pyramid" and "servant leadership". Both of these metaphors are attempts to modify the shepherd-warrior-king myth. But as useful and meaningful as such imagery is for many people—and significantly liberating and reorienting for some—it still retains a focus on a presumed hierarchy of control (and the servant imagery has limited attraction for women and minorities). What we seek in a more adequate myth of leadership is a wealth of inspired stories and images that rigorously and deftly portray the practice of adaptive leadership within the uncertainty of swamp conditions. As one seasoned practitioner put it, "In today's commons every issue is a swamp issue. When you really don't know what to do, all you can do is become an artist. The notion of creative leadership is not a matter of whimsy, it is a matter of survival—making the future work."[10]

Rigorous in its Own Terms

From the perspective of professional practice, a mythic shift is long overdue. In attempts to understand leadership, a persistent conundrum is that professional knowledge as often conceived and taught, coupled with the heroic leadership myth, simply does not address the complex, unstable, unpredictable, and conflictual worlds of practice. Yet some professionals—whether they are business executives, lawyers, engineers, policy makers, physicians, journalists, or clergy—are manifestly more effective than others in their ability to work out useful solutions and ways of proceeding in indeterminate zones that lie beyond the boundaries of conventional professional knowledge. "The difficulty," Donald Schon wrote, "is not that critics fail to recognize some professional performances as superior to others—on this point there is surprisingly general agreement—but that they cannot assimilate what they recognize to their dominant model of professional knowledge. So outstanding practitioners are not said to have more professional knowledge than others but more 'wisdom,' 'talent,' 'intuition' or 'artistry.'" He goes on, however, to observe, "Unfortunately, such terms as these serve not to open up inquiry but to close it off. They are used as junk categories, attaching names to phenomena that elude conventional strategies of explanation." He then argues, "Artistry is an exercise of intelligence, a kind of knowing, though different in crucial respects from our standard model of professional knowledge. It is not inherently mysterious; it is rigorous in its own terms . . . "[11]

Within this larger frame, the yet deeper significance of the approach to the formation of leadership that Heifetz and his colleagues have developed can be recognized. They call forth a practice of leadership that is less like command and control and more like artistry. What they are practicing in both theory building and case-in-point teaching is best understood as akin to processes of creativity—evoking innovative and more adequate ways of seeing and responding within organizations, communities, corporations, societies, and cultures in a time of extraordinary cultural change. By definition, adaptive leadership mobilizes people to address the toughest of problems that require new learning; such learning is driven by a potent mix of constraint and curiosity, and it spawns new capacities, competencies, strategies, a clarified set of values, and new organizational and institutional forms within the context of the particular adaptive challenge being engaged. (Note that this is a very different process than merely identifying an example of best practice or industry standard from another context and attempting to plug it into the context at hand—a technical solution.) On-the-ground creativity is integral to such learning.

Indeed, though they have not argued for a mythic shift from hero to artist per se, Heifetz and Linsky have described leadership as "an improvisational art," and their approach to teaching leadership is aligned with that perspective.[12] Heifetz and his colleagues do use language that is associated with command-and-control models such as strategy and tactics. But we have also heard a cascade of language that explicitly evokes a practice of artistry in the service of adaptive leadership: innovation, dance floor, tuning, improvisation, singing, pressure cooker, walking the razor's edge, courage, orchestrating the conflict, listening and thinking musically, and creative deviance on the front line—all pointing to an understanding and practice of leadership that are rigorous in their own terms.

Leadership as Artistry

How a new, more adequate myth of leadership may finally be named remains to be seen. The phrase "the art of leadership" is certainly well worn. But consciously recognizing the practice of leadership as artistry has received little attention.[13] For now, I simply suggest that art, artist, and artistry be given a more prominent place within the lexicon of leadership theory and practice.

Affirmation and Resistance

The image of artist, cast as a metaphor for those who provide acts of leadership, immediately evokes two primary responses—affirmation and resistance. Those who think of themselves as artists in the conventional sense of the word—for example, painters, sculptors, musicians, writers, architects, photographers, and some athletes and gardeners—may pick up the metaphor with ready enthusiasm, recognizing that incorporating their artist-self into their practice of leadership opens into a horizon of powerful possibilities. But those who suffered through their last required art project in school, or who hold the stereotype of an artist as nonrational, asocial, marginal, or soft—may cast a more jaundiced eye upon this metaphor.

It is highly likely, however, that the jaundiced eye belongs to someone who in some aspect of his or her professional or personal life exemplifies the power and qualities of an artist: the ability to work on an edge, in an interdependent relationship with the medium, with a capacity for creative improvisation. (Entrepreneurs and some politicians, physicians, and educators, for example, are akin to artists, seeking to bring into being what has not yet taken form.)

Working on an Edge

Within any profession or sector, one of the primary characteristics of the artistry of leadership is the willingness to work on an edge—the edge between the familiar and the emergent. Heifetz honors this edge when he speaks of the capacity to lead with only good questions in hand—and that acts of leadership require the ability to walk the razor's edge without getting your feet too cut up—working that edge place between known problems and unknown solutions, between popularity and anxious hostility. Artistic leadership is able to remain curious and creative in the complexity and chaos of swamp issues, often against the odds. As we have seen, those who practice adaptive leadership must confront, disappoint, and dismantle and at the same time energize, inspire, and empower. The creativity that emerges from working on this paradoxical edge is integral to adaptive work, building out of what has come before, yet stirring into being something new and unprecedented—the character of leadership that is needed at this threshold time in human history.

Interdependence with the Medium

Artists work within a set of relationships that they cannot fully control. In regard to the practice of leadership, one of the most potent features of thinking like an artist is that the artist necessarily works in a profoundly interdependent relationship with the medium—paint, stone, clay, a musical instrument, an orchestra, a tennis court, a slalom run, or food. Artists learn "everything they can about the medium(s) with which they work . . . what they can expect from it and where it will fall short."[14] A potter, for example, must learn that clay has its own life, its own potential and limits, its own integrity. The potter develops a relationship with clay, spending time with it, learning to know its properties, how it will interact with water, discovering that if you work it too hard, it will collapse, and if you work with it, it will teach you its strength, your limits, and the possibilities of co-creation. "Even in drawing," notes an architect, "though we think of the artist as imposing something arbitrary on the page, when you draw even a single line on the page, it begins to speak back to you. The kind of pencil you use and the tooth of the paper will affect the message. The design emerges in the dynamic interaction of the relationships among architect, pencil, paper, client, site, building materials, budget, and contractor."[15]

The practice of adaptive leadership requires the same awareness of working within a dynamic field of relationships in which the effect of any single action is not entirely controllable because in a systemic, interdependent reality, every action affects the whole. On the other hand, if one learns to understand the nature of the system that needs to be mobilized (the underlying structure and patterns of motion), he or she can become artfully adept at intervening in ways that are more rather than less likely to have a positive affect in helping the group to move to a new place, creating a new reality.[16]

Linda St. Clair, who served as a highly successful personnel manager for manufacturing in a major technology firm, is keenly aware of how her earlier experience as an artist-director of theater productions informed her practice of leadership within a corporate context. "When I was at my best in the corporation," St. Clair tells us, "I helped the people who reported to me get what they needed to be effectively creative. Over time I got to help select a talented team, but it remained my responsibility to be clear about what we were supposed to be doing as an organization and enable every person within the system to know how the work of each one contributes to the whole."[17]

Heifetz and his colleagues regard giving the work back to the group as a hallmark of adaptive leadership, and recalling her experience in the theater, St. Clair confirms the same: "More even than a captain of a team or the conductor of an orchestra, in a theater production at some point the director has to let go and know that the cast will make critical decisions." But the director isn't the only one who has to learn how to give the work back. There is a whole constellation of artists who are giving the work back to the group, within a system in which no one is fully in control. The playwright gives the play to the producer, who gives it to the director, and thus, St. Clair contends, the director has a sense of stewarding something. "You are not the playwright, the producer, or the actors. Something came before you and will come after you. It doesn't mean that you don't have a critical contribution to make and gifts to give. The same is true in a corporate context."

"A part of your role," she continues, "is to practice an anticipatory imagination, asking the question: 'What will be needed to get there with comfort?'" Which means, in part, attention to timing—or to what Heifetz refers to as 'pacing the work.' There is a set date for the opening night. "By the time dress rehearsal arrives," says St. Clair, "the director has given the work away, becoming an observer, taking notes, but talking about it later—becoming less 'a director' and more a coach, guide, mentor, companion, ally."

In Heifetz's terms, a director in a theater production must exercise both the functions of authority—maintaining equilibrium within the social group—and the practice of leadership—mobilizing the social system to create a new reality. "One of the vital tasks of the director," St. Clair continues, "is to comprehend a dynamic complex of interactions." This includes appreciating the artistry of many others: set design, lighting, casting, acting, costuming, make-up, sound engineering. Each and all must create something new. While helping each part to move in a common direction, the director needs to be mindful that every part needs to be as creative as possible, honoring everyone's artistic power—and all the conflict thereof. Tough decisions have to be made, and the director (authority) must be willing to do so—jointly when possible—which means a lot of interaction and process.

"Rehearsals can be a dynamic, creative time," she says, "and good directors hold back from making 'world-without-end' decisions early on so that unforeseen possibilities have room to emerge." Good directors dwell in a significant measure of ambiguity—again, that edge between the known and the unknown. "We have to play a bit—practice," says St. Clair.

Later, in the corporate context, this concept of rehearsal and practice remained central. She continually reminded her people, "Try it out. We aren't making decisions yet, we can try out 'what ifs.'" The day came when the sign on the corporate "war room" was changed to "music room." "You have to get the metaphors right," she insists. "We are trying to create something, not destroy something."

Theater, leadership, and teaching are all communication arts requiring constructive feedback in a demanding, consultative mode. St. Clair sees parallels with jazz. "As you are playing, you are listening to one another, intuitively modulating into new possibilities, a more effective product, and a more successful organization."

Improvisation

Whether adaptive leadership is practiced in the corporation, the neighborhood, or within an international alliance, it does, indeed, require something very much like the artistry of skilled jazz musicians—bringing tradition, intuition, technique, and the power of imagination and innovation to that edge where the toughest challenges and greatest possibilities are located. Similarly, when describing the art of teaching adaptive leadership using case-in-point, Heifetz frequently has invoked jazz as a metaphor to convey the strength of the framework, the demand for improvisation, and what it is like to work on an edge within a field of interdependent relationships. He muses,

> Case-in-point teaching is similar to the experience of an improvisational jazz group. Jazz musicians will select a structure to work within. The structure might be a set of key changes—"we're going to move from this key to that key to that key." It might be a structure where "we're going to start with this tune and then do variations on that tune, and everybody is going to get their turn improvising and providing a variation on that theme." It may be a structure in which "we're going to first do a trumpet solo, and then a drum solo, and have an order in which each takes a turn." If it's blues, it's not going to be Bach. So the musicians have created for themselves all sorts of boundaries and limits within which they improvise.
>
> Any jazz musician is good at experiencing moments of doubt and confusion—moments of, "Wait a second, this guy just threw me a phrase, and I don't know what to do with it, and I'm going to just play with it until I figure out something to do, or I'm going to let somebody else catch the ball until I can come up with something." There's always these moments of doubt, action, doubt, action, what's the next action? It's part of the adventure, and what adventure doesn't have uncertainty and doubt in it? Adaptive leadership asks for that capacity to move from doubt to action and back to doubt again and again. Similarly, teaching case-in-point is filled with uncertainty and doubt—but

there is a framework, a structure, a discipline within which you work.[18]

Interestingly, when Dean Williams speaks of his experience of case-in-point teaching, he also uses a metaphor from the arts:

Teaching case-in-point is like there is a canvas, and you are going to create on that canvas, but it's neither arbitrary nor capricious. There is a design underneath it all—the framework we're working with, but the manifestation of that framework is new every time. So, as with any artist, you don't create out of nothing. Artists have their palette, their tools, and their orientation. There is spontaneity and improvisation, but underneath that is the design, the model, the skill, the technology that allows us to do it relatively well.

Developing the Courage to Create

Because creativity requires a disciplined relationship with a dynamic medium and the ability to improvise on the edge of the unknown, and because many people in today's society have been led to believe that they are neither creative nor artistic, the call to be an artist can seem to be merely one more difficult expectation, and the invitation to be truly creative can be scary.[19] In PAL-101, a few weeks into the term, the theme for the week is creativity. How do you teach creative, adaptive leadership using case-in-point within the confines of a lecture hall?

Dean Williams begins the class session by simply playing a tape that combines African wedding music and classical European choral music—but he says nothing to the class about the music. When the tape has finished, he is quiet and gives space for the students to respond, which they do in varying ways. About a third of the way into the class session, Williams comments that the students appear to be responding in accordance with their preset roles (as students, various ethnicities, professional or nonprofessional musicians) and the constraints posed by the norms of how they think they should be responding in a classroom dialogue. This observation is prompted in part by a student's observation that being in a classroom may have "sucked some of the creativity out of work that we could be doing."

"Yes, so there's a prevailing paradigm that holds the system," responds Williams. "So how does someone come in and disrupt the paradigm? Who is ever willing to do that, to see if maybe they can shift that prevailing worldview to a different location? That requires enormous creativity, and the world is scared to bits of creativity. This group is scared to bits of creativity."

Josh disagrees:

"I don't think we are scared—"

"I think you're scared. I think you're really scared," Williams interrupts.

Josh insists,

"We're not scared at all. I just think . . . "

"I think you're terrified of it. [Laughter] And you more than anyone, probably," Williams persists.

Shifting his stance a bit, Josh hangs in:

"Perhaps, but perhaps that is because I'm scared that other people here take themselves too seriously. As soon as we stop talking across each other and start talking to each other as a class, we will stop being scared. And then the creativity will come out. The essence of creativity here is to define our objective."

Williams picks up this additional thread:

"So that's what you think, Josh. You're still stuck in that view that once you define the objective, only then does the creative process begin."

Maria asks,

"Can I speak for a moment please?"

Williams responds,

"You're free to speak at anytime in this class."

Somewhat surprised, Maria asks,

"Oh, we can just jump in, that's the rule? Okay."

"No, it's not a rule," Williams clarifies. "But you are free to speak at any time in this class." [In other words, he is suggesting that Maria may discover that as a creative agent she is less encumbered by rules than she supposes.]

Whether or not she truly grasps this, Maria continues,

"In relationship to the paradigm that you were talking about, I think that what I would like to offer the class is this. According to Thomas Kuhn [one of the readings for the day], societies change when groups of people are pushed by competitive pressures.[20] Now if we look at what Heifetz wrote about Ruckelshaus and the EPA, I think the intervention that Ruckelshaus made was because he saw that there was a possibility that this society could think differently because they were pushed beyond passivity, under enormous strain.[21] He intervened to try to manage the pressure and frame issues so that the competitive pressure could move to a shift in paradigms, if you like, or creative outcomes. So essentially, maybe if we were all pushed in some particular way, and if we could allow people to frame issues differently, we might actually be more creative and less like rats in a maze."

Williams responds,

"Well, that's part of the challenge, isn't it, Maria? I mean, what does that challenge look like inside this room? Everyone talks about it, as you just did, by repeating the case study, or the quotes from the book, but it's impossible to manifest it in this room."

Donna picks up the challenge:

"Well, I think it's exactly what you're trying to do, Dean. You're trying to push us into some kind of competitive pressure to shift the environment, hoping that while you're pushing us we will just break out of these constraints."

The conversation continues including several additional voices, and then yet another student remarks,

"I'm still way back stuck on the horns of the dilemma of creativity as an essentially singular, personal act, and then how does it end up hanging out with the group? . . . I mean, I know how to create off in my own little private Idaho. But I haven't got a frickin' clue about how to use this group as a canvas."

The Social System as a Canvas

The instructor is artfully working on the edge of what the students assume about leadership and creativity and what can emerge as they begin to experience themselves as artists working interdependently with the medium of the social system. What new reality can be created within the collective field? An artistic practice of leadership recognizes that the process of sociopolitical-cultural creativity is mediated through the human imagination. Moreover, the canvas of the social system is composed within each individual's imagination and also within the imagination of the group as a whole. The capacity of a person to work creatively within the potential of the collective imagination (in contrast to his or her own little private Idaho) lies at the heart of the practice of adaptive leadership.[22]

Imagination—A Dynamic Process

The art of leadership can be illuminated by using a model of the process of creativity, understood here as the process of imagination. Imagination is not the same as mere fantasy. As Samuel Taylor Coleridge and others have observed, imagination is the highest power of the knowing mind—integral to reason, perception, understanding, judgment, and conscience. The human mind is not a very good transmitter but it is a powerful transformer, continually composing reality from the many elements of our experience.[23] The work of the imagination is to grasp what is real and to create new, more adequate compositions of reality—that is, more truthful, viable patterns of knowing and acting.

The work of the human imagination may be understood as a dynamic process composed of five moments, and the practice of artist-leadership continually moves among them. These are the following: (1) conscious conflict (held in relationship), (2) pause, (3) image or insight, (4) re-patterning, (5) interpretation/testimony and testing.[24] The framework of ideas and the pedagogy developed by Heifetz and his colleagues can be understood as a way of encouraging the process of the individual and collective imagination.

Conscious Conflict

The creation of something new emerges from what isn't working or fitting—from dissonance, doubt, confusion, irritation, opposition, devastation, gaps between values and practice, or the unexpected curiosity appearing on the horizon that has all the properties of the proverbial Trojan horse. As Alma Blount tells her students,

> Your first clue to adaptive work is when there is resistance or conflict. Then learning how to read conflict so that you don't get stuck on the surface conflict leads you to where the underlying, hidden issues are—it's a kind of intelligence. It's a capacity you develop by doing it, and especially by doing it with others—it takes the whole group to do it. It's like peeling away layers, but as the hidden issues appear (along with the work avoidance) and you orchestrate them, the group can begin to move.[25]

This phase of the imagination process requires wading into the swamp of conflicting passions, forces, values, perspectives, personalities, and factions. It requires also creating a container (time, place, norms of working) in which the conflicts can be orchestrated to become productive. Orchestrating the conflict requires naming the truth and uncovering the work that needs to be done—however attractive or painful it may be—at a rate that can be borne, and regulating the heat that is being generated. It depends on a practice of presence that makes it possible to build trust, partnerships, and alliances within the conflicted field and to clarify the purpose and future prospect that make the current anguish and angst worthwhile.

In the class we just observed, we can see that the instructor is provoking (or recognizing when others provoke) some kind of conflict or question that can become what Leonard and Swap have termed "creative abrasion" that can catalyze the reimagination of the practice of leadership.[26] The instructors are particularly artful in reading the expected norms, disappointing them, and managing the consequent stress and conflict in ways that will be productive, using the course design and a trustworthy rapport between instructor and students as a container—a crucible—for the transformation of assumption, habit, and default settings. The discovery that there are always conflicting factions within any social group ensures that a creative possibility is also present—if a worthy framing of the conflicts (the adaptive challenge) can be surfaced and worked constructively.

At the close of the class, Williams presses this point—and the depth of the challenge that it represents:

> "The factions are an element of group reality. There's no singular group. There are going to be multiple, conflicting factions all over the place. And part of the challenge is to move those factions to do adaptive, creative work, to get them learning. Who has to learn what? And it's not simply a case of society progressing by having a discussion and building upon people's good ideas and things will work out well. Some of those factions will have to give up an awful lot.

> "I was just down in Atlanta, Georgia, and saw the Confederate flag—the Stars and Bars—flying on the State House again. That's offensive to an awful lot of people who see it as nothing more than a symbol of oppression, not only in Atlanta, but also throughout Georgia and maybe the world. So how do you get people to give up that symbol when their granddaddy fought for that flag, and maybe died for it? That's pretty painful work. That's not simply a discussion. They've had discussions until they are blue in the face. It's going to be tough work, because it's really embedded in people's values around what they consider important. The moment you start messing with people's real values, that's bound to generate conflict."

Janos asks,

> "Are there benefits? When you challenge what people hold, what they own, their wealth—whatever is dear to them—when your creative ideas are dangerous to them, that's when you really run into problems."

Williams responds,

"Absolutely. And so polite disagreement can turn into violent riots very fast the moment there's something considered sacred embedded in what it is you're trying to take away. When progress was made in civil rights in this country, a lot of ordinary men and women came out to do that work. The real work isn't the passing of a technical law. Rather, who's working the values? This is the tough work, the difficult work. This requires enormous creativity, to get people's attention and then to get their engagement so they start to at least explore what it is they hold precious, what it is they're willing to give up, and what it is they are willing to modify.

"As both Rollo May and Thomas Kuhn [course readings] have said, you're not going to get much creativity unless there is some degree of encounter, opposition, and something to bang up against. You don't create in a vacuum. And so if you are going to have that kind of encounter, particularly in a social setting, it's going to be fraught with conflict, or—to use our more technical word—a lot of disequilibrium will be generated when you start doing this adaptive work. And that can be very painful and difficult. And there you are, your heartstrings are resonating, and you get caught up in all that, and you lose sight of even how to intervene anymore. Or you get sucked back into your own particular group dynamic, your faction, and just start representing that faction."

Then Williams says something unexpected:

"It would be enormously creative to step outside your faction and put yourself in another faction and get a sense of their reality, and start intervening from that position."

The class is quiet as this reality sinks in.

Williams concludes,

"We'll see you Wednesday."

Pause

When the conflict or the gap has become clarified, as in the previous conversation, it is time to pause. This is the moment in which the active mind steps back, so a deeper process can shift into gear. What is needed is a waiting and, as it were, a scanning for an image or insight (a pattern within the chaos) that will simplify and unify the disparate elements of the conflict. The pause may last for only a few seconds or several years. The pause may take the simple form of putting things on the back burner, or it may require enduring a sense of impasse and a long dark night of the soul. In a world gone busy, moments of pause in which the contemplative, deep mind can be at work (within an individual and within the group) are perilously scarce, threatening our capacity to create meaningful responses and make progress on adaptive challenges. As long as leadership is assumed to be manifest primarily in being decisive and taking action, the critical capacities to be present to the complexity in ways that hold the tension, uncertainty, and ambiguity and simply protect the space for heretofore unknown solutions to emerge are thwarted and the opportunity costs are significant.[27]

Thus, Heifetz and his colleagues create space for pause—sometimes including, as we have observed, a surprising use of silence. Note the opening of the first class (chapter 2), when Heifetz begins with a long silence in which he simply looks around the room, holding the group with only his presence, engaging people through eye contact, catching conventional expectations off-guard, making room for something new.

The primary way, however, in which this approach makes provision for pause is in the repeated injunction to go to the balcony to contemplate the action on the dance floor. Whenever one is swept up in the dance, attempts to lead are all too readily blindsided by larger patterns and forces. For that reason it is essential to acknowledge the role of pause in the process of adaptation—the reimagination of self and world.

Image or Insight

This is the moment of "Ah-ha!" or "Oh, I get it!"—the gift of the pause.[28] Here the conflict comes to resolution (or at least to a new horizon of insight) in a form that meets us with a sense of reality—an image, a concept, a framework, a theory, a way forward. Heifetz and his colleagues seed this possibility by providing images, metaphors, stories, concepts, and frameworks conveying insight. But foremost, they create the conditions that serve the internal process of the students' imagination so that they begin "to see for themselves what they most need to see"—that is, students begin to generate their own fabric of images, metaphors, stories, and concepts to interpret their experience of themselves and their interactions within the systems in which they attempt to lead. They deepen their capacity to be artists.

Re-patterning

In the fourth moment, previous assumptions are recomposed in the light of the new insight. This doesn't happen automatically. The linkages between the new insight in one domain of experience and the implications for practice at another point in time have to be consciously forged. While the moment of image comes as a gift, the process of re-patterning is hard work. But this connective work, revealing the emergent, more dependable patterns, is an integral part of what artists do. They assist us in seeing the connections among things and in building a systemic awareness—a larger consciousness that helps the group to find the room in which to move to a new place. M. C. Richards, potter, poet, and teacher, suggests that this function is embedded in the word "art" itself:

> When we trace it to its origins as best we can, we find an old Indo-European syllable, *ar*, which meant "to fit together, to join." An example would be the word "harmony" which comes from the Greek word *harmos*, which means "shoulder where two bones are fitted together." The idea of art being the practice of finding connections, of fitting things together is very open indeed . . . a wholeness made of diverse elements.[29]

Heifetz and his colleagues have designed modes of practice by which people become strengthened in their capacity to see the connections—the patterns—among things and therefore are able to see and think more systemically and creatively. As students reflect on their own cases of leadership failure, grapple with the questionnaires, uncover hidden issues, and trace the connections between their interventions and the progress of the group, they are able over time to perceive patterns of connections that they were blind to earlier. They discover that they are working within a larger, more complex and challenging field of action. Their working reality is reconfigured in more adequate terms.

Interpretation/Testimony and Testing

In this fifth moment, the new pattern of perception and action is brought to an interested public for confirmation—or contradiction. This is vital for two reasons. Articulating a new perception completes and anchors an inner process of learning as one bears witness to what one has come to see as true. But that learning, that new truth, must also be tested if we are to be saved from our own subjectivity. We could be wrong. We may have made an erroneous connection or failed to recognize critical linkages, thus forming a distorted perception. Anyone attempting to practice adaptive leadership needs communities of confirmation and contradiction.

As we have seen, through case-in-point teaching practiced within the structure of the six studio-labs, Heifetz and his colleagues provide rich testing ground for discerning what will and will not work in one's practice of leadership. Students are encouraged over and over again to intervene in the system by making observations regarding what they think is going on—if they think that it will be useful to the progress of the group. Every time they do so, and every time the instructor does so, it is a moment of both testimony and test. The group serves as a community of either confirmation or contradiction. "Yes, life is like that—this fits," or "No, life is not like that—this doesn't work" (or ambiguous shades in between calling for further discernment).

There is no guarantee that one's interpretation and intervention will be timely and useful in the collective imagination of the group and serve to create new realities. Again quoting Alma Blount,

> You are creating as you go along, and in adaptive challenges you don't know for certain what it is that you're growing into together—what you are learning your way into. It has to be an art, because what you do is always just going to be your best guess. What you have to do is test it out. This is what is meant by the notion of making an intervention, asking a question, or providing an insight and then watching what unfolds in the social system. And then there is the companion notion of holding steady in this dynamic process. There is a whole subset of skills and competencies that come along with working in this way.[30]

The Artistry of Adaptive Leadership

Understood in the light of this model of the imagination process, there is a strong resonance between the process that artists undergo, the practice of adaptive leadership, and case-in-point teaching. For in the end, both the artistry of leadership and the artistry of teaching recognize the opportunity within the *conflict*—the gap between how things are and the needs and aspirations of the social system— the adaptive challenge. One learns, not only how to take action and intervene, but also how to *pause*, to wait, to pace the work to let a process the leader cannot fully control work its way to new *insight*. The one who would lead allows the insight to *re-pattern* perception in the cauldron of public learning—typically marked by the *testing*, gyrating energy of confirmation and contradiction in the pull and push of the search for a new equilibrium that will hold. This process takes time—sometimes quick time, more often long and labored.

Working with Fire

In the long and labored work of adaptive leadership, the artist-leader, like the potter, works in relationship to fire. Potter and clay are both tested in the risk and promise of a co-creative relationship with fire. Fire can be both foe and friend. In the ongoing creative process, when the clay has been shaped, dried, fired, glazed, and fired again, the complex potter-clay-fire relationship becomes at once vivid and invisible. In the fire, the work may become a grotesque distortion of the artist's hope, it may be transformed into splendor beyond what the artist could envision, or it may be reduced to simple shards. Over time, the artist can learn much about the way of fire and strategically interact with its power. Nevertheless, when the potter opens the kiln, it is always a revelatory, learning moment.

Acts of leadership that address adaptive challenges are also tested in fire—the fire of competitive markets, the fire of the boardroom, the fire of the legislative process, the fire of office morale, the fire of public scrutiny, the fire of organizational dysfunction—the fire of failure. Fire tempers arrogance, shatters illusion, threatens destruction, bears gifts, keeps us open to complexity, ambiguity, and mystery—and makes the ongoing creation of life possible.

There is also another kind of fire. It is the fire of inspiration that sustains the practice of adaptive leadership. Writers speak of the role of the muse. They acknowledge that there is something that, as it were, moves them, moves through them, and fires their imagination. Without inspiration, their art feels flat, fixed, lifeless—no matter how fine their technical competence. Likewise, those who would lead can only move people and encourage their commitment over the long haul when they themselves are moved, inspired, inspirited. There is an energy that prods and sustains. Attuning to that energy, that spirit, is the spiritual dimension of leadership. Mere ambition, fear, or desperation can temporarily pass for inspiration. But authentic inspiration arises from a depth of worthy purpose and is the energizing (though often demanding) force that evokes possibility and fuels the capacity to stay the course. Inspiration is the wellspring of courage, arising from a way of seeing—or seeing through—that transcends and thus resists inadequate solutions that pose as ultimate. Inspiration nourishes a conviction of worthy possibility in the face of the unknown.

Investment of Self

As is implied throughout this exploration of the experience of the artist as a primary metaphor for the reimagination of leadership, to be an artist is to be invested in the work. An artist is willing to struggle (and if necessary to feel the pain) to bring forth the truth of the imagination. Similarly, the art of adaptive leadership requires a willingness to invest oneself in bringing forth the potential that is within the group, organization, or society.

Artists Within Heroes and Heroes Within Artists

Perhaps it has become apparent that the search for a more spacious and adequate myth of leadership may not require an either-or stance in relationship to these two sets of metaphors—artists and heroes. What does appear to be useful is a mindful shift of field and ground. When we look carefully at the heroic model, we often find considerable artistry within it. David, the Hebrew shepherd-warrior-king, for example, was also a harpist, interpreter of dreams, and purported composer of more than half of the biblical psalms. Alexander the Great was a master of the arts of oratory, ceremony, and theater.[31] When we reexamine the Lone Ranger myth, we see that the image never captured the reality. The "Lone" Ranger was not alone. Tonto was there. Tonto and the Lone Ranger shared a profoundly *inter*dependent partnership. But Tonto was a person of color, and in Spanish his name means "stupid." Yet the truth is that the white heroes who made names for themselves in the Wild West of the United States were often accompanied by darker natives whose multilingual facility, sensitivity to the environment, and superior tracking skills proved essential to success and survival.[32]

Just as the artist is embedded in the heroic-commander myth, the hero is embedded—albeit in transformed ways—in the artist. The artistry of adaptive leadership requires the ability to respond to high ground, technical issues as well as to swamp-like adaptive challenges. Strong in a differing way, adaptive leadership often shoulders authority—formal or informal—using it as a resource, bearing significant responsibility, and acting heroically in the sense of acting courageously.

Nevertheless, Heifetz and his colleagues are solidly located among those who are challenging the conventional, prevailing myth of heroic leadership in the service of an enlarged and more viable myth and practice of leadership in alignment with the realities of a changing world. Students of this approach are not only being initiated into creative, adaptive work on behalf of their organizations and societies. Seen from this perspective, they are a part of a growing field of inquiry and experimentation that is contributing to the adaptive work of transforming the prevailing myth of leadership itself.

When we speak of the art of leadership, therefore, we are not speaking of art as merely a mirror (reflecting the times), art as a hammer for social protest, art as furniture (something to hang on the walls), or art as only the search for self. When the practices of leadership and teaching are recognized as art and artistry, we are honoring the capacity of every human being to respond to the cries and wonder of the world *as an artist* and to co-create with others; that is, to cultivate a collective creativity—a shared excellence in the art of life—a practice rigorous in its own terms.[33]

CHAPTER TEN

Leadership Can Be Learned

Strengths and Limitations of This Approach

WARREN BENNIS has observed that the art of leadership is arguably difficult to teach, but it can be learned.[1] Though difficult to teach, if leadership can be learned, how well does the approach described here serve the formation of the capacity to practice the art of adaptive leadership on behalf of the common good in today's world? What are the central strengths of this approach, what are its limitations, what questions remain for further inquiry? and vulnerabilities?

Central Strengths

A central strength of this approach is that a theory of leadership and a way of teaching have been woven into a seamless whole. A set of ideas that usefully describes key features of a practice of leadership has been wedded to a way of teaching that tightly corresponds to those ideas. From this base, Ron Heifetz and his colleagues are pressing the edges of what can be learned about how to work effectively in changing and challenging conditions. They have re-defined leadership as the activity of engaging the important but confounding conditions in multisystemic domains that are neces-sarily undergoing profound change—devoting their efforts to the formation of adaptive leadership that can take the whole field of action into account. This approach, therefore, brings a needed competence to the formation of leadership for the common good, which must take into account a larger whole—today's new com-mons. In this new and more complex context, adaptive leadership, most profoundly understood, poses a response to the need to dis-mantle current, inadequate arrangements while animating the cre-ation of more adequate patterns of life.[2]

The case-in-point mode of teaching that Heifetz and his col-leagues have developed provides a challenging context in the class-room itself that mirrors the larger field of action. Students are invited to learn from their own immediate and past experience, and as a consequence, the traditional roles of both teachers and learners are reconfigured to good effect. As the meaning of leadership is shifted from a narrow focus on an individual's exercise of individual talent and power and turns toward mobilizing the group to make progress on their toughest problems, the individual learner becomes more than a mere consumer of knowledge and technique and be-comes instead an actor in a complex system and an active partici-pant in her or his own learning.

In tandem, case-in-point teaching also shifts the locus of action from the teacher to the group—from the individual to the system and the issues at stake. This mode of teaching reveals the multifaceted role in the social system of the teacher, who is at once a teacher giving access to key ideas and frameworks, an authority maintaining equilibrium in the group, and a practitioner in the service of making progress on the adaptive work of learning the art and practice of adaptive leadership. Thus, the teacher is a co-learner and at the same time a model, practicing authority and leadership in public so that others may eavesdrop, watch, contend with, and learn.

Unmasking the Power of Teachers

In all educational experiences, people to one degree or another model themselves after the teacher, learning things that are not in the explicit content of what is being said or read, but that are implicit in the way the teacher goes about teaching. It is easy for teachers to underestimate how much is taught about "how to be" that goes unexamined. Students unconsciously drink in, for example, the way a teacher models the resolution of conflicts in class, solves problems, handles the introduction of deviant, innovative, troubling, or confusing points of view, and exercises authority. Lessons about professionalism and expertise are absorbed and reinforced class after class—year after year. Especially in a course in leadership, where people come to it most frequently with the assumption that leadership is a set of formulas and personality characteristics, students of whatever age are vulnerable to taking in what the teacher says and does, independent of the ideas or the theory. The modeling becomes as significant as the explicit conversation.

"I think," says Heifetz, "that it becomes a moral challenge to us as educators to discover the ways in which we are unwittingly modeling and thus teaching lessons through our behavior that are not a part of what we've designed in our deliberate planning of the course." Case-in-point teaching (where the teacher's behavior is subject to scrutiny) makes it possible for unconscious modeling to become conscious rather than remaining unexamined. Thus, just as the theory at play in this approach is particularly competent in revealing the power of the currents just under the surface of the social system (and how to constructively work with them), a strength of this approach is its capacity to unmask the power that all teachers have in their role as the authority in the classroom. Reflecting on the importance of the instructor taking responsibility for the appropriate use of authority in any classroom, a doctoral graduate who had been a student in PAL–101 said,

> I had never really thought about how important it was to that class, to any classroom, to have somebody standing up front. That person is the teacher—that person wears a tie, that person is paid by the school to teach this group of people—how important it was for that person to maintain the discipline of that class. That was amazing, and it was the first time I'd ever really thought about a commonly held norm that was clearly held also by the other ninety people in the class.

The same awareness was echoed in the reflections of a woman in mid-career:

> I remember that once a man came into the class to fix the thermostat, and Heifetz just stared him out of the room. He said, "May I help you?" whereas I think most professors would have just ignored it. And the man said, "Well, I'm here to fix this thermostat." Heifetz said, "You can do that later," and the guy just left. That function of letting the group know that you're going to protect the boundaries [so the class can do adaptive work] has never left me.

On the other hand, precisely because a teacher holds the formal authority and can so significantly shape the norms in the classroom, teachers are vulnerable to protecting themselves and their students from the discomfort of confusion, anger, and disturbing perspectives.

Case-in-point teaching invites a more visceral and courageous engagement on the part of both teachers and students.

The Self—Within and Transcending System

This approach continually encourages the development of a deepened understanding of self as both an individual and an "embeddual"—a socially embedded being.[3] Because this approach is intended to foster learning at the level of default settings, even those who have studied and worked with organizational behavior, psychological models, or political systems discover that they are not as exempt from being acted upon by external forces as they may have presumed. This revelatory discovery of the multiple interdependent, dynamic systems in which all human beings are embedded is a key element in gaining a more complex and fitting understanding of the reality in which leadership is practiced.

Barbara Kellerman, exploring critical questions of leadership education for the twenty-first century, asks whether as a society we are failing to address the problems that are not fully public-, nor private-, nor independent-sector issues—for example, poverty and education. This macro level is where she perceives most leadership education to fall "woefully short." When the formation of leadership does not address in a comprehensive way the complex political, economic, ecological, technological, religious, and social challenges that require transsectoral work, she argues, those who would lead are unpracticed in what she calls the "tactics of transcendence" and are unable to address those challenges that are most chronic and complex.[4] A key value of the approach to leadership education that Heifetz and his colleagues have developed is that in its radical grounding in systems and multisystemic consciousness and in its capacity to address multiple sectors within a single learning context, this approach can serve as a strong response to the call for the formation of cross-sector leadership.

A More Effective Deployment of Self

The work of this approach, in both the large class and the small groups, invites students and teachers alike to teeter on their own growing edges, peer into murky depths, and wade into unfamiliar swamp-like territory, unexpectedly squinting at a tangled and hazy new horizon within their own selves. Blind spots are discovered, along with more competent ways of responding to complex situations. As one educator and administrator reflected,

> By far, the biggest aspect of the class is the whole notion of the power of the group and . . . of learning to use yourself. One of the great things about it was to learn to use my own reactions and to interpret myself—that when I'm angry or cynical, it's not just me. There's something "out there" that I am a part of. I can blurt it out, so to speak, in whatever way I will, but that's not necessarily good for the group. That's just playing a reflexive, reactive role in some sort of unconscious drama. The point is to make it conscious and to do it in a useful way.

This is one way of speaking about a more effective deployment of self, especially as a consequence of a wider range of choice. As we have seen, this more effective deployment of self is cultivated by a potent set of concepts, metaphors, and practices. These foster the formation of five central competencies:

ANALYZE. The ability to clarify a sense of worthy purpose, to see the factions, forces, and other systemic patterns within the relevant group, to identify the adaptive work and where it is located, to discern who holds the functions of authority both formally and informally, to understand the history of the issue, to discover where new movement and innovation are possible, and to recognize work avoidance activity such as scapegoating and attempts at assassination.

INTERVENE. The ability to enter and act within the system in a way that will help the group or organization to make progress on the adaptive work—recognizing points of leverage, how to ripen an issue, attract attention, build trust, surface hidden issues, orchestrate the conflict, regulate the heat to create new realities, walk the razor's edge without getting your feet too cut up, show people the future that makes the current work worthwhile, and lay the past to rest lest it become an improper guide.

COMMUNICATE. The ability to attract and hold the attention and anxiety of the group, to speak clearly, to know the power of words and gestures and to use them strategically and compellingly, and to challenge, comfort, and inspire. This includes the ability to listen and to take the pulse of the group. As a former student now heading a state agency confirmed, "I constantly find that in my job here, no matter what the group, no matter what the issue, if I don't have the pulse of the group, I'm very uncomfortable. In giving a speech, in trying to make decisions, I need to know where they are. Not that where they are is where I'm going to let them stay, but I need some common feeling and understanding about where the group is, and then I plot a better course for leading them."

PAUSE, REFLECT, PACE. The ability to get on the balcony in the midst of the action, to reflect on the effect of one's intervention and attempts to communicate, to tolerate and use silence, and to pace the work so that people are disappointed at a rate they can stand. This is a particularly critical capacity in the midst of competitive pressures and the fast-paced, busy, often perilously unreflective, and action-oriented norms of today's societies across all sectors.

TAKE THE HEAT AND HOLD STEADY. The ability to bear the stress of doubt, dissonance, and chaos in the necessary disequilibrium—the place between a familiar pattern that is no longer adequate, and a new, more viable pattern of shared life within an organization, community, or enterprise that has not yet taken form. In other words, to be fully present in a compassionate, trustworthy, strategic, disciplined, and inspiring manner.

Learning from Experience on One's Own Horizon of Readiness

Another primary strength of this approach is that essentially all the learning is designed to take place in relationship to the actual, lived experience of the learner. Though there are reading assignments and concepts to be mastered, these are deemed valuable only to the degree to which they interpret the puzzles that arise from each learner's current grappling—either with previous experiences of attempting to lead or with the experience that is taking place immediately in the large class and the small group sessions. Students are continually having the opportunity to engage in what is truly alive for them.

This engagement with one's own lived experience (and the sometimes quite powerful vicarious effect of hearing about the experience of other students), combined with access to a compelling framework and a set of metaphors to hold and interpret it, has the effect of meeting students on the horizon of their own readiness to learn. Each student engages and develops what is just rising to the surface of his or her own awareness, or lurking at the periphery of their attention. As a consequence, in its best practice, it is consistently notable that each student learns somewhat different things than do other students in the class. Although this is the case in most educational contexts, it is striking the degree to which—among a wide diversity of students—each comes away having been met on their own growing edge in a manner that appears to be particularly fitting for her or him at that point in time. The course functions as a very rich brew that has something for almost everyone.

Learning Below the Neck

This approach provides an unusual degree of repetition of concepts and metaphors as they are used to interpret recurring phenomena that arise in the often emotionally charged work of the course—especially when the group itself functions as a case-in-point. Repetition acknowledges that most learners either initially resist new ways of seeing or simply do not fully absorb them the first time around. Repetition serves the necessarily slow process of dissolving the resistance to the new, emerging reality. Then, further iterations drive the new learning deep into the realm of those default settings, offering preferred alternatives to business as usual. It becomes possible to see what one needs to see and to feel a corresponding reordering of gut assumptions that can yield new behavior and an enhanced sense of conscious choice about how to respond. The necessity of repetition (in relation to reflection on one's own experience) underscores the role of provocation, persistence, and patience in sponsoring lasting behavioral change. Thus, the approach is a practice of what it seeks to teach about the nature of adaptive leadership. As one student put it,

> I think I would partly define a leader as someone who's not afraid to push things into an uncomfortable range for a group, who's not afraid to bring up something that the group is not ready to deal with and not let it drop, who doesn't just articulate a common vision that's comfortable for everybody, but articulates a vision for the group that moves the group to do some work that they may not be comfortable with, but that in the end, proves to be the most creative kind of work that they could be doing.

The capacity of this approach to push things into an uncomfortable range is another feature of its competence in facilitating learning below the neck. It does, however, create tension between two characteristics of an effective learning environment: safety and challenge. Parker Palmer has eloquently argued for the practice of "creating a hospitable space" for learning.[5] Aware of Palmer's work, Richard Broholm, who on behalf of the Lilly Endowment, visited several of the large class sessions, later wrote, "Ron Heifetz wants students in his class to reflect deeply about important questions. He's not afraid to push them to do so. At times I wondered if he was pushing too hard." Broholm then raises the question of whether a pressure cooker is a hospitable space for learning. He explores but does not resolve the tension in the question, and then he concludes,

> I have observed a remarkable integration of theory and ped-agogy—not perfect but incredibly honest and powerful—in which students were encouraged to move deeply into their own experience and grow. I know that for myself, this class has been the most provocative and stimulating of any in my academic career.[6]

Addressing these same issues, a former student who is now an assistant professor of public policy, has said, "What I learned from Heifetz is how much students really do want to be challenged."

Ethical Valence

Although there is an ongoing, hearty debate about whether or not *leadership* is a value-free word, the approach described here holds the conviction that acts of leadership are inevitably steeped in ethical choices and that the hunger for leadership is at its core a hunger for moral commitment—for leadership that serves the common good in contrast to personal gain or aggrandizement alone. The question of purpose that is posed at the heart of every case analysis, the aspiration of finding ways to lead in the heart of danger while retaining a commitment to life, the critical reflection on the appropriate and inappropriate use of authority, the honoring of grief and loss, the call for compassion in the face of adaptive work, the invitation to reflect on one's ambitions and aspirations and set them in conversation with each other, and the recognition of the consequences of one's action (or failure to act) in real time—all are manifestations of the ethical fiber that is woven into the fabric of this approach.

A man who attended an executive session led by Heifetz titled "Cutting Edge Leadership," reflected two years later that it had helped him to become convinced that he could have a positive impact on the institutions to which he was related—in both his "day job and in his volunteer work." Returning to his notes to see what he felt "was important enough to write down," he discovered phrases such as: "maintain innocence amid betrayal," "avoid cynicism but still be able to doubt," "be compassionate," "preserve the values and loyalties that are most precious to you," "celebrate the fruits of your labor." Then he reflects, "There is definitely something spiritual about his take on leadership." That which is authentically spiritual always has an ethical core.[7]

But the ethics aren't simple. Within the cadre of people who work with the ongoing development of this approach, ethical questions regularly surface and there is a good deal of wrestling with them. For example, Hugh and Alma have questioned whether putting purpose at the heart of a student's case analysis necessarily yields—without more exploration than is often pursued or even possible within the discussion of a single case—the ethical consciousness and conscience that can serve as good enough moorage in the complex conditions of practicing leadership in today's world. Human motivation is complex, and such questions are not easily resolved, but the ongoing grappling with them is one of the strengths the approach evokes—as every class and case can be worked as an ethical case-in-point.

Beyond the Traditional Case Method

The virtues of the traditional case method are that it deals with an actual situation that has happened in the past (though it is occasionally used for a case that is unfolding in the present), has been well researched, and can serve as an example of the kinds of situations that the learners have or might experience. The instructor can anticipate the multiple facets of the case that may be useful to student learning and pose study questions in advance of the case discussion. Students can then develop their own insights and pose questions of their own. The case itself, however, is typically at a safe remove from the student's own felt experience.

A standard outcome of the traditional case method is that students become adept at critiquing what someone else has done in the past, but do not as readily gain insight into how they themselves do or do not respond in complex situations. Case-in-point methodology not only offers a set of ideas but sets them in direct dialogue with the student's own episodes of failure, reconsidered within their own immediate experience of the ever-changing dynamics of the group as a social system trying to make progress. As such, these cases are more likely to stir the kind of cognitive, emotional, visceral engagement that precipitates and sustains transformative learning.

Engagement and Creativity

At its best, this approach forges a bond between a high level of engagement and a new capacity for creative response. David Whyte writes,

> Every organization serious about its place in this new moveable world is asking desperately for more adaptability, vitality, and imagination . . . But it is just as difficult for any individual to find their own creative powers as it is for an organization. When it comes to the moment of truth, both the organization and the individual are equally afraid of the creativity, the passion, and the courage that accompany those powers hidden within them and that are central to

their vitality. This meeting place of creative anticipation and fearful arrival is the elemental core of a new conversation in the workplace.[8]

This approach is a contribution to that new conversation on the edge of creative anticipation and fear of arrival. The teaching and learning process is designed to bring teachers and students into a field of experience that is at once both uncomfortable and potentially productive for the creation of a revitalized imagination and artful leadership. In concert with the call to direct engagement that case-in-point teaching fosters, additional design elements that foster the development of a robust imagination and a capacity for the artistry of creative leadership include the following:

- A context in which students are placed in dialogue with different kinds of people, encountering disturbing points of view, uncertainties, and surprising commonalities.

- The instructor's refusal to duck paradoxes or to provide easy answers, choosing instead to respond obliquely, evoke puzzlement, curiosity, and mystery, and provoke or surface conflict—all of which develop a stomach for chaos and tolerance for working on an emergent edge.

- Access to images—language, concepts, and experience—that encourage toleration of discomfort, engagement with conflict, innovative experimentation, and new insight.

- The offering and validation of many forms of pause, space, and silence that are essential to the creative process.

- Disciplined practice in reflection and analysis—an invitation to recognize and forge connections among previously under-recognized elements within the field of action.

- The development of knowledge, skills, and technique—recognizing that the artistry of leadership requires not only a sense of worthy purpose but also well-honed competence with which to realize it.

- Affirmation of experimentation—failure and success.

There is, however, a yet deeper distillation of what this approach offers at its essence in a time in which the vocation of the human as a creative agent is both imperiled and required. An exceptional artist in five mediums, Martha Mood was asked what it required to do her work. Her response: "A seeing eye, an open mind, and a little courage." Borrowing from her insight and setting it in conversation with the formation of adaptive leadership, I suggest that at the essence of the contribution of this approach are three key provisions that must be considered in any effort to teach the art of leadership that can serve the common good in a time of heightened complexity and change: the formation of *a seeing heart, an informed mind, and a little courage.* This requires learning how to pay attention with compassion; access to illuminating concepts and embodied models—forms that can seed a more adequate imagination and repertoire of behaviors; and the will to practice in the face of repeated discouragement, failure, and ambiguous success.

A Seeing Heart—Learning to Paying Attention

Attracting sustained attention is one of the greatest challenges for any teacher and for anyone attempting to practice adaptive leadership. This is especially true in societies where most people are subject to varying forms of systemic distraction and are tempted to seek it out when confronted with the conflict and loss that usually accompany adaptive work.

Paying attention, as the phrase suggests, requires an active investment of self—and a certain vulnerability to the phenomenon at hand. It asks us simultaneously to be awake, to be present, to observe, to see, to listen, to hear, and to feel. When a woman who followed a successful career by taking up painting in her late fifties was asked why it was so important to her, she immediately responded, "Oh, I see things I never saw before. You assume," she continued, "that you know what a human hand, especially your own, looks like. But when you attempt to draw it, you see elements and relationships that you never 'saw' before." [9]

The challenges of the twenty-first century require a radical openness to seeing what we've never seen before, and a willingness to be affected, to be moved. The artistry of leadership requires the capacity to see with a compassionate heart, taking in the current reality without either being overwhelmed by it or by cynically and dismissively blaming the system.[10] Only from this posture can an adequate conviction of possibility take form and a new orientation emerge from within today's complex milieu.

Like all artists, those who offer this kind of leadership are often regarded as prophetic. They are credited with a sense of vision. But they do not have a crystal ball. Rather, they serve a prophetic function because they pay such careful attention to what is happening in the present, while others are looking through the spectacles of the preceding age. "To perceive . . . liberated from the consensus reality is the first task of any artist." [11]

Heifetz and his colleagues have developed a live model of learning and teaching leadership that encourages this quality of paying attention to the deep master currents of the social system and fosters the hard, creative work required to forge the common cords that can be woven into a more worthy future. As Robert Bellah and his colleagues have suggested, democracy itself is a matter of paying attention.[12] Thus, something important is happening when people find themselves in a learning milieu in which they begin to let their attention be arrested by the discovery of ways of seeing that cut through distraction and spin and give rise to a new imagination of leadership.

An Informed Mind—Seeds of Possibility

A powerful learning milieu provides revelatory processes for seeing reality more adequately, and offers explicit content. Frameworks, concepts, images, insights, language, and actual embodied behaviors offer models and possibilities for creating alternatives to what is. A strong learning milieu in*forms* the mind, seeding new ways to think, imagine, and work.

By strength of discipline and spirit, an artful practice of leadership is attuned to those forms that honor the deepest yearning of a people and serve as harbingers of cultural possibility. This is the artist to whom Marshall McLuhan referred when he asserted that the artist is the one most needed in the global village. Great artists are engaged in making live models of situations that have not yet matured in society at large.[13] In their artistic play, they develop a way of seeing and knowing that has its own genetic code that lives first in the consciousness of a few individuals and communities. They create and demonstrate the possibilities that begin as heresy and end up as heritage.

Heifetz and his colleagues are engaged in making live models of understanding, practicing, and teaching leadership that serve as harbingers of possibility and modes of engagement that are powerful but unpracticed in society at large.

A Little Courage—Commitment to Practice

If leadership is finally an art that cannot be conventionally taught but can be learned through the artistry of the right kind of coaching, then a commitment to practice must dwell at the core of the learning process. One of the most important features of this approach is that it has gone a long way in creating a context that recognizes the value of practice and makes it normative for both teachers and students. This approach counters the notion that leaders are born and contends that the art of leadership is never fully mastered. It is in this sense that we speak of the *practice* of medicine, law, politics, religion—and leadership.

One of the perils in this era of dramatic change is that as our current social and economic arrangements become ever more brittle, there is little tolerance for practice. Leaders and their colleagues are supposed to get it right the first time even in the midst of the unknowns and muck of swamp conditions. In contrast, in this approach, it is assumed that practice is an integral feature of effectiveness and that you never fully arrive. The instructors themselves are subject to critique and more practice, students are set to work in studio-labs where practice is required, and reflection on past practice is incessant. It encourages the gradual discovery that the artistry of adaptive leadership requires the understanding that clarity of purpose and skillful intervention in the social system yield practical, life-bearing progress only in the hard work of practice and reflection and new practice—over time.

Karen Thorkilsen has written,

In our present era, with its sense of profound transition, we yearn with special intensity for a powerful synthesizing vision of what we, and our life with each other might be . . . To try to name, to give definition in any way to that which we sense to be emerging is to experience the process of form-giving. It may seem that giving formal expression to a compelling image or intuition is something only those we call "artists" do . . . But there are many day-to-day ways in which all of us participate in creative expression . . . [giving] shape to what we are trying to know, what we believe, and who we are trying to be. We need to understand more clearly that there can be much at stake in each of these efforts, that each can be sacred creative work, reaching toward a threshold we have not crossed before . . . yet we are so insistently called to keep trying because what is at stake is the shape of our lives . . .

Thinking about how artists proceed in their work, I am struck by how much time is devoted to practicing. Months of rehearsal precede a single performance; dozens of discarded lines finally yield the one that completes the poem; and isolated movements exercised over and over again gradually cohere into liquid dance . . . In the hours of rehearsal one is continually coming up against what one cannot quite do . . . and then, on a subsequent try, moving beyond that point to another. It is a halting, often frustrating process, but it certainly builds patience, and it builds courage in the face of awkwardness . . . From practice then, from a commitment to work at the edge, comes the gift of eloquence—in movement, in color, in clay, or in song.[14]

The approach to learning adaptive leadership that we have described here is predicated on the bone-deep assumption that it will take a commitment to practice to create truly fitting responses to the hungers of our time for leadership. And that practice will require courage. Courage, from *coeur*, shares the same root as heart, which brings us full circle back to the seeing heart from which the courage to practice comes—courage even in the face of the demands for conclusive expertise, instant solutions, and robotic efficiency. Heifetz and his colleagues have developed an approach that provides an initiation into the humility and courage that practice requires.

Contribution to a New Myth

In these and other ways, this approach to the formation of a practice of leadership is both inspired and muscular enough to fuel creative, adaptive responses to the call for a new myth of leadership—another strength of this approach. Whether the recognition of the artistry of leadership contributes to a new myth or a reconfiguration and rebalancing of elements embedded in the more familiar heroic myth is as yet unclear.[15] But in a changing world where creative solutions have become critically urgent across every sector of the commons, the recovery of the human as an engaged, creative, responsible agent is vital.

Haunting Questions

Those who practice this approach to leadership tend, as artists do, to allow important questions to haunt them: What are we missing? What's still not working? Thus, the development of this approach continues to find that edge place of ongoing, creative inquiry. Heifetz has suggested that this work is something like building a house:

> I think we've got the foundation piece . . . But I think there are a lot of rooms to be built in this house so we can discover more about how leadership may be exercised differently in different contexts—cultures, policy areas, different kinds of business organizations. I think we have further to go in areas such as curriculum design, use of field experience, an understanding of teaching as mentoring, and further development of the competencies this approach requires.

Similarly, each person we spoke with who is using this approach in a primary way in his or her professional life is extending the inquiry and the experimental reach into additional domains—each responding to differing, haunting questions that arise from their distinctive experience of the adaptive work they have engaged. For example, working with people in East Timor, a fledgling democracy, Dean Williams is aware that many students leave PAL-101 with a new understanding of the importance of creating disequilibrium to move adaptive work. But he observes that when a new government is barely taking form and inevitably mistakes abound, creative alliance and the capacity to honor an emergent, fragile equilibrium may be as vital to adaptive work as creative deviance may be at an earlier point in the process. "And so," he wonders, "what will that mean for how we practice and teach?"[16]

One Good Approach—Only

William G. Perry Jr., one of Harvard's master educators, was often heard to remark: "To have any idea of what is going on in a situation, you need at least three good theories." By that he implied that if there is only one theory in play, a person might be overly confident in his or her interpretation. If there are only two theories, then whatever is occurring is apt to be reduced to either this or that. If three theories are at work, then it becomes easier to be open to other yet unrecognized possibilities. The approach we have described here is just that—one approach, one theoretical-pedagogical perspective.

Thus, as with any educational endeavor, this approach to learning and practicing leadership, though powerful, does not exhaust all that is needed or can be understood regarding the practice of leadership. What, then, are the companion theories and points of view that may be required for one's particular practice of leadership? This approach, for instance, does not address per se the political arts of institution building, constituency and coalition building, and negotiation. And as acknowledged earlier, although this approach has an ethical valence, it may not work as deeply as is needed to achieve its own aspiration that adaptive leadership be aligned with worthy purposes. Thus, those who teach this approach (as is often the case with any powerful perspective or skill) must wrestle with the question of how it may be used for unworthy ends.

Partial Learning

Precisely because the approach is effective in meeting people in their own place of readiness for learning at a given moment in time, an individual learns aspects of the approach but rarely the totality of its interdependent elements. Most people leave the course with both new strengths and partial knowledge, that is, with powerful ideas that remain untempered by the course material they were unable to absorb. Though more confident, they may yet remain perilously vulnerable. One person we interviewed, for instance, had effectively grasped an understanding of adaptive work, but did not recognize the importance of knowing the history of the issue—though this is one of the concepts available in the course. In her subsequent attempt to make progress on an adaptive challenge within her organization, she was significantly blindsided by her inattention to the history of the issues involved.

When former students inevitably and sometimes significantly mess up, what is the responsibility of those who have taught them leadership? As this approach evolves, two key questions that remain alive at the heart of the work are these: How can this pedagogy continue to develop so that it provides a yet stronger hedge against people reverting to their former default settings in a crisis? How can learning from this perspective be continued over time? Two avenues of response present themselves. First, there is an implied call for continual enhancement of curricular design, short-term executive-alumni sessions, and consulting practitioners who take this approach into the workplace. Second, former students in self-organized small groups may continue to work cases of failure to deepen their insight and enhance their competence.

Vulnerabilities of Case-in-Point Teaching

Despite its obvious strengths, there are several ways in which case-in-point teaching is limited and its effectiveness can be compromised. To identify a few:

A DEMANDING PROCESS. This pedagogy is not for the faint of heart. As we heard in both chapters 7 and 8, it asks a great deal of both teachers and students when it is used as the exclusive method throughout a course, seminar, or consultation. One instructor acknowledged that though she had used it in its fullest form several times, she later moved to a modified form because she had to balance several major professional responsibilities. Having to hold steady through the period when students are bewildered, frustrated, and complaining can be daunting for both teachers and students. One student remembers,

> Heifetz would literally just sort of say, "Well, where are we today?" And then there would be these incredible, painful pregnant pauses, and we would feel like, "Oh, I can't take this any more, I just can't do this." And it was the pressure that actually revealed the learning I had to do. But I was sort of like, "Well, what are we paying you for? You're supposed to be entertaining me with great lectures."

NOT FOR EVERYONE. Not only does this pedagogy require a real measure of courage, it is not for everyone. It may require instructors who are particularly amenable to practices of reflection, who have developed a significant measure of self-knowledge, who have a certain turn of mind that honors the reality of inner experience and the existence of hidden issues both within and without that lead to conflict. Further, these sensibilities must be linked with a well-developed systemic consciousness, the capacity for patience with the processes of learning in both self and others, and the willingness to step into the unknowns inherent in working on a creative edge. All these capacities are unevenly manifested among educators as a group and within any individual teacher.

CAN MASK LACK OF PREPARATION. Ironically, though case-in-point teaching is a demanding art when practiced well, another vulnerability of this pedagogy is that it can serve as at least a temporary cover for a lack of preparedness on the part of either the instructor or the students. And because everything that happens is potentially grist for the learning mill, in irresponsible hands, almost anything can be justified in the name of a learning opportunity.

POSSIBLE HURT. In this approach, on the one hand, the teacher protects the boundaries of the holding environment to create a trust-worthy environment for learning. On the other hand, the norms of discourse in the traditional classroom are loosened, permission is given to confront and provoke, and thus there is the possibility of hurt. A question I asked repeatedly in this study is whether or not people have been hurt by the use of this approach. In the end, evidence of any significant or long-term hurt was very hard to find. In an educational process, however, people are vulnerable to uncomfortable feelings. Changing our minds and our practice is often a discouraging as well as an encouraging adventure—"challenge" and "hurt" are sometimes difficult to distinguish. In PAL-101, some find themselves going through some rough, soul-searching days. But sustained wounds, though not completely absent, appear to be reduced to very small percentage. (The 1989 survey report found that 3 to 4 percent of the students remain upset by the course to some degree.) Though I asked former students directly not only about their own experience but also about their perceptions of the experience of others who had taken the course, I have found only one specific report of hurt that may have been unconstructive, and that came from Heifetz himself who has kept the conversation with that student open long after the completion of the course, reportedly to good effect over time.

Marty Linsky was one of the first other than Heifetz to use this approach including case-in-point (teaching courses in politics) and he continues to use and develop this approach, now as a part of Cambridge Leadership Associates. He is keenly attuned to this issue and a closely related question that all who would lead face. He reflects,

> One of the razor edges that I and others who use this approach tread is whether to accept casualties in a course or

program in the interests of maximizing the learning of the rest. This is a vulnerability of this teaching method. There are always going to be people who will be left behind—which is almost always inevitable also when you are exercising leadership. Being compassionate, however, is not inconsistent with "accepting casualties." It means taking responsibility for their loss, but not avoiding progress for the group as a whole. Those I know who have long experience in teaching this way have never experienced a significant percentage of people being as lost—and angry—at the end of the course as they may have been on the first or second day. And we certainly have stories of people who months or years later say they profited enormously, and they are sorry they gave a low ranking on the evaluation at the time. But we still wrestle with the question of whether there is a way to teach this approach that is as effective without some of the discomfort.[17]

TENSION BETWEEN COMPETITION AND COLLABORATION. Related to the questions just posed, although a primary contribution of this approach and pedagogy is its dedication to leading to stay alive and to create new realities and to give purpose and hope, the culture's fascination with power, death, and violence gives enormous fuel to the themes of assassination, conflict, and the dangers of leading, which the course necessarily takes up. Holding the tension among these themes in the service of a postmodern, postnuclear understanding of leadership (transforming war rooms into music rooms without denying the positive features of competitive pressures) is a part of the adaptive work of today's societies (and, as we have seen, differentially resolved by the instructors we have observed). It will probably remain a central challenge in the ongoing practice of this approach for some time to come.

In sum, as with any teaching method, the particular talents, pre-occupations, and judgments of the teacher make a significant difference in this approach. Because this pedagogy is less practiced than other, more established pedagogies, evaluation against the norms of best practice is difficult. But the high quality of scores on standard course evaluations, the number of times students affirm "that was my best course" or "one of my most influential courses"—across several institutional contexts and different instructors, along with the findings from the in-depth interviews and observations I have made—suggests that this approach when well practiced is highly valuable.

Leadership for the Common Good

Perhaps the central strength of this work for today's world is located in its laser-beam focus on the systemic, interdependent reality of which we are each a part and within which each of us has the opportunity, therefore, to exercise leadership from wherever we sit. This approach to the formation of leadership serves as a solvent on the leader-follower dichotomy and thus is exceptionally well tuned to the aspirations of the democratic impulse throughout the whole of our shared commons—embracing both the private and the public sector. This approach to the practice of leadership has a distinctive capacity both to enhance the freedom and effectiveness of the individual and the capacity of the whole group to create more vibrant and viable patterns of life. Without being naive and, indeed, addressing some of the most fraught features of the human experience that repeatedly appear to stymie efforts to make meaningful progress on critical issues, this approach responds to calls for leadership in today's world because it provides ways of learning how to uncover illusion, name what is otherwise unrecognized, and build a new contract of engagement and creativity that can contribute to the awakening of the minds, hearts, and affections of workers and citizens in ways that are not easy but are grounded in the reality of what is and can be.

This approach to learning, practicing, and teaching leadership is, finally, therefore, an invitation to recognize that those who would lead are always swept up in complex systems larger than themselves. We cannot control but we can creatively intervene in these systems, offering acts of leadership—sometimes going beyond our authorization—that assist in reshaping the life of the commons in ways that create a more just, sustainable, peaceful, and prosperous world.

In doing so, we continually discover that a key feature of the art of leadership is the ability to give the work back to the group so that it can learn and adapt to make progress on our toughest challenges. This is the core strength underlying this response to the question "Can leadership be taught?" It offers a compelling response to the hungers in our time for an understanding and practice of leadership informed by a consciousness of the complexity of our new global commons, inspired by a commitment to the common good, and manifest in the competence to engage the adaptive challenges of today's world.

The practice is ongoing.

Notes

CHAPTER ONE

1. "In the course of history, there comes a time when humanity is called to shift to a new level of consciousness, to reach a higher moral ground . . . That time is now." Wangari Maatthai, lecture upon receiving the Nobel Peace Prize, 2004.

2. Laurent A. Parks Daloz, Cheryl H. Keen, James P. Keen, and Sharon Daloz Parks et al., *Common Fire: Leading Lives of Commitment in a Complex World* (Cambridge, MA: Beacon Press, 1996), 1–19.

3. David Garvin, "Barriers and Gateways to Learning," *Education for Judgment: The Artistry of Discussion Leadership*, ed. C. Roland Christensen, David A. Garvin, and Ann Sweet (Boston: Harvard Business School Press, 1991), 11.

4. See Terry Tempest Williams, *The Open Space of Democracy* (Great Barrington, MA: Orion Society, 2004), 59.

5. The twenty-first century calls for a new kind of management-practitioner. See Peter M. Senge, *The Fifth Discipline: The Art and Practice of the Learning Organization* (New York: Doubleday/Currency, 1990), 15. "Leadership scholars need to develop a new leadership narrative with revised myths and rituals that fit the postindustrial paradigm. And practitioners of leadership need to adopt postindustrial leadership models that help them make sense of what they do as leaders and followers . . . Only with these transformed leadership models in their minds will they be able to develop the skills—the practical ways of doing leadership—that are necessary to help make the future work." Joseph C. Rost, *Leadership for the Twenty-First Century* (New York: Praeger, 1991), 36.

6. Donald A. Schon, *Educating the Reflective Practitioner: Toward a New Design for Teaching and Learning in the Professions* (San Francisco: Jossey-Bass, 1987), 17.

7. Ronald A. Heifetz, *Leadership Without Easy Answers* (Cambridge, MA: The Belknap Press of Harvard University Press, 1994; Ronald A. Heifetz and Marty Linsky, *Leadership on the Line: Staying Alive through the Dangers of Leading* (Boston: Harvard Business School Press, 2002).

8. David A. Garvin, "Making the Case," *Harvard Magazine*, September–October, 2003, 56–65 and 107.

9. Ellen Schall, "Learning to Love the Swamp: Reshaping Education for Public Service," *Journal of Policy Analysis and Management* 14, no. 2 (1995): 203.

10. The reader may recognize a resonance between "technical problems and adaptive challenges" and the discussion of "transactional and transformational leaders" as discussed by James MacGregor Burns and others within the field of leadership studies. As we shall see, the distinction Heifetz makes extends the conversation in ways that address the leader-follower dichotomy and other issues that Burns's call for a general theory of leadership requires. See James MacGregor Burns, *Transforming Leadership* (New York: Atlantic Monthly Press, 2003), especially 22–25.

11. Dean Williams helpfully delineates six different forms of adaptive challenges: the development challenge, the transition challenge, the maintenance challenge, the crisis challenge, the creative challenge, and the activist challenge. Dean Williams, *Real Leadership: Helping People and Organizations Face Their Toughest Challenges* (San Francisco: Berrett-Koehler, 2005).

12. Ronald A. Heifetz, Riley M. Sinder, Alice Jones, Lynn M. Hodge, and Keith A. Rowley, "Teaching and Assessing Leadership Courses at the John F. Kennedy School of Government," in *Curriculum and Case Notes, Journal of Policy Analysis and Management* 8, no. 3 (1989): 536–562.

13. The study informing this book is grounded in qualitative research methods and served as formative evaluation, meaning that it has contributed to the development of the work in process as well as yielding a summative analysis and assessment. During a concentrated five-year period, I observed twice and in depth every facet of the primary course in which this approach to leadership is taught (and occasionally thereafter). I interviewed twelve students for the pilot study, twenty-four students pre- and postcourse, fifteen former students who had taken the course three to ten years previously (along with interviewing ten corroborating witnesses), and conducted one group interview with nine graduates. The analysis of these interviews has been carried out with the assistance of my research associate, Karen Thorkilsen, who serves also as a second reader. I have also interviewed current instructors and teachers who are using the approach at Harvard and elsewhere. (More informally, I interviewed a few of their students and three other students from the Harvard course). Thus, we have sixty-five formal, transcribed interviews. These interviews as a group represent a broad diversity in ethnicity, gender, geographical location, and professional responsibility. The interviewees range in age from twenty-four to sixty-five, with most in mid-career. I have observed the approach in several other contexts and have used aspects of the approach in my own teaching, consulting, and theory building. In sum, the study on which this publication is based represents more than a decade of observation, study, analysis, assessment, and practice.

Notes

CHAPTER TWO

1. The class sessions are recorded and the tapes are available in the library during the term in which the course is offered so that students can review the process of the conversation or learn about what occurred if they were absent. This chapter is an edited version of a transcribed tape of an opening class.

CHAPTER THREE

1. Colleen Burke, "Tulips, Tinfoil, and Teaching: Journal of a Freshman Teacher," in *Education for Judgment: The Artistry of Discussion Leadership,* ed. C. Roland Christensen, David A. Garvin, and Ann Sweet (Boston: Harvard Business School Press, 1991), 40–41.

2. See William G. Perry, Jr., *Ethical and Intellectual Development in the College Years: A Scheme* (San Francisco: Jossey-Bass, 1999); Robert Kegan, *The Evolving Self: Problem and Process in Human Development* (Cambridge, MA: Harvard University Press, 1982) James W. Fowler, *Stages of Faith: The Psychology of Human Development and the Quest for Meaning* (San Francisco: Harper & Row, 1981); Carol Gilligan, *In a Different Voice: Psychological Theory and Women's Development* (Cambridge, MA: Harvard University Press, 1982); Laurent A. Parks Daloz, Cheryl H. Keen, James P. Keen, and Sharon Daloz Parks, *Common Fire: Leading Lives of Commitment in a Complex World,* (Cambridge, MA: Beacon Press, 1996).

3. See Kegan, *The Evolving Self.*

4. The word *tribe* is used advisedly, but throughout most of human history, all people have been dependent on tribes—networks of belonging that provide identity and orientation. See Daloz et al., *Common Fire,* 55–79.

5. See Sharon Daloz Parks, "It Matters How We Think," in *Big Questions, Worthy Dreams: Mentoring Young Adults in Their Search for Meaning, Purpose, and Faith* (San Francisco: Jossey-Bass, 2000), 53–70; and Mary Field Belenky, Blythe McVicker Clinchy, Nancy Rule Goldberger, Jill Mattuck Tarule, *Women's Ways of Knowing: The Development of Self, Voice, and Mind* (New York: Basic Books, 1986), 35–51.

6. Robert Kegan, *In Over Our Heads: The Mental Demands of Modern Life* (Cambridge, MA: Harvard University Press, 1994)—especially 320–322; See also Ken Wilbur, *A Theory of Everything: An Integral Vision for Business, Politics, Science, and Spirituality* (Boston: Shambala, 2000).

7. David Gergen, *Eyewitness to Power: The Essence of Leadership* (New York: Simon & Schuster, 2000), 349.

8. Peter M. Senge, *The Fifth Discipline: The Art and Practice of the Learning Organization* (New York: Doubleday/Currency, 1990), 68–69.

9. See Marco Iansiti and Roy Levien, "Strategy as Ecology," *Harvard Business Review* (March 2004): 69–78.

10. See Daloz et al., "Habits of Mind," in *Common Fire*, 102–124.

11. See George C. Lodge, *The New American Ideology* (New York: Knopf, 1983).

12. See Thomas R. Piper, Mary C. Gentile, and Sharon Daloz Parks, *Can Ethics Be Taught? Perspectives, Challenges, and Approaches at Harvard Business School* (Boston: Harvard Business School Press, 1993), 29–30.

13. See Kegan, *In Over Our Heads*, 94–95, and Parks, *Big Questions, Worthy Dreams*, 54–70.

14. See Daloz et al., *Common Fire*, 116.

15. Kegan, *The Evolving Self*, 115.

16. The teaching assistants in the course at the Kennedy School are often doctoral students in political science, education, law, business, or divinity who have previously taken the course and are keenly interested in leadership, usually in relationship to a particular issue—an adaptive challenge to which they are committed.

17. See Ronald A. Heifetz, *Leadership Without Easy Answers* (Cambridge, MA: Harvard University Press, 1994); and Ronald A. Heifetz and Marty Linsky, *Leadership on the Line: Staying Alive Through the Dangers of Leading* (Boston: Harvard Business School Press, 2002).

18. Ellen Schall, "Learning to Love the Swamp: Reshaping Education for Public Service," *Journal of Policy Analysis and Management* 14, no. 2 (1995): 203.

19. Interview with Dean Williams, Cambridge, MA, June 2003.

20. Heifetz, *Leadership Without Easy Answers*, 37–40.

21. Heifetz and Linsky, *Leadership on the Line*, 11.

CHAPTER FOUR

1. Quoted from a set of interviews of entering MBA students conducted by the author at Harvard Business School. See Thomas R. Piper, Mary C. Gentile, and Sharon Daloz Parks, *Can Ethics Be Taught? Perspectives, Challenges, and Approaches at Harvard Business School* (Boston: Harvard Business School Press, 1993), 13–72. On the other hand, one may privately take on a disproportionate measure of shame and guilt as a means of protecting others or simply failing to recognize the fact of limited power in the face of overwhelming forces. As one wise man put it, "It is sometimes easier to feel guilty than to have been helpless."

2. Students are usually assigned two or more films, each serving as a case of leadership success or failure. Film offers yet more compelling and complex material, including conflicting emotions (motivations, values, forces, longings, jealousies, idealism, ambitions, fears, and hopes) that are often beneath the surface but driving the action. Film also provides a balcony perspective and an occasion to work with the concepts of the course—factions, blind spots, pressures, the history of an issue, the practice of authority, and so forth. The films used have varied and remain an area of experimentation. Two that have worked well are *Lean*

on Me and *The Gate of Heavenly Peace*. *Lean on Me* is based on actual events in a high school in New Jersey. It tells the story of a bold attempt to foster adaptive change under the enormously difficult conditions of urban decay. Joe Clark, a former teacher who was always regarded as a liberal, is appointed principal. He exercises his formal authority in surprisingly dramatic, forceful, and disturbing ways, significantly affecting every aspect of the school and drawing fire from the town. The outcome is a controversial mix of success and failure. *The Gate of Heavenly Peace*, introduced into the curriculum by Dean Williams, another instructor who teaches this same course at the Kennedy School (see chapter 8), portrays the story of the Tiananmen Square uprising. Williams asks students to provide written responses to two of nine questions after viewing the film. Four of the suggested questions are the following: (1) Imagine that you are consulting to Chai Ling and Wang Dan during the demonstrations. The documentary provided a great deal of information, but you would probably want additional information to consult to them during those weeks. What clarifying questions would you want to ask them? What default assumptions would you want to question? What key concepts would you want to teach them? Why? (2) What conflicts existed among the students in regard to purpose, strategy, or tactics? (3) Please comment on the authority dynamics between students and government—dependency, counter-dependency, and inter-dependency. What issues were the students embodying in the society and what pressures do you think they were experiencing? What pressures do you think government officials were experiencing? (4) Comment on how the students and the government each managed or mismanaged the holding environment. Make a timeline of the key events. What were the major decision points for the demonstrators? What were the major decision points for the government? Along with the timeline, trace the changing levels of dis-equilibrium. The final paper provides an opportunity to reconsider again one's own case of leadership failure or another issue in the light of the learning of the entire course.

3. To be fair, the work does require time and focus. A mid-career, international student was not alone when he protested: "There's a lot of hard work. For instance, those questionnaires—I don't know how Heifetz thinks it takes just two hours to write them. It takes a minimum of four to five hours. I don't think my English is bad. It's not a lack of command of the language that makes me spend [all this time] . . . I have checked with my other friends, including Americans, who say, 'Yes, it has taken a very long time.' Because you have to reflect on each sentence, each question, and make sure it is consistent with what you have written and what you feel."

4. For each week of the course, there are two to seven readings of varying lengths drawn from the social sciences, leadership theorists, significant public addresses, and occasionally poetry and other literature from the humanities. These correlate with the theme for the week and are continually changed in the ongoing evolution of the course.

5. Note similarities between the characteristics of real teams as described by Richard Hackman and the design of this small group process: "Real work teams in organizations have four features: a team *task*, clear *boundaries*, clearly specified *authority* to manage their own work processes, and membership *stability* over some reasonable period of time." J. Richard Hackman, *Leading Teams: Setting the Stage for Great Performances* (Boston: Harvard Business School Press, 2002), 41.

6. See also Robert Kegan and Lisa Laskow Lahey, "The Real Reason People Won't Change," *Harvard Business Review* (November 2001): 84–92.

7. Ronald A. Heifitz and Marty Linsky, *Leadership on the Line: Staying Alive Through the Dangers of Leading* (Boston: Harvard Business School Press), 188.

8. Conversation with Judy Bunnell, Whidbey Institute, Clinton, WA, July 31, 2003.

9. Ronald A. Heifetz, *Leadership Without Easy Answers* (Cambridge, MA: Harvard University Press, 1994), 276.

CHAPTER FIVE

1. Peter Senge and his colleagues refer to this dimension of presence as a state of "letting come" crucial to leadership that can serve an emergent future that both entrepreneurs and those adept in spiritual consciousness know, albeit often in different expressions. See Peter Senge, C. Otto Scharmer, Joseph Jaworski, and Betty Sue Flowers, *Presence: Human Purpose and the Field of the Future* (Cambridge, MA: Society for Organizational Learning, 2004), 10–12.

2. Note that this corresponds with the etymology work in the weekly questionnaires (see chapter 6).

3. See also, Parker J. Palmer, *The Courage to Teach: Exploring the Inner Landscape of a Teacher's Life* (San Francisco: Jossey-Bass, 1998) 156–161; and Donald L. Finkel, *Teaching With Your Mouth Shut* (Portsmouth, NH: Heinemann, 2000).

4. See the value of "encounters with otherness" in Laurent A. Daloz et al., *Common Fire*, 55–79.

5. Joan Chittister, *Illuminated Life* (Maryknoll, NY: Orbis Books, 2001), 106–107.

6. Ibid., 108.

7. When this occurs at the group level, Senge and his colleagues describe this emergent possibility as "the field of the future." Peter Senge et al., *Presence*, 10–11.

8. For the insight regarding pairings, I am indebted to Karen Thorkilsen.

CHAPTER SIX

1. Former students were interviewed in Bolivia, Indiana, Massachusetts, Michigan, Minnesota, Washington, and Washington, D.C. Two working in New York City were interviewed in Cambridge, Massachusetts. I also conducted a

group interview in the Midwestern United States, and a colleague interviewed a former student in New Zealand and another in Australia. Note that as indicated earlier, this qualitative study followed the survey research described in chapter 1.

2. All of these interviews were taped. Twenty-five of these (including the ten corroborating interviews) were transcribed for analysis and read by a second reader.

3. The one exception among those I interviewed was a very fine executive in a government context who essentially "sat out" the large group experience; the instructor and TAs all failed to recognize that he was doing so and did not engage him in the learning system as a whole. Though he did have some memorable moments of insight in the small group, it would be wrong to report that his leadership practice has been significantly affected by his participation in the course.

4. See Robert E. Horn, *Visual Language: Global Communication for the 21st Century* (Bainbridge Island, WA: MacroVU, 1998), 21.

CHAPTER SEVEN

1. See May Sarton, *The Small Room* (New York: Norton Library, 1976).

2. See Sharon Daloz Parks, "How Then Shall We Live? Suffering and Wonder in the New Commons" in *Living the Questions: Essays Inspired by the Work and Life of Parker J. Palmer*, ed. Sam M. Intrator (San Francisco: Jossey-Bass, 2005, 298-320.

CHAPTER EIGHT

1. Dean Williams, *Real Leadership: Helping People and Organizations Face Their Toughest Challenges* (San Francisco: Berrett-Kohler, 2005).

2. Ibid., chapter 4.

3. Alma, like Hugh, believes it is important to strengthen the attention to purpose when she is using this approach—especially because she is working with undergraduates. "I have found that my students are looking for something to latch onto that's outside themselves, and that's a primary reason to want to be interested in politics and public life. As Ronald Heifetz does, I have my students write about their ambitions and aspirations. But then I take it a step further and have them craft a purpose statement for themselves. I also give them readings and other ways of finding the people and resources that will help them discern a worthy sense of purpose. This is the contextual piece that is critical to the ethical dimension of this approach and that is vital for students to be grounded in, the piece that for me comes out of what I call 'the service and social justice tradition.'" See also Sharon Daloz Parks, *Big Questions, Worthy Dreams: Mentoring Young Adults in Their Search for Meaning, Purpose, and Faith* (San Francisco: Jossey-Bass, 2000).

4. For another description and interpretation of the SOL program at Duke University, see Ann Colby, Thomas Ehrlich, Elizabeth Beaumont, and Jason Stephens, *Educating Citizens: Preparing America's Undergraduates for Lives of Moral and Civic Responsibility* (San Francisco: Jossey-Bass, 2003), 154–156.

CHAPTER NINE

1. "Orders derive much of their force from the aura of mystery, more or less strong, with which the successful commander, more or less deliberately, surrounds himself; the purpose of such mystification is to heighten the uncertainty which ought to attach to the consequences of disobeying him." John Keegan, *The Mask of Command* (New York: Viking Penguin, 1987), 315–316.

2. Beneath the Lone Ranger image is another more ancient but powerful image—the image of the shepherd. The mythic voice of the shepherd-leader still speaks through features of a cultural inheritance shared by Jews and Christians, grounded in the stories of Abraham and Moses, shepherds who became leaders of their people. From earliest times, there is an intimate link among the images of the shepherd, the warrior, and the monarch who are identified, in part, as protectors of the defenseless. For example, David, the simple but courageous *shepherd* boy, becomes the young *warrior*, and then is chosen by God to become *king*. Alexander the Great assured his troops, "I will make of shepherds, warriors!" Joan of Arc, a shepherdess, became a warrior-leader. This imagery is also strongly linked with Jesus, whose birth is attended by both shepherds and kings, and he is described later as both shepherd and king. This same sequence is echoed in a primary myth underlying the history of political leadership in the United States, where men from humble origins become military men and then presidents.

3. Joseph C. Rost, *Leadership for the 21st Century* (New York: Praeger, 1991), 94–95.

4. A growing discomfort with the heroic myth of leadership emerges from at least four points of awareness: (1) the heroic myth suggests that leaders are all-knowing and that followers are radically dependent—hardly an adequate assumption in increasingly educated societies that aspire to democracy; (2) the heroic myth feeds an illusion of control that fails to consider the decentralization of knowledge spawned by Internet technologies, an explosion of information, and the embeddedness of any single individual or organization in an expanding, dynamic network of complex interdependencies (systems); (3) the flock-of-sheep image suggests a homogeneity that masks the need for a practice of leadership that can function within increasingly diverse, multifunctional, and multicultural organizations and communities; (4) the heroic, shepherd-warrior-king myth is grounded in a willingness to die (or require the death of others)—metaphorically or actually. In the heroic model, the leader makes a pact with death—to destroy or be destroyed. The good shepherd was willing to lay down his life for his sheep, protecting them against all predators. In turn, the warrior-king can only maintain power by sharing, or at

least appearing to share, the risk of death that his or her followers are expected to undergo. This aspect of the heroic myth grasps certain features of the risks inherent in the exercise of authority and leadership. It also tends to eclipse the critical ability to stay alive in the midst of unprecedented and dangerous conditions in order to preserve life and to do the hard work over the long haul of creating new realities that will heal, productively sustain, and encourage life within our new commons to flourish.

5. See also Leo Braudy, "An Army of One?" *Compass: A Journal of Leadership* 1, no. 2 (Spring 2004): 20–22.

6. The value we have placed on the power of the individual is not misplaced. A recognition of the inalienable rights and potential contribution of every individual is an enormous achievement of civilization. But this value has given rise to an ideology of individual*ism*, which, as George Lodge prophetically insisted, obscures the critical fact of our necessary and growing interdependence within the natural, social, and global reality. See George Cabot Lodge, *The New American Ideology* (New York: Knopf, 1975).

7. Warren G. Bennis and Robert J. Thomas, *Geeks & Geezers: How Era, Values, and Defining Moments Shape Leaders* (Boston: Harvard Business School Press, 2002), 101.

8. David Whyte, *Crossing the Unknown Sea: Work as a Pilgrimage of Identity* (New York: Riverhead Books, 2001), 240–241. In my own teaching, I have found that though many may initially resist the image of themselves as artists, the artist in each of us is revealed when I invite each person to name the kind of artist they would be if they were an artist.

9. M. Mitchell Waldrop, *Complexity: The Emerging Science at the Edge of Order and Chaos*, (New York: Touchstone, 1992); Margaret Wheatley, *Leadership and the New Science*, (San Francisco: Berrett-Koehler, 1992); John Kotter, *Force for Change: How Leadership Differs from Management* (New York: The Free Press); Peter M. Senge, *The Fifth Discipline: The Art & Practice of the Learning Organization* (New York: Doubleday, 1990); Geoffrey Bellman, *Getting Things Done When You Are Not in Charge* (San Francisco: Barrett-Koehler, 1992); Jean Lipman-Blumen, *The Connective Edge: Leading in an Interdependent World* (San Francisco: Jossey-Bass, 1996); Dee Hock, *Birth of the Chaordic Age*, (San Francisco: Berrett-Koehler, 2000); Debra E. Meyerson, *Tempered Radicals: How People Use Difference to Inspire Change at Work* (Boston: Harvard Business School Press, 2001).

10. Conversation with Tom Ewell, March, 2004.

11. Donald A. Schon, *Educating the Reflective Practitioner: Toward a New Design for Teaching and Learning in the Professions* (San Francisco: Jossey-Bass, 1987), 12–13. For an accounting of the kind of wisdom to which Schon refers as modeled within the business context, see the account of Level 5 leadership in Jim Collins, *From Good to Great* (New York: HarperCollins, 2001), 17–40.

12. Ronald A. Heifetz and Marty Linsky, *Leadership on the Line: Staying Alive Through the Dangers of Leading* (Boston: Harvard Business School Press), 73.

13. See Rosabeth Moss Kanter, *The Change Masters: Innovation and Entrepreneurship in the American Corporation* (New York, NY: Simon & Schuster, 1983) especially pp. 48–49, 304–305; Peter B. Vaill, *Managing as a Performing Art: New Ideas for a World of Chaotic Change* (San Francisco: Jossey-Bass, 1989); and Stephen D. Brookfield, *The Skillful Teacher: On Technique, Trust, and Responsiveness in the Classroom* (San Francisco: Jossey-Bassm 1990);

14. Richard Goll, "Artist as a Metaphor for the Youth Worker," unpublished paper, January 2004, Hampton, VA.

15. Conversation with Donald L. Hanlon, Associate Professor of Architecture, University of Wisconsin, Milwaukee, June 15, 2003.

16. "Nancy J. Adler, Professor of Management at McGill University, has been creating watercolors for more than a decade as a recognized artist. She is exploring the relationship of art and management. She writes, 'Invited by the blank paper, the best of my intentions and experience enter into a dance with uncontrollable coincidence. Neither the process nor the resulting art are ever completely defined. Which way will the colors run? . . . I purposely use water-based media that don't stay put where I place them on the paper. There's never any illusion that I control the process. I only enter the dance . . .' She is learning how things move—yet recognizes that the more technical knowledge and experience you have to bring to the work the better." Artist Statement, Galerie Espace, Montreal, 2003.

17. Author's interview with Linda St. Clair, Gabriola Island, British Columbia, April 28, 2003.

18. See also Sharon D. Welch, *After Empire: The Art and Ethos of Enduring Peace* (Minneapolis: Fortress Press, 2004), 182–184.

19. Whyte, *Crossing the Unknown Sea*, 237.

20. Thomas S. Kuhn, *The Structure of Scientific Revolutions* (Chicago: University of Chicago Press, 1962).

21. See Ronald A. Heifetz, *Leadership Without Easy Answers* (Cambridge, MA: Harvard University Press, 1994) 88–100.

22. See Robert Kenny, "The Science of Collective Consciousness," *What Is Enlightenment?* May–July, 2004, 78–79.

23. See Suzanne Langer, *Philosophy in a New Key: A Study of Symbolism of Reason, Rite, and Art* (Cambridge, MA: Harvard University Press, 1942), 42.

24. See James E. Loder, *The Transforming Moment: Understanding Convictional Experiences* (San Francisco: Harper & Row, 1981), 31–35; Laurent A. Parks Daloz, Cheryl H. Keen, James P. Keen, and Sharon Daloz Parks, *Common Fire: Leading Lives of Commitment in a Complex World,* (Cambridge, MA: Beacon Press, 1996). 125–153; Sharon Daloz Parks, *Big Questions, Worthy Dreams*, 104–126. See also the resonance between these descriptions of the process of imagination and the model of discernment and emergence in Peter Senge, C. Otto Scharmer, Joseph Jaworski, and Betty Sue Flowers, *Presence: Human Purpose and the Field of the Future* (Cambridge, MA: Society for Organizational Learning, 2004), 83–92.

Notes

25. Alma Blount, transcribed interview, Whidbey Island, November 2002. See also Robert Greenleaf: "As a practical matter, on most important decisions there is an information gap . . . between the solid information in hand and what is needed. The art of leadership rests, in part, on the ability to bridge that gap by intuition . . . The person who is better at this than most is likely to emerge the leader because he [or she] contributes something of great value . . . Leaders, therefore, must be more creative than most; and creativity is largely discovery, a push into the uncharted and the unknown . . . [A] leader finds himself [or herself] needing to think like a scientist, an artist, or a poet." from Robert Greenleaf, *The Servant as Leader* (Indianapolis: The Greenleaf Center for Servant Leadership, 1982).

26. See Dorothy Leonard and Walter Swap, *When Sparks Fly: Igniting Group Creativity* (Boston: Harvard Business School Press, 1999).

27. See Richard Florida, "America's Looming Creativity Crisis," *Harvard Business Review* (October 2004): 122–136; and Steven J. Tepper, "The Creative Campus: Who's No. 1?" *Chronicle of Higher Education* (October 1, 2004), 122–136.

28. See Rhea Y. Miller, *Cloudhand—Clenched Fist: Chaos, Crisis and the Emergence of Community* (San Diego: LauraMedia, 1996), 48.

29. M. C. Richards, "Toward M. C. : A Monograph by M. C. Richards," *Studio Potter* 14, no. 1 (1985): 2.

30. Alma Blount, transcribed interview conducted by Sharon Daloz Parks, November, 2002.

31. When, for example, he faced the adaptive challenge of incorporating Persians into the Macedonian army (a kind of merger) and some veterans in command who had been with him from the first were threatening to turn the army against him rather than yield to retirement as Alexander proposed, he reminded them that once they had been only shepherds who had become warriors and citizens: "Philip, [my father], found you vagabonds and helpless, most of you clothed in sheepskins, pasturing a few sheep on the mountain sides, and fighting for those against Illyrians, and Triballians and Thracians; Philip brought you down from the hills to the plains, made you doughty opponents of your enemies, so that you trusted not to the natural strength of your own villages but to your own courage. More, he made you city dwellers and civilized you." This speech was "only the opening act of a three-day drama" including the staged death (and return) of Alexander himself. It reveals Alexander's keen awareness of the interdependencies within the whole system and the need for improvisation. Thus, the artistry of leadership is revealed, even in a citadel of the command and control myth. See Keegan, *Mask of Command*, 57–58.

32. This dynamic appears also in the Gilgamesh epic—a classic myth including the essential bond between a cultural "lighter" brother and his darker, wilder, and more in-touch-with-life brother. The same is found in the relationship of Sacagawea and Lewis and Clark.

33. Suzi Gablik, formerly the London correspondent for *Art in America*, observed that only in relatively recent times has the artist sought an asocial role, eschewing communication with a public, asking no question, making no statement, offering no information, message or opinion, totally self-possessed, self-reliant, free, autonomous. It is only a certain generation of artists who as something of an enigma have doubted that art was ever meant to be integrated into the work of society. In modernism's "demystified" art, she observed, what is "conspicuously missing . . . is the sacramental vision that had been present in art for nearly all of human history." As the dangers to planetary survival escalate, she finds the notion that art might answer only to its own laws to seem more than a bit ingenuous. Along with growing number of others, she calls for a recognition of the principle of interrelatedness and the renewal of the relationship between artist and society in which the artist is self-consciously planting images of reality that awaken us to our present condition, including images that empower the confidence that we can shape a positive human future. From *Lightworks: Explorations in Art, Culture, and Creativity*, ed. Milenko Matanovic (Issaquah, WA: Lorian Press, 1985), 8–14.

CHAPTER TEN

1. Warren Bennis, "Learning to Lead," *Executive Excellence* (January 1996): 7.

2. See Walter Brueggemann, *The Prophetic Imagination*, 2nd ed. (Minneapolis: Fortress Press, 2001).

3. See Robert Kegan, *The Evolving Self: Problem and Process in Human Development* (Cambridge, MA: Harvard University Press, 1982), 31–32.

4. Barbara Kellerman, *Reinventing Leadership: Making the Connection Between Politics and Business* (Albany, NY: State University of New York Press, 1999), 188.

5. Parker Palmer, *To Know As We Are Known: A Spirituality of Education* (San Francisco: Harper & Row, 1983), 73–74. Palmer argues for creating a hospitable space "where obedience to truth may be practiced."

6. Richard C. Broholm, memorandum, "Report to the Leadership Education Committee," The Lilly Endowment, January 4, 1992.

7. When I was first invited to undertake this study and assessment, I was told that an apparent effect of the course was that a small but noticeable number of students appeared to seek out for the first time or to re-engage religious interest and commitment. It was not clear why, and I made no particular effort to study this in the interviewing process. I did, however, observe that as the course progresses, students are implicitly pressed to recognize the intensification of the dynamic complexity of life, and to ask essential questions about power and about trust. As the finitude and limits of presumed authorities are revealed, as students discover new dimensions of their own vulnerability, and as they are invited to take risks on behalf of their own deep purposes and aspirations, we begin to see how, as Alfred North Whitehead put it, "The essence of education is that it be

religious." That is, at its best, education draws forth the great questions about the whole of life—Who are we? What is our purpose? What is the character of the force field of life in which we dwell? What is the scope and nature of our individual and collective power? Who or what can we trust? How are we to live? These are all moral, ethical questions, and the test of religion is the adequacy of its ongoing process of inquiry and discovery in response to these questions. See also Anthony B. Robinson, Transforming Congregational Culture (Grand Rapids, MI: Eerdmands Publishing, 2003), chapter 2.

8. David Whyte, *Crossing the Unknown Sea*, 236–237. See also Robert Fritz *The Path of Least Resistance: Principles for Creating What You Want to Create* (Salem, MA: DMA, Inc., 1984).

9. Conversation with Emily Sander, Iona, Scotland, May, 1997.

10. See Ronald A. Heifetz and Marty Linsky, *Leadership on the Line: Staying Alive Through the Dangers of Leading* (Boston: Harvard Business School Press), 225–236.

11. Milenko Matanovic, Lightworks: Explorations in Art, Culture, and Creativity (Issaquah, WA: 1985) 4.

12. Robert Bellah et al., *The Good Society* (New York: Knopf, 1994), 60.

13. Marshall McLuhan, Understanding Media (New York: McGraw Hill, 1964), 65.

14. Karen Thorkilsen, "The Edge of Knowing," *In Context*, no. 5 (Spring 1984): 4–5.

15. See Sr. Theresa M. Monrow, "The Practice of Authority," *Leading Ideas, The Newsletter of Trustee Leadership Development*, vol. 1, no. 2 (Winter 1996): 3–4.

16. See Dean Williams, *Real Leadership: Helping People and Organizations Face Their Toughest Challenges* (San Francisco: Berrett-Kohler, 2005).

17. Marty Linsky, personal communication, December, 2004.

Index

Index

Index

entertainment, class as, 25
epistemology, shift in, 51–56
equilibrium, efforts to maintain, 91–92
Erhard Seminar Training, 157–158
ethics
  common good, 3–4, 255–256
  ethical valence, 240–241, 250
  reexamination of, 55–56
  religious interest and, 241, 268*n*
etymology of words
  "art," 225
  hidden issues and, 131–132
  "manager," 205
  in questionnaires, 262*n*
Ewell, Tom, 265*n*
executive coaching, 195–197, 241
expectations, 19–43, 46
  about course, 21–22
  about instructor, 20–21, 28–29, 61
  changing, 35–36
  conflict of, 45–49
  differing, 25–26, 32
  frustration of, 50–51
experience
  direct, learning from, 7, 196, 238
  life experience of teachers, 154–158
  of students, differing, 49
experimentation, 36, 131, 179, 213
expertise, 73–74

factions
  alienating, 23
  bridge-building and, 112–113, 174
  changing factions, 222
  changing patterns and, 85
  identifying, 13, 60, 138
  in orchestrating conflict, 65, 220–221
  as social pattern, 63–64
failure. *See also* leadership failure cases
  difficulty recognizing, 73–74

  learning from, 42, 73–97, 244
  systemic analysis of, 74
fear, 182, 186. *See also* courage
The Fifth Discipline (Senge), 206, 265*n*
films, 79, 260*n*–261*n*
Finkel, Donald L., 262*n*
fire, working with, 227–228
"flattening the pyramid," 207
Florida, Richard, 266*n*
Flowers, Betty Sue, 262*n*
Force for Change (Kotter), 206, 265*n*
formal authority, 9
  autonomy and, 54–55
  pressures to finesse failure, 73–74
  of teacher in classroom, 234–235
formal authorization, 39
Fowler, James W., 259*n*
framework for learning, 60–61
  four critical distinctions, 8-11
  four key questions, 191
framework for systemic thinking, 158–159
Fritz, Robert, 268*n*

Gablik, Suzi, 267*n*
Galamian, Ivan, 33
Garvin, David A., 257*n*, 258*n*
The Gate of Heavenly Peace (film), 260*n*, 261*n*
gender, 182–183, 207
Gentile, Mary C., 260*n*
Gergen, David, 53, 259*n*
Getting Things Done When You Are Not in Charge (Bellman), 206, 265*n*
Gilligan, Carol, 259*n*
giving work back to group, 97, 186
  example of, 141–142
  as hallmark of adaptive leadership, 212, 256
  importance of, 132–133
  in small group consultation, 77–78
Goldberger, Nancy Rule, 259*n*

About the Author

SHARON DALOZ PARKS is Director of Leadership for the New Commons, an initiative of the Whidbey Institute in Clinton, Washington. She teaches also in the Executive Leadership Program at Seattle University. She received her doctorate from Harvard University, where she subsequently—for more than sixteen years—held faculty and research positions in the schools of divinity and business, and the Kennedy School of Government. She is a coauthor of *Common Fire: Leading Lives of Commitment in a Complex World* (Beacon Press, 1996) and *Can Ethics Be Taught?: Perspectives, Challenges, and Approaches at Harvard Business School* (Harvard Business School Press, 1993). Parks also authored *Big Questions, Worthy Dreams: Mentoring Young Adults in Their Search for Meaning, Purpose, and Faith* (Jossey-Bass, 2000). She lectures, teaches, and consults nationally, with particular interest in the formation of leadership and ethics within the changing contexts of organizations and cultures. She and her husband, Larry Daloz, live on Whidbey Island in Washington state and in Vermont.